# THE DANGEROUS DOCTRINE

## National Security
## and U.S. Foreign Policy

# About the Book and Author

Ever since President Truman invoked the words "national security" to launch the U.S. side of the cold war, government officials have used the phrase to explain, justify, or excuse executive actions that were dubious, illegal, or, as Senator Sam Ervin said during the Watergate hearings, "on the windy side of the law."

National security does not simply connote ideological anticommunism. Actions taken in the name of national security are placed above and beyond the reach of the law and the Constitution. In *The Dangerous Doctrine,* Saul Landau reviews the history of national security doctrine from Truman's declaration that national security was at stake in Iran, Greece, and Turkey to subsequent national security justifications of CIA operations in Iran and Guatemala under Eisenhower, Kennedy's fiasco at the Bay of Pigs, Johnson's phantom Tonkin Gulf incident, Nixon's secret bombing of Cambodia, the CIA's role in the 1973 coup in Chile, and the Reagan administration's scandal-ridden policy toward Central America.

Congress's role in previous national security scandals, argues Landau, has been not only to investigate covert action and violations of congressional mandates but to help restore credibility and integrity within the system. The unfortunate result, however, has been to recreate conditions that allow the next administration to abuse the law by appealing to the vagaries of national security interests. Ultimately, he contends, the United States needs to return to the system of law upon which its constitutional government is based and to put an end to the system of permanent exception to that law that the doctrine of national security represents.

Saul Landau is a senior fellow at the Institute for Policy Studies and a member of the Executive Board of Policy Alternatives for the Caribbean and Central America. He has written widely on U.S. policy toward Latin America. He and John Dinges won the Edgar Allen Poe Award for their book *Assassination on Embassy Row.*

# THE DANGEROUS DOCTRINE

## National Security
## and U.S. Foreign Policy

### Saul Landau

## A PACCA BOOK

## WESTVIEW PRESS
### BOULDER AND LONDON

Copyright © 1988 by Saul Landau

Published in 1988 in the United States of America by Westview Press, Inc.; Frederick A. Praeger, Publisher; 5500 Central Avenue, Boulder, Colorado 80301

Library of Congress Cataloging-in-Publication Data
Landau, Saul.
  The dangerous doctrine.
  Bibliography: p.
  Includes index.
  1. United States—National security.  2. United
States—Foreign Relations—1945—    .  I. Title.
UA23.L25  1988    355′.033073    87-31635
ISBN 0-8133-7506-1
ISBN 0-8133-7508-8 (pbk.)

Printed and bound in the United States of America

 The paper used in this publication meets the requirements of the American National Standard for Permanence of Paper for Printed Library Materials Z39.48-1984.

10    9    8    7    6    5    4    3    2    1

# Contents

# Preface

*Thus far our fortune keeps an upward course,*
*And we are graced with wreaths of victory.*
*But in the midst of this bright-shining day,*
*I spy a black, suspicious, threatening cloud,*
*That will encounter with our glorious sun,*
*Ere he attain his easeful western bed.*
—King Edward from *Henry VI, Part III*

In 1984, close to the Nicaraguan border, a journalist came upon a Honduran peasant. From his small parcel of land where he grew corn and coffee the peasant could see the radar antennas of a nearby U.S. airbase. For the past year, he had watched in awe as sophisticated aircraft landed and took off. The journalist asked the farmer what he thought about this expensive new equipment and the contra troops and Honduran soldiers who had moved into this previously tranquil area. The farmer chuckled and pointed to his wife. "She plows sometimes; sometimes I plow." The farmer explained that he could not afford to buy an animal to help with plowing, much less a tractor. Yet within eyesight were hundreds of millions of dollars of military equipment. In fact, several of his neighbors had been evicted when the base was built on their land.

Nearby, the peasant acknowledged, the contras had set up a base camp from which they carried out raids into nearby Nicaragua. He had seen *gringos* enter the area, but he did not know that they were officials of the National Security Council and the CIA as well as retired military officers, all of whom were working overtime to supply the contras, despite a U.S. law forbidding such activities. Just as the small peasants of the area had little concern outside of the effect on their lives of the politics of this affair, so, too, did the fast-moving

U.S. officials pay scant attention to the results of their actions on the local population.

Lieutenant Colonel Oliver North, then an obscure NSC staff member, felt such an urgency to supply the counterrevolutionary troops with weapons that he did not think about the consequences of such pressures on the Honduran population. His job, indeed his mission, was to stop the Nicaraguan revolution at all costs. For North, the suppression of the Sandinista revolution was so high a priority that he circumvented U.S. laws and engaged leaders of other nations to do his anti-Sandinista bidding. North had organized not only the contras' resupply organization; he had organized groups of specially trained forces to enter Nicaragua surreptitiously in order to destroy buildings and installations and to kill people.[1] From 1981 on, the U.S. government had been at war with Nicaragua, although Congress had not declared any such war.

In July 1986, at the United Nations, Nicaraguan president Daniel Ortega charged U.S. president Ronald Reagan with violating the basic rules of international behavior by forming a mercenary army called the contras (Spanish shorthand for *contrarevolucionarios,* or counterrevolutionaries) who under U.S. orders destroyed Nicaraguan property, mined Nicaragua's harbors, killed and kidnapped its people, and even instigated a rebellion among members of the indigenous Indian population. In a 1984 lawsuit brought by the Nicaraguan government, the World Court had found for the Sandinistas and ordered Reagan to desist. But he did not. He told the U.S. public that he had a higher cause, that of stopping communism, a word that he, Colonel North, and many others had come to confuse with popular revolution in Third World countries.

In 1776, the British Crown acted on the basis of its higher cause, as imperial states did against colonies. Among the charges that Thomas Jefferson leveled against King George III were that he had "plundered our seas, ravaged our coasts, burnt our towns, and destroyed the lives of our people." The Declaration of Independence accused the king of "transporting large armies of foreign mercenaries to complete the works of death, desolation, and tyranny, already begun with circumstances of cruelty and perfidy scarcely paralleled in the most barbarous ages, and totally unworthy of the head of a civilized nation." The declaration also expressed indignation regarding the British policy of stirring resentment among the Indian nations against the settlers.

When these historic charges are compared with the accusations made by Daniel Ortega against Ronald Reagan at the U.N. in 1986, a remarkable parallel emerges. King George III responded with imperial righteousness against the upstarts in the colonies, who put forth ideas about nationalism and revolution that made the rulers of the British Empire shudder, and he predicted a parade of horrors should the colonies succeed in gaining independence.

Like King George III more than two hundred years ago, U.S. foreign policymakers cringe when Third World leaders speak in "liberationist" terms, and the foreign policy elite postulates a parade of horrors should such "liberation" be achieved. This elite foresees falling dominoes, a loss of U.S. credibility, and the installation of enemy bases. Nevertheless, after two centuries of nationhood, the United States must deal with the nationalism of other peoples and be able to apply to others the ideals of its own Declaration of Independence, which called revolution an inalienable right.

In this book I attempt to show that contrary to its ideals, U.S. policy since the late eighteenth century has seen revolutions in other places as threats. But only for the past forty years have the formal and informal leaders of the country declared that the nation has a mission to stop revolutions, almost all of which are identified with a fiendish enemy that is out to destroy the United States at all costs.

In fact, the United States emerged from World War II to dominate an immense overseas empire. But its leaders did not refer to this control of vast territories all over the world as an empire. The United States was fighting for "freedom," its presidents declared, as they dispatched troops and CIA officers to Asia, Africa, and Latin America.

The public, while ingesting the ideology of anticommunism for four decades, nevertheless has been reluctant to abandon the republican fabric of society and allow a president to simply govern with an imperial mandate. Consensus still has to be attained through a difficult persuasion and bargaining process. The media have maintained their rights to publish; Congress has insisted on certain of its prerogatives. No institution has been willing to cede its rights so that the United States could become a formal empire.

This book argues that an unwillingness or inability on the part of U.S. policymakers and party leaders to offer an honest choice to the public—imperialism or republicanism—led to the rise of the doctrine of national security, the unofficial and often "higher" cause that has guided U.S. policy for the last forty years. This political finesse of real choice in turn has undermined the very republican principles it was supposed to protect and has menaced the foundations of democracy abroad and at home. Using as justification the vague words *national security,* presidents and appointed officials repeatedly have declared crises and emergencies that in effect have removed

U.S. government officials from the civilized precepts and limits imposed by both divine and natural law.

This usurpation of power reached new depths during the Reagan years. As the president failed to forge a consensus on his policy to destroy the Nicaraguan revolution, a military junta grew up inside the government to carry out the imperial agenda. Led by the director of the CIA and staffed by military and former military officials both in and out of government, this cabal amassed a fleet of planes and ships and an army drawn from veterans of old wars and covert actions. The members of this junta also accumulated a private treasury, which they used to transact business under the name of the U.S. government, but which was unauthorized by Congress and indeed was unscrutinized by official executive monitoring agencies.

The full agenda of William Casey, Oliver North, Richard Secord, and company was not revealed in the lengthy 1987 congressional investigation. Nevertheless, the public was shocked by the fact that these men carried substantial policy portfolios, directed the contra war and the invasion of Grenada, swapped arms for hostages with Iran, plotted coups, and tried to manage the media—all in the name of national security.

The U.S. public must understand how and why this has happened if it is to restore the principles upon which the United States was founded. For those who wish to change policy, it is important to know and acknowledge the past and see how it has shaped the present in order to be better prepared to shape the future.

*Saul Landau*

### Notes

1. See Peter Kornbluh, "Ollie's Follies: What North Might Have Wrought," *The Nation*, June 27, 1987, p. 887. Also see Peter Kornbluh, *Nicaragua: The Price of Intervention* (Washington, D.C.: Institute for Policy Studies, 1987), pp. 88–89.

# Acknowledgments

Scores of friends and colleagues helped me write this book. Bob Stark gave me his understanding, his commitment to justice and equality, his constructive nagging, and ultimately his knee as a sacrifice to the cause of good works. I appreciate him. Jim O'Connor offered his marvelous imagination and his deep insights; his ability to critique ideas is unsurpassed. Walter LaFeber not only wrote the best book on U.S.-Central America policy, but offered immensely helpful suggestions on this manuscript. Richard Barnet, Bob Borosage, Richard Fagen, Bill LeoGrande, Phil Brenner, Marcus Raskin, Fred Halliday, John Dinges, and Dan Siegel took time to read early drafts and offer extremely helpful and creative suggestions. Ken Sharpe offered excellent reorganizing suggestions on Chapter 9. Michael Robins, Angela Blake, and Julia Sweig did research, solid editing, and countless other tasks in helping me to finish the manuscript.

Peter Kvidera and Birgitte Mortensen did outstanding and diligent research. Michael Ashford, Michael Hardt, and Patrick Wictor helped on footnotes. Colin Danby was a thorough and efficient editor. Melessa Hemmler offered intellectual and physical help when it was badly needed. Evan Schaeffer, Scott Brookie, and Mike Cohen introduced me to the labyrinth of computers and to electronic mail. Jim Abourezk made possible the writing of the book with his generosity and his teaching skills. Susan Szabo helped me with the word processing in the early stages, and the late and dear Peggy Vecchione helped type some of the early chapters. My faculty colleagues at the University of California at Santa Cruz, where I was a visiting professor, and many of the citizens of that great city, offered me assistance, constructive ideas, and an intellectual climate that helped me to work. Rebecca Switzer pushed me to finish, criticized my sloppy thinking and writing, and provided untold help.

I am grateful for the aid and comfort all these friends and colleagues offered at various points in the writing. My colleagues at the Institute for Policy Studies in Washington, D.C., and at the Transnational Institute in Amsterdam provided me with rich intellectual stimulation and enormous insights into politics and life. I owe them and those two great institutions an enormous debt.

Some of the material that formed the background for Chapter 7 came from conversations I had with Fidel Castro during the course of filming sessions in 1968, 1974, 1977, and 1987. I also have relied on conversations with other Cuban officials. I learned from my filmic sessions with the late Dr. Salvador Allende and with Michael Manley important lessons about the meaning of independence and nationalism in the Third World. Both men are models of integrity, and they opened democratic socialist paths that still stand as important experiments from which current and future generations can learn.

The original inspiration for this book came from William Appleman Williams, who, as a professor at the University of Wisconsin, taught me and other eager graduate students how to deal with ideas in history and to take seriously and skeptically the words that political and intellectual leaders say and write. I am responsible, however, for any and all the errors as well as the opinions that appear in the final product, no matter how much I borrowed or squeezed out of others.

S.L.

SIR THOMAS MORE: . . . I know what's legal, not what's right. And I'll stick to what's legal.

WILLIAM ROPER: So now you'd give the Devil benefit of the law?

MORE: Yes. What would you do? Cut a road through the law to get after the Devil?

ROPER: I'd cut down every law in England to do that.

MORE: Oh? And when the last law was down and the Devil turned round on you, where would you hide, the laws all being flat?

—Robert Bolt, *A Man for All Seasons*

# CHAPTER 1

# From Anticolonial to National Security State: Continuity and Change

*The national security of all the Americas is at stake. . . . Who among us would wish to bear responsibility for failing to meet our shared obligation?*
—Ronald Reagan, Address before a joint session of Congress on Central America, April 27, 1983

On February 24, 1984, General Paul Gorman, commander in chief of the U.S. Southern Command, brought a distracted audience of senators and public to attention. "Mexico," he said, could become "the number one security problem for the United States in the next decade." Not Moscow or Havana, Gorman declared to the Senate Armed Services Committee, "but the capital of Mexico is the hub of subversion for all of Central America."

U.S. officials offered immediate denials while the Mexican Foreign Office sounded appropriately indignant, but the assembled senators recognized that the general had meant what he said. Nor was he the first important official to say it in recent years. Central Intelligence Agency (CIA) director William Colby, in his 1976 retirement speech from the Agency, also had pointed to Mexico as the most serious national security threat to the United States. Both men were talking about the danger of the spread of revolution in the Western Hemisphere.

Neither Gorman nor Colby told their audiences exactly what "national security" meant, nor how the spread of revolution from

Mexico could affect U.S. interests. The meaning of these two words and the reality of the threat to the United States were taken for granted by these officials and their audiences. Yet the government's refusal to define national security and the loose and elusive way in which it is used should make us look twice at this powerful phrase.

How can something so vaguely defined be achieved in practice? How can the lay public, or even U.S. senators, grapple with a topic that is discussed in generalities such as "credibility," symbols such as "dominoes," vague menaces such as "threats to vital shipping lanes" and "missile gaps,"[1] and lurid nightmares such as being overrun by "floods of refugees" or invaded by the Russians?[2]

The United States has legitimate security concerns. Indeed, in order to make their case for a new constitution, the authors of *The Federalist Papers*—Alexander Hamilton, John Jay, and James Madison (the man who also drafted the U.S. Constitution)—attacked the vagueness of the Articles of Confederation in the areas of defense and foreign policy.[3] In the debate about the Constitution, the Founding Fathers grappled with the question of how to build a strong and enduring state without depriving the citizens of their inalienable rights. Among the answers that emerged from this debate was the idea of a democratic empire, one that would recognize societal and individual rights. According to this view, the new state had to be accessible to society and had to guarantee citizen participation in the governing process.

It was, after all, the colonists' experience with the English Crown and their reading of history that led them to mistrust centralized states. This suspicion found its way into the Constitution, which gave limited powers to the government and divided those powers among different branches. In addition, citizens were protected, in principle, from the state by the Bill of Rights.

Suspicion of unchecked centralized government remains an axiom of U.S. politics, and indeed most civil liberties cases revolve around the state-citizen conflict. But through the creation of an outside and centralized enemy state, the Soviet Union, with its "atheistic" and "communistic" ideology, the brunt of historic suspicion in effect was transferred from the U.S. central government to the Soviet state. Security as protection from the evil central government came to mean protection from the expansionist impulses of the Soviet bear.

### The Emergence of the National Security State

Until the 1950s, the U.S. public generally understood security to mean the preservation of the country's territorial integrity, the well-being of its citizens, and the strength of its democratic institutions.

Although territorial expansion played a large part in achieving this security up through the 1890s, few U.S. citizens ever equated security with the nineteenth century imperialism of England, France, Russia, or Japan. It was widely assumed that contiguous territory rightfully belonged to the United States and that expansion did not interfere with the society's access to the state. Indeed, new lands were seen as beneficial. The process of acquiring them involved a minimum of hocus-pocus and did not require a draft or other accoutrements of military governments.

How is it that national security has become a widely accepted explanation for questionable, and often highly illegal, government activities at home and abroad? As will be shown, eighteenth and nineteenth century expansionism spilled over into imperialism in the early decades of this century, as the United States extended its power to Latin America and Asia, areas for which Europe could not compete militarily. Moreover, the oceans protected the United States from the powerful nations of Europe and their destructive wars. Until President Woodrow Wilson involved the United States in "world" (European) affairs as a war partner, "isolationism" (noninvolvement in European affairs) had prevailed.[4]

From World War I on, the government began to change as the United States became a global power. Before then, the majority of the U.S. public generally had accepted wars as just or, at least, as cruelly necessary. But after World War I, in which 125,000 U.S. troops died for what seemed a remote cause, there was a reaction. The U.S. population suspected that it had not been told the real reasons for U.S. entry into World War I, and through Congress, public opinion forced the state to pull back and confine its intervention to Latin America and Asia. Even there, when body counts grew (for example in Nicaragua in the late 1920s and early 1930s), popular pressure induced Congress to bring the troops home.[5]

After the United States emerged from World War II as the strongest economic and military power in the world, key government and industrial leaders saw the opportunity for a world empire. Urged on by the business elite, which sought to maintain and expand its advantaged status, U.S. leaders constructed, from the expansionist past and the World War II organization, a national security state to deal with global affairs.[6] The concept of national security, which was never defined clearly or explained, became the overriding concern of the state, at the expense of other long-held traditions and practices. The concept also became dominant in domestic affairs; it governed political debate and rationalized restrictions on the individual's constitutional freedoms. The National Security Act of 1947 (which was secret at the time) and subsequent amendments and decrees placed the governance of critical foreign and defense policies in the hands of new institutions: a national security apparatus run by national security managers.[7]

The national security myth required changes in political language because, given the implications of the undefined notion "national security," the president simply could announce that a crisis existed and that U.S. national security required him to commit armed forces to, for example, Iran, Greece, or Korea. The president did not explain "why" because clear explanations might violate another national security requirement: secrecy.

Secrecy became an obsession. It was not just the "enemy," however, that could endanger national security through knowledge of national security operations. *No one* outside the newly formed national security elite could be trusted. Thus, national security became a justification for withholding information of the kind that previously had been available to the public.[8] By keeping the citizenry in the dark, the national security elite forestalled debate and participation.

In the course of less than five postwar years, U.S. leaders made George Washington's "no permanent alliances" dictum obsolete and engaged in military pacts with scores of nations around the world. At the same time, the federal government began interfering in previously sacrosanct domestic areas.[9] Once established, the national security bureaucracy not only perpetuated itself, but also spread its hegemonic authority to the point of warping the basic idiom of political debate.

In less than forty years, the national security state elite has obfuscated traditional values by claiming even higher values—the security of the nation. This elite has not offered basic security or enhanced the national well-being. Instead, the elite's members have defined a dominant worldview under which we must live, in constant and precarious tension, uncertainty, and social unrest, and under the threat of nuclear obliteration. The national security managers have prevented public and congressional debate about major policy decisions, which violates the spirit of the Constitution and indeed limits each citizen's democratic rights.

A demonic view of the world that requires hundreds of billions of dollars to be spent every year for "defense" unrelated to the nation's established territorial boundaries must be questioned. The worldview that sees all anticolonial and anti-imperial revolutions as a communist threat to U.S. security also must be challenged because the United States won its own independence in a bloody revolutionary war that provided an example for many that followed.[10]

## Central America and National Security

The current conflict in Central America provides an ideal opportunity for challenging the taboo on discussing national security. The United States does have real concerns about Central America, but the prevailing definition (or lack thereof) of national security does not address the issue of real security. In fact, the current definition produces ongoing anxiety.[11]

Former speaker of the House Thomas P. "Tip" O'Neill has predicted that this escalation of military activities and supplies will culminate in the use of U.S. troops in Central America. This is not idle speculation. O'Neill has observed that for more than sixty years presidents have sent U.S. armed forces to intervene in Third World nations after they were declared vital to U.S. national security.[12]

The former House speaker also was aware of the sizable domestic and international opposition to U.S. policy on Central America, one that is becoming more active and militant as Washington's actions in the region become more aggressive and less lawful. Since the early 1980s, there has been much organized opposition from churches, labor unions, and community groups, and Washington, D.C., has hosted numerous protests against the administration's national security policies in Central America.

From 1981 to 1985, Congress responded to this opposition by refusing to grant carte blanche to President Ronald Reagan's alarmist Central America policies.[13] Yet despite polls indicating overwhelming public opposition, Congress approved $100 million aid in the summer of 1986 for an effort to overthrow the revolutionary government of Nicaragua, after the administration virtually charged that opponents of the policy were soft on communism.[14] One member of the House described the effects of forty years of national security policy on the debate about contra aid:

After [Nicaraguan president Daniel] Ortega went to Moscow, no one in the House would be caught dead saying anything good about Nicaragua no matter what good things they did down there. And they are doing some. The only issues we could stand up on was aid to the contras and even there the goddamned national security language gets shoved down our throats. Every time one of these rinkydink nations starts a revolution or independence movement, the Congress gets bludgeoned over the head by national security crap. It means we have to sit by and watch the taxpayers' money get spent on a bunch of thugs who kill, torture, rape and steal from poor people, whether it's Nicaragua or Angola.[15]

Once invoked, the national security rhetoric becomes difficult for publicly elected officials to oppose. The result is that at decisive moments, debate is cut off. In the name of national security, the administration and a majority in Congress have declared support for counterrevolutionary wars in Asia, Africa, and Latin America.[16] But little discussion has taken place in Congress or in the press on the likely consequences of such action.

Whether or not Tip O'Neill's dire prediction of U.S. troop intervention in Central America before Reagan leaves office is correct, real national security itself requires a debate on the meaning of the concept. The guidelines for such discussion should emerge from the experience of the past, from the Declaration of Independence— which declared the right to revolt when there was no "just consent" of the governed—and from the lessons learned and forgotten or still unlearned from the war in Vietnam. The history of the United States and that of other peoples and nations must become the context for such discussion—not a history that is stored in the White House attic, to be rewritten by the president's speechwriters.

## Notes

1. For a critique of the "missile gap," a phrase invoked by John F. Kennedy in the 1960 presidential campaign, see Desmond Ball, *Politics and Force Levels* (Berkeley: University of California Press, 1980), and Edgar M. Bottome, *The Balance of Terror* (Boston: Beacon Press, 1980). On the "window of vulnerability," a term used by critics of the SALT II treaty and picked up by Ronald Reagan in his 1980 campaign, see Strobe Talbott, *Deadly Gambits* (New York: Random House, 1986).

2. According to Senator Jesse Helms, republican of North Carolina, "There are ten million people between our borders and the Panama Canal. If we sit back and allow communism to take over, how many of those ten million do you expect to flood across the border into the United States? Look back at what happened in Cambodia. Those people had only leaky boats. . . . The Soviet strategy is, and always has been, to encircle the United States with socialist nations. I wonder if I'm allowed to say this anymore. It's a strategy that was made possible, my friends, by the giveaway of the Panama Canal." (From the film *Quest for Power: Sketches of the New Right,* produced and directed by Saul Landau and Frank Diamond, 1983, pp. 36–37, of the transcript.)

3. *The Federalist Papers* was a series of essays written by Alexander Hamilton, James Madison, and John Jay to convince the public to adopt the Constitution of the United States. See Alexander Hamilton, James Madison, and John Jay, *The Federalist Papers* (New York: Mentor, 1961).

4. Even after the war, the Senate refused to accept Article X, the enforcement clause of the League of Nations, which, in Wilson's words, was

"the heart of the enterprise. . . . [It] says that every member of the League . . . solemnly engages to respect and preserve as against external aggression the territorial integrity and existing political independence of the other members of the league." For further discussion, see William Appleman Williams, *The Tragedy of American Diplomacy* (New York: Dell, 1967).

5. Walter LaFeber, *Inevitable Revolutions* (New York: W.W. Norton, 1983), p. 67; Peter Kornbluh, "U.S. Involvement in Central America: A Historical Lesson," *USA Today* (September 1983):45–47.

6. For studies of the national security elite, see Richard Barnet, *Roots of War* (Baltimore, Md.: Penguin, 1973); Lawrence Shoup and William Minter, *Imperial Brain Trust: The Council on Foreign Relations and United States Foreign Policy* (New York: Monthly Review Press, 1977); John C. Donovan, *The Cold Warriors: A Policy-Making Elite* (Lexington, Mass.: D. C. Heath, 1974); and Holly Sklar, ed., *Trilateralism* (Boston: South End Press, 1980).

7. Enacted July 26, 1947, the act established the National Security Council (NSC) and under it the Central Intelligence Agency and created the office of secretary of defense to oversee the Departments of the Army, Navy, and Air Force. The act's intent was "to provide a comprehensive program for the future security of the United States; to provide for the establishment of integrated policies and procedures for the departments, agencies, and functions of the Government relating to the national security."

The NSC includes the president, the secretaries of state, defense, army, navy, and air force, and a few other top officials. Among the NSC's duties are "to assess and appraise the objectives, commitments, and risks of the United States in relation to our actual and potential military power, in the interest of national security, for the purposes of making recommendations to the president." For further discussion of the act, see Alan Wolfe, *The Limits of Legitimacy* (New York: The Free Press, 1977), pp. 186–213.

8. On the secrecy of the CIA's budget, see Robert Borosage, "The King's Men," in Robert Borosage and John Marks, eds., *The CIA File* (New York: Grossman, 1976), p. 133; and U.S. Senate, *Hearings before the Select Committee on Intelligence: Whether Disclosure of Funds Authorized for Intelligence Activities Is in the Public Interest,* 95th Cong., 1st sess., April 27 and 28, 1977. On the concealment of atomic testing, see Paul Jacobs, "Clouds from Nevada: A Special Report on the AEC's Weapon Tests," *The Reporter* 16, 10 (May 16, 1957):29; and Paul Jacobs, "Precautions Are Being Taken by Those Who Know: An Inquiry into the Power and Responsibilities of the AEC," *The Atlantic* 227, 2 (February 1971):45–56. For more on nuclear testing, see Harvey Wasserman and Norman Solomon, eds., *Killing Our Own: The Disaster of America's Experience with Radiation* (New York: Delta Books, 1982), pp. 3–102.

9. On CIA economic analysis, see John Ranelagh, *The Agency: The Rise and Decline of the CIA* (New York: Simon and Schuster, 1986), p. 220. On the Agency's LSD testing, see John Marks, *The Search for the "Manchurian Candidate": The CIA and Mind Control* (New York: New York Times Books, 1979), pp. 53–86.

10. From the Declaration of Independence: "Prudence, indeed, will dictate that governments long established should not be changed for light and transient causes; and accordingly all experience hath shown that mankind are more disposed to suffer while evils are sufferable, than to right themselves by abolishing the forms to which they are accustomed. But when a long train of abuses and usurpations, pursuing invariably the same object, evinces a design to reduce them under absolute despotism, it is their right, it is their duty to throw off such government, and to provide new guards for their future security." Merrill D. Peterson, ed., *The Portable Thomas Jefferson* (New York: Viking Press, 1975), pp. 235–236.

11. See Joshua Cohen and Joel Rogers, *Inequity and Intervention: The Federal Budget and Central America* (Boston: South End Press, 1986), for an analysis of the costs of the current U.S. policy in Central America; the authors put the cost at $9.5 billion annually. Michael Klare, "The U.S. Defense Commitment in Latin America, *The Tribune,* April 19, 1984, p. B4, estimated the total expenditure to be twice that figure.

12. A document submitted by the then-secretary of state Dean Rusk to the Senate Foreign Relations Committee on September 17, 1962, listed 158 occasions on which U.S. troops were used overseas between 1798 and 1945; all but 20 or so were Third World interventions. U.S. Senate, *Instances of the Use of United States Armed Forces Abroad, 1798–1945: Hearing before the Committee on Foreign Relations and the Committee on Armed Services,* 87th Cong. 2nd sess., September 17, 1962.

On April 23, 1971, Senator Barry Goldwater submitted to the Senate Foreign Relations Committee, in the course of testimony on war powers legislation, U.S. Senate, *A Chronological List of 153 Military Actions Taken by the United States Abroad Without a Declaration of War: Hearings before the Committee on Foreign Relations,* 92nd Cong., 1st sess., April 23, 1971. Both lists excluded wars fought against Indian nations on the landmass that now makes up the United States.

13. Since taking office in 1981, the Reagan administration has spent hundreds of millions of dollars on the Nicaraguan contras, a small part of which has been publicly approved by the Congress. In 1982, Representative Edward Boland, a Massachusetts Democrat, successfully proposed an amendment prohibiting the expenditure of funds "for the purpose of overthrowing the government of Nicaragua." The amendment remained in effect until the end of fiscal year 1983. In 1983, $24 million in contra funding was approved for fiscal year 1984; no further money was formally authorized until $27 million in "humanitarian assistance" (nonlethal or logistical aid) was approved in 1985. In June 1986, the House of Representatives voted a further $100 million for the contras. It is clear, however, that the Boland Amendment was honored mainly in the breach and that if the total cost of the contra operation is figured in, including the building and maintaining of a logistical infrastructure in Honduras, the transfer of weaponry from the Pentagon in ways that do not show up on the contra funding accounts, the provision of "political aid" by the CIA, and multitudinous other means of laundering

funds, the yearly total would substantially exceed $100 million. After the June 1986 vote, *Newsweek* reported that the CIA, newly unleashed to run the contra operation, "is preparing to provide the rebel forces with covert logistical support, training, communications, and intelligence worth the equivalent of $400 million." Tom Morgenthau et al., "Rekindling the Magic," *Newsweek*, July 7, 1986, p. 20.

14. See the syndicated column by White House communications director, Patrick Buchanan, in which he presented the White House line. "With the vote on contra aid, the Democratic Party will reveal whether it stands with Ronald Reagan and the resistance—or Daniel Ortega and the communists." "The Contras Need Our Help," *Washington Post,* March 5, 1986. Also see the nationally televised address Reagan gave on March 16, 1986: "Clearly the Soviet Union and the Warsaw Pact have grasped the great stakes involved, the strategic importance of Nicaragua. The Soviets have made their decision— to support the Communists. . . . Now Congress must decide where it stands."

For a detailed account of the propaganda war that was directed from the White House, see Peter Kornbluh, *Nicaragua: The Price of Intervention* (Washington, D.C.: Institute for Policy Studies, 1987), pp. 205–211.

15. Personal communication with the author, May 1985. Nicaraguan president Daniel Ortega had flown to Moscow shortly after the House had voted against further contra funding. What Ortega did not announce was that the Mexican government had demanded that Nicaragua pay for its oil imports, a change in Mexican policy that resulted from U.S. pressure. The Soviets agreed to provide the Nicaraguan government with oil after Ortega explained to Mikhail Gorbachev the nature of the Nicaraguan dilemma. Ironically, after Ortega returned from the Soviet Union, the Mexicans reversed their position. See Kornbluh, ibid., pp. 117, 119.

16. As of late 1987, there were four major "covert" programs to support anticommunist insurgencies. The two principal beneficiaries were the Afghan insurgents, receiving in excess of $250 million annually, and the Nicaraguan contras. The National Union for the Total Independence of Angola (UNITA) and a coalition of three Cambodian forces were getting much smaller amounts.

# CHAPTER 2

# The Origins of the National Security Doctrine

*We are as a city set upon a hill, in the open view of all the earth, the eyes of the world are upon us, because we profess ourselves to be a people in Covenant with God.*
—Reverend Bulkeley[1]

In an ironic twist of history, the defeat of English imperialism on U.S. soil in 1783 cleared the way for the rise of a native U.S. imperialism that in less than one hundred years extended the thirteen colonies into a vast continental nation, with interests in overseas territories as well. By 1945, the United States had transformed itself into a world empire. This process of growth involved continuous military interventions and wars, followed in most cases by the expansion of the U.S. economic system into conquered territories. After the contiguous land was occupied, the United States extended its control to the Caribbean, Central America, and parts of Asia. This expansion was viewed by U.S. leaders as both just and necessary.[2] Unless we attribute U.S. expansionism to higher powers or aimless stumbling, we need to look at this pattern in order to explain today's policies.

An ambiguous relationship between the society and the state emerged from the American War for Independence. The soldiers in George Washington's army viewed a strong state as antithetical to a free society. The first U.S. constitution, the Articles of Confederation, reflected that sentiment; the articles lodged political power in the thirteen states and their assemblies. The men who crafted the articles' replacement, the 1787 constitution, knew that there had to be clear limits placed on the central government's powers. To postcolonial U.S. citizens, central government was an object of mistrust, to be limited, monitored, and checked.

The revolutionaries viewed the state as fundamentally incompatible with societal liberty, hence never quite legitimate. The colonists had ingested these attitudes well before Paul Revere took his famous ride. "What do we mean by the Revolution?" John Adams asked rhetorically in a letter to Thomas Jefferson. "The war? That was no part of the Revolution; it was an effect and consequence of it. The Revolution was in the minds of the people, and this was effected from 1760 to 1775, in the course of fifteen years, before a drop of blood was shed at Lexington."[3]

Revolutionary agitators and pamphleteers spoke and wrote about notions that went beyond the rights of individual citizens; these writers suggested that the citizenry in its collective form, the society, also had rights. According to this view, the state essentially contracted with this abstract collective and received the minimal and enumerated powers necessary to maintain social order. The Articles of Confederation expressed this popular understanding, to which John Adams referred, but so fettered the central government that it could not carry out the function of expanding the territories.

The revolutionary aspect of the social contract worked out by the colonists after their successful break with the British Crown carried over to the 1787 Constitution as well. This document contended that state legitimacy derived from the society, and the implications of that contention carried over into the new government as well. Although the nature of the social contract had changed, the mistrust of central authority, fear of its repressive possibilities, remained. The national government, even headed by the beloved George Washington, never achieved full legitimacy.

Although the Constitution created a central government capable of carrying out an expansionist policy, the stain of illegitimacy written into the parchment of the document could never be entirely washed away. Those who guided the state began to make policy in the context of a culture that was deeply suspicious of centralized power. The slogan "Give Me Liberty or Give Me Death" had lasting effects. It meant that natural rights were axiomatic, that the social body held these, and that the state could not take them away—a concept quite new to the historical process. The king as God's representative did not exist in the new world as of 1776; thus, the national government had to find its legitimacy in acceptance by the social order.

The question then was: What would the national government have to do to prove itself to the suspicious populace? The government's contract with society was interpreted from the outset as providing the social body with new wealth and resources, rather than taking from existing parts and redistributing to other segments. This expansionist quality was both conscious and necessary. James Madison, who wrote some of the most persuasive arguments for adopting a national government, exhorted his fellow citizens to "extend the sphere" as the one solution to the endemic problem of republics: the social struggles regarding the distribution of wealth.[4] When Madison suggested extending the sphere, he meant not only bringing in more citizens, but more social wealth also. Expansion was not only inherently rewarding to the citizenry, but offered protection against oligarchy as well.[5] So ingrained was the idea of expansion westward and the God-given task of taming the wilderness, that a Virginia nationalist, Thomas Jefferson, drafted a series of ordinances in the 1780s that allowed for new western territories to become states after a determined number of white males established residence.

James Madison, Alexander Hamilton, John Jay, and the other Founding Fathers had studied Greek democracy and European history and had culled the key lessons that they believed would allow the U.S. citizenry to enjoy a tranquility and a stability that had eluded both ancient and European societies. Even Thomas Jefferson, who at the end of his life still identified himself as first and foremost a citizen of Virginia, reflected, "I am persuaded that no Constitution was ever before as well calculated as ours for extensive empire and self-government"[6]

The expansionist motif, like the mistrust of state power, had become part and parcel of colonial culture by the 1770s, and those who subsequently inhabited the offices of decisionmaking internalized both aspects of the history and culture of the young nation.

## Zion in the Wilderness

The Seventeenth Century Puritans believed that they were "God's chosen people" who had been sent to build a "Zion in the wilderness." The colonists' idea that they had come to the "promised land" developed into more secular notions of power and empire, which took the form, among others, of popular and religious justifications for occupying Indian lands to the west. The historian James Truslow Adams highlighted one such justification when he cited a settler in the early nineteenth century who remarked, "It was against the law of God and nature that so much land should be idle while so many Christians wanted it to labor on and raise bread."[7]

U.S. expansionism, from the inception of the nation, differed from European models in part because of geographic circumstances. The colonists had fought a revolutionary war against European colonialism and forged an independent identity, and there were no powerful neighbors to menace U.S. borders. George Washington's farewell words to the nation, warning of the dangers inherent in "permanent alliances," became a key foreign policy guideline. It was logical and practical, given the conditions. The nation kept to its side of the Atlantic, moved its frontiers westward, and staked claims in more remote areas.[8]

By the 1820s, a consensus had formed that the United States had permanent and special interests throughout the Western Hemisphere, and President James Monroe gave notice to the European powers to keep out of this unilaterally defined sphere. The 1823 Monroe Doctrine pretentiously pledged, in exchange, that the United States would keep out of European affairs.[9] This audacious assertion of U.S. power was not backed at the time by a large military, but rather was shielded by vast distances and inter-European rivalry.

However, the Monroe Doctrine did demonstrate an attitude that U.S. leaders intended the world to know. Written by Monroe and Secretary of State John Quincy Adams,[10] the doctrine claimed an area of influence far beyond the borders of the United States—from the tip of Patagonia to the icebergs of Hudson Bay. In an earlier version of Monroe's claims, Thomas Jefferson had remarked, in the 1780s, that the United States wanted Spain to maintain its hold on Latin America "till our population can be sufficiently advanced to gain it from them piece by piece."[11]

Within the United States, the western lands served a variety of functions in preserving internal harmony. The West was won with relative ease in wars with Indian nations and later with Mexico and by purchasing lands from Europe. The new territories offered for the older society a seemingly endless supply of new wealth and resources; the territories also became a "safety valve," not in the sense of providing land and opportunity for the overflow working class, but for farmers who had used up their soil, for immigrants, and for speculators.[12]

## Manifest Destiny

Since the landings of the English settlers in the early seventeenth century, there had been a steady and constant movement to the

West. By the mid-nineteenth century, this trend was two hundred years old and for much of the population had become an axiom of U.S. life. When an ideology emerged that not only explained westward expansion as natural and good but indeed godly, it was met with popular enthusiasm. Manifest Destiny was the notion that a higher design mandated white Americans to move their frontiers rapidly westward.[13] Manifest Destiny expressed as well as resolved a tension that had existed from the birth of the nation. On the one hand, those values deemed necessary to foster a healthy and free society entailed a restrained and relatively weak central government. On the other hand, the need for and promise of more wealth for the society required a strong and flexible state. Manifest Destiny (as well as other patriotic ideologies filled with "destiny" and "freedom" rhetoric) helped to paper over this latent antagonism.

Those ideologies that became endemic to expanding U.S. culture offered not only explanations for the continual westward expansion but also justifications for the white American's "progress"; these justifications were based on ethnocentricity, racism, and the feeling, present since the Puritans, that the United States had a "special" destiny.[14] As the nineteenth century progressed, this became a justification for wars against the Indians and Mexicans that added to the territory of the United States; Manifest Destiny also provided impetus for initiatives to wrest colonized territory away from vulnerable European powers.[15]

## Coming of Age

The Civil War of 1861–1865 represented a conflict regarding the institution of slavery, a struggle between the largely preindustrial economy of the South and the developing industrial capitalism of the North. The Civil War also was a test of the authority of the federal government. The North's victory in the Civil War led to an acceleration of economic growth. Northern capital flowed not only into the previously slave South and the remaining western lands, but also began to find its way to Latin America. The expanded role of the president, thanks to the powers that Abraham Lincoln had claimed and won from Congress and the courts, would serve as precedent for future leaders who needed to push constitutional limits when the nation encountered "crisis."

By the 1890s, the foreign policy assumption of the Monroe Doctrine—that the United States would and should be supreme in the Western Hemisphere—had become commonly accepted, as had the implications of Manifest Destiny. Indeed, the importance of the labor, markets, and resources of the Latin territories and other areas were recognized by leading policymakers,[16] even though European banks and corporations remained dominant in certain Latin American countries well into the twentieth century. The equation of U.S. freedom and prosperity with expansion overseas became almost axiomatic by the mid-1890s.[17]

But the landmass between the Atlantic and Pacific oceans had been occupied. Frederick Jackson Turner, in his famous 1893 essay, "The Significance of the Frontier in American History,"[18] declared the frontier closed, and this recourse for ameliorating domestic miseries and solving factional problems—the reliance on new, contiguous territories with their inherent wealth and possibilities—ceased to exist. But even as the country sank into the depression of the 1890s and the government, with expectations of massive labor unrest, built armories in cities, Brooks Adams (the grandson of John Quincy Adams), Admiral Alfred T. Mahan (the naval strategist), and others proposed that James Madison's exhortation to "extend the sphere" be carried abroad.[19] They looked beyond the continental United States to China and the vast Orient as well as to the more accessible areas of Central America and the Caribbean.

The nineteenth century wars fought with the British and with the Indian nations had taken place on U.S. soil. By the mid-1890s, the nation's leading intellectuals, politicians, and businessmen felt that the time had come to test the country's strength abroad. Indeed, they counted on foreign markets and resources to help stimulate the economy and thus "solve" the depression.

In the last few years of the nineteenth century, the debate that took place in Congress, the press, and policy circles centered around how and where the United States should extend its influence, not whether expansion should take place. But unlike old-fashioned, European-style colonialism, the new foreign policy would maintain a formal commitment to the principles in the Declaration of Independence and democratic traditions. By avoiding cumbersome colonial administrations, the new foreign policy also would be less expensive. The new expansionism was announced formally after the policy actually had been adopted in the form of Secretary of State John Hay's "Open Door Notes."[20] The note of 1899 announced the primacy of U.S. interests in far-off Asia and neighboring Central America and the Caribbean. The "Open Door Notes" were "designed to establish principles, or rules of the game," wrote William Appleman Williams, "which Americans considered essential for the immediate and long-range effectiveness of the expansion of their political economy."[21] By the time Hay had delivered the last of these proclamations, the United States had become a formidable military and economic power with a variety of military expeditions under its belt, including the Spanish-American War.

Using the pretext of supporting Cuban independence, the United States pushed Spain out of the Americas and the Pacific Ocean and replaced the faded European colonial power with a new system of government that was neither colonial nor republican. It was a new form of empire, one that denied imperial intentions while practicing them with vigor. By 1900, the United States had developed an economy and a military of sufficient strength so as to be able to force open doors in several less-developed nations for its investors, merchants, bankers, and missionaries. Missionaries often served both as cultural emissaries and as links for U.S. business.[22] Although untested in war, the United States had emerged as a global power. Manifest Destiny had been extended overseas and justified as a divinely inspired mission to uplift dark-skinned peoples, thereby saving them from themselves and the decadent colonial powers.[23]

Historian Walter LaFeber called U.S. policy in the Caribbean and Central America in the 1890s "setting up the system."[24] This system, which allowed U.S. business easy access to the region, also avoided serious clashes with tradition. By prudent use of dollar and gunboat diplomacy, U.S. presidents established a unique kind of protectorate, one for which they assumed little responsibility.[25] U.S. business exploited the region's land, labor, resources, and markets, with military protection, while Washington avoided any obligations to these small nations.

By the time the United States entered World War I to test U.S. global might, the nation's forces had intervened in Central America and the Caribbean forty-five times. U.S. investors had gained control of vast amounts of foreign wealth, and no serious political candidate or party in the region could aspire to power for any length of time without the consent of the United States. Although publicly adhering to the sentiments embodied in the Declaration of Independence, the United States had added an informal and unstated clause to its basic policy document: For the Caribbean and Central American republics, "independence" meant asking U.S. permission before making any changes in economic or foreign policy. An illustration from U.S.-Nicaraguan relations dramatizes the general picture.

In 1909, Nicaraguan president Jose Zelaya, a "relatively benevolent, modernizing, authoritarian nationalist," withdrew certain business concessions that he had granted to U.S. concerns and brought in European and Japanese firms to aid Nicaraguans in building a canal through the San Juan route. He also began to negotiate a loan with a British bank.

Secretary of State Philander C. Knox labeled Zelaya's actions "European infiltration." He demanded that the Nicaraguan government cede to the United States a ninety-nine-year lease for a naval base in the Gulf of Fonseca and rights of permanent access for a canal through the San Juan del Sur route and that Nicaragua cancel its loan negotiations with the Bank of England and grant the United States a virtual monopoly on Nicaraguan borrowing and lending. Knox also accused the Nicaraguan president of "keeping Central America in tension of turmoil."[26]

Zelaya refused, and the United States organized the equivalent of a contra force against him. U.S. nationals participated in the anti-Zelaya forces, and two of them were captured, tried, and executed, after they were caught trying to blow up Nicaraguan ships. The United Fruit Company contributed $1 million to the attempt to oust Zelaya.

Zelaya was deposed, and Adolfo Diaz, the new U.S.-backed president, canceled the concessions Zelaya had granted to non-U.S. businesses and opened the way to a transfer to U.S. banks of more than 50 percent of Nicaraguan national bank assets. In addition, he gave the United States "rights in perpetuity" to the San Juan Canal route.

But finding a stable puppet acceptable to Nicaraguans proved to be more difficult than the economic takeover of the country. Because the Nicaraguan puppet government and its leaders, who were handpicked by the U.S. State Department, did not forge a consensus and maintain minimal order, President William Taft dispatched U.S. Marines to police the country, which they did until 1925. In 1926, still unable to find a suitable means of native rule, President Calvin Coolidge sent the troops back into Nicaragua. Between 1927 and 1933, when Congress cut off the funds for the occupation troops, the marines unsuccessfully chased the Nicaraguan resistance leader, Augusto Cesar Sandino, and his guerrilla bands and successfully trained a local gendarmerie, which emerged as the National Guard.

Thus, the essence of the "system" devised by the United States to maintain unfettered access to the labor, markets, and resources of Central America required a twofold process: tacit alliance with a governing class that was willing to accept or encourage U.S. supervision over its affairs with the quid pro quo of becoming junior partners and the understanding that Washington would use military force if U.S. interests were threatened. After he retired, General

Smedley Butler of the U.S. Marine Corps summed up his experience in protecting those interests:

> During [my thirty-three years in the Marine Corps] I spent most of my time being a high-class muscle man for Big Business, for Wall Street, and for the bankers. In short I was a racketeer for capitalism. . . . Thus I helped make Haiti and Cuba a decent place for the National City Bank to collect revenues. . . . I helped purify Nicaragua for the international banking house of Brown Brothers in 1909–1912. I brought light to the Dominican Republic for American sugar interests in 1916. I helped make Honduras "right" for American fruit companies in 1903.[27]

Butler also wrote that "corporations and banks that began with cautious entrepreneurial ventures in Central America and the Caribbean had by World War I become established giants in the area, and, in turn, had used their wealth and influence to gain the equivalent in political power." This commander of more than ten interventionist forces concluded that "the United States had established a tacit protectorate over the region."[28]

## Notes

1. James Truslow Adams, *The Epic of America* (Boston: Little, Brown, 1931), p. 45.
2. John Gallagher and Ronald Robinson, "The Imperialism of Free Trade," *Economic History Review* 6 (August 1953):5–6.
3. Bernard Bailyn, *The Ideological Origins of the American Revolution* (Cambridge, Mass.: Belknap Press, 1967) p. 1.
4. Alexander Hamilton, James Madison, and John Jay, *The Federalist Papers* (New York: New American Library, 1961), p. 83.
5. Ibid., no. 14.
6. From a letter to President Madison, April 27, 1809. H. A. Washington, ed., *The Writings of Thomas Jefferson* (New York: H. W. Derby, 1861), vol. 5, p. 444.
7. James Truslow Adams, *The Epic of America* (Westport, Conn.: Greenwood Press, 1980), p. 67. With similar reasoning, on February 16, 1835, Andrew Jackson wrote to the Seminole Indians in northern Florida: "The white people are settling around you. The game has disappeared from your country. Your people are poor and hungry. All this you have perceived for some time. . . . I tell you that you must go, and that you will go" (in Paul Jacobs and Saul Landau, *To Serve the Devil, Natives and Slaves* [New York: Random House, 1971], vol. 1, pp. 63–65. In 1815, on orders from Jackson, the Seminoles were wiped out by Gerard Gaines' forces. Henry Trumbull, *History of the Indian Years* (Boston: George Clark, 1841).

8. Alexander Hamilton and other of the more crusty Federalist party leaders considered forging an Anglo-U.S. entente so as to more efficiently assert their combined imperial urge, while placing a check—through the English monarch—on the pronounced democratic tendencies of the state legislatures. Hamilton urged an allilance with Britain to help in a war against France and an invasion to conquer parts of South America. William Appleman Williams, *Contours of American History* (Cleveland: World Publishing, 1961), pp. 174–175.

9. The War of 1812, in which the United States tried to take Canada from England, demonstrated to U.S. leaders that the new nation did not yet possess sufficient military might to challenge existing European control. But they also learned that the Atlantic Ocean's distance made it difficult for Europe to fight wars in the Western Hemisphere.

10. Adams also saw the perils of expansion, particularly the danger it posed to the framing of public policy. See J. Lloyd Mecham, *A Survey of United States-Latin American Relations* (Boston: Houghton Mifflin, 1965) pp. 29–36; Charles Francis Adams, ed., *Memoirs of John Quincy Adams* (Philadelphia: J. B. Lippincott, 1875), vol. 5, p. 176; and Dexter Perkins, *A History of the Monroe Doctrine* (Boston: Little, Brown, 1963), pp. 25 and 372.

11. From a letter to Archibald Stuart, January 25, 1786, in Julian P. Boyd, ed., *The Papers of Thomas Jefferson* (Princeton, N.J.: Princeton University Press, 1954), vol. 9, p. 218.

12. The territories also allowed the state to maintain a precarious equilibrium between the nation's two antagonistic labor systems. At those moments when the slave and nonslave systems appeared headed for inevitable conflict, the western states were offered as temporary sops, as in the compromises of 1830 and 1850. The compromise of 1850 provided for the admission to the Union of California as a free state, admitted Texas and New Mexico to the Union "without restriction" on slavery, strengthened the Fugitive Slave Act, and abolished the slave trade in the District of Columbia without prohibiting the owning of slaves. See Glyndon Van Dusen, *The Life of Henry Clay* (Boston: Little, Brown, 1937), pp. 399–413; Holman Hamilton, *Prologue to Conflict* (Lexington: University of Kentucky Press, 1964), pp. 133–188; and Ludwell H. Johnson, *Division and Reunion: America 1848–1877* (New York: John Wiley and Sons, 1978), pp. 14–20.

Ironically, slavery may well have prevented U.S. territorial expansion into Central America. Some Central American leaders saw the anticolonial United States as a potential protector from rapacious Mexico and approached the United States for possible statehood in 1849. However, northern antislavery advocates saw the move as benefiting their southern rivals and therefore opposed Salvadoran incorporation. See Steffan W. Schmidt, *El Salvador* (Salisbury, N.C.: Documentary Publications, 1983), p. 36; Mario Rodriguez, *El Salvador* (Englewood Cliffs, N.J.: Prentice-Hall, 1965), p. 62; and Walter LaFeber, *Inevitable Revolutions* (New York: W. W. Norton, 1983), p. 25.

Moves by U.S. politicians to make Cuba a state also encountered suspicion and opposition by antislavery exponents. The various unsuccessful attempts

THE ORIGINS OF THE NATIONAL SECURITY DOCTRINE

to annex Cuba, however, only dramatized the vital role of new territories in maintaining stability in a nation that housed two antagonistic production systems.

13. See Albert Weinberg, *Manifest Destiny* (Baltimore, Md.: Johns Hopkins University Press, 1935); and Wayne S. Cole, *An Interpretive History of American Foreign Relations* (Homewood, Ill.: Dorsey Press, 1974), pp. 85–146.

14. John Winthrop, governor of Massachusetts, wrote in 1630: "We shall find that the God of Israel is among us, when ten of us shall be able to overcome a thousand of our enemies; when we shall make us a praise and a glory. . . . For we must consider that we shall be as a City upon a hill." Robert C. Winthrop, ed., *Life and Letters of John Winthrop* (New York: Da Capo Press, 1971), vol. 2, p. 19.

15. Thomas Jefferson bought the Louisiana Purchase for little money when Napoleon was unable to defend the area because of military commitments elsewhere. William Seward bought Alaska knowing that Russia could not fight for it. The U.S. attack that precipitated the Spanish-American War occurred when Spain was weak.

In 1861, William Henry Seward, Lincoln's secretary of state, unsuccessfully advocated going to war with the French in Mexico as a way to unify North and South. In 1866, he again demanded that the French pull their troops out of Mexico. Instead, they installed the Austrian archduke Maximilian as the country's ruler. Lincoln then aided Mexican nationalist Benito Juarez in his efforts to expel the French. Juarez succeeded in 1867. See Cole, *An Interpretive History of American Foreign Relations,* p. 179; Thomas M. Leonard, *Central America and United States Policies, 1820s–1920s* (Claremont, Calif.: Regina Books, 1985), pp. 42–47; and Milton Plesur, *America's Outward Thrust* (Dekalb: Northern Illinois University Press, 1971), pp. 157–158.

16. The United States was not able to dislodge the English from their primary economic position in much of Latin America, but the English tacitly agreed to U.S. political control of the region. In 1895, for example, the United States sided with Venezuela in a boundary dispute with British Guiana, and Secretary of State Richard Olney wrote to the British foreign secretary on July 20, 1895, that British claims violated the Monroe Doctrine. Olney added that "today the United States is practically sovereign on this continent and its fiat is law upon the subject to which it confines its interposition." Lord Salisbury replied that the conflict was none of the United States' "damned business," but after Washington threatened war, the British backed down and submitted to arbitration. See Thomas A. Bailey, *A Diplomatic History of the American People* (Englewood Cliffs, N.J.: Prentice-Hall, 1980), pp. 438–447.

17. See William McKinley's war message of April 1898 and Lewis Gould, *The Spanish-American War and President McKinley* (Lawrence: University of Kansas Press, 1982), pp. 47–53. Also see Williams, *Contours of American History,* pp. 263–370, on McKinley; and William Appleman Williams, *The*

*Tragedy of American Diplomacy* (New York: Dell, 1967), pp. 53–83, on Theodore Roosevelt. Williams noted that for Roosevelt "it was America's 'duty toward the people living in barbarism to see that they are freed of their chains, and we can free them only by destroying barbarism itself.' Roosevelt believed that 'peace cannot be had until the civilized nations have expanded in some shape over the barbarous nations.' The inherent requirements of economic expansion coincided with such religious, racist, and reformist drives to remake the world" (p. 57).

18. Reprinted in William E. Leuchtenberg and Barnard Wishy, eds., *Frontier and Solution* (Englewood Cliffs, N.J.: Prentice-Hall, 1961), p. 37.

19. See Williams, *The Tragedy of American Diplomacy,* pp. 22–25, for a discussion of the thinking of these "expansionist intellectuals."

20. These were a series of circular notes sent by Secretary of State John Hay to all powers, September 6, 1899, and July 3, 1900, seeking equal commercial opportunity in China.

21. William Appleman Williams, *Empire as a Way of Life* (New York: Oxford University Press, 1980), p. 129; and William Appleman Williams, *America Confronts a Revolutionary World, 1776–1976* (New York: Morrow, 1976), pp. 134–138. Also see Gabriel Kolko, *Main Currents of American History* (New York: Harper & Row, 1976), pp. 42–49; and Cole, *An Interpretive History of American Foreign Relations,* pp. 268–281.

22. On the role of U.S. missionaries in Korea, see Fred Harvey Harrington, *God, Mammon, and the Japanese* (New York: Arno Press, 1980), pp. 125–143. On missionary activities in China, see Williams, *The Tragedy of American Diplomacy,* p. 55.

23. William McKinley said in 1898, "I walked the floor of the White House night after night until midnight; and I am not ashamed to tell you, gentlemen, that I went down on my knees and prayed Almighty God for light and guidance more than one night. And one night it came to me . . . first, that we should not give [the Philippines] back to Spain—that would be cowardly and dishonorable; second, that we could not turn them over to France or Germany—our commercial rivals in the Orient—that would be bad business and discreditable; third, that we could not leave them to themselves—they were unfit for self-government, and they would soon have anarchy and misrule over there worse than Spain's was; and fourth, that there was nothing left for us to do but to take them all, and to educate the Filipinos, and uplift and civilize and Christianize them, and by God's grace do the very best we could by them, as our fellow-men for whom Christ also died. And then I went to bed, and went to sleep and slept soundly." Quoted in Leon Wolff, *Little Brown Brother* (Garden City, N.Y.: Doubleday, 1961), p. 174.

24. LaFeber, *Inevitable Revolutions,* p. 9. See Chapter 7 for a discussion of the Roosevelt corollary and the Platt Amendment.

25. For a discussion of the case of Puerto Rico, a partial exception, see Landau and Jacobs, *To Serve the Devil,* pp. 271–279.

26. On the Zelaya-U.S. conflict, see Walter LaFeber, *Inevitable Revolutions,* pp. 38–48, and for Knox to Nicaraguan chargé, December 1, 1909, p. 322.

The United States also continued to try gaining financial supremacy, indeed monopoly, from England. See Thomas W. Walker, *Nicaragua: The Land of Sandino* (Boulder, Colo.: Westview Press, 1981), pp. 15–20.

27. Quoted in Jenny Pearce, *Under the Eagle* (Boston: South End Press, 1982), p. 20. Also see Lloyd Gardner, Walter LaFeber, and Thomas McCormick, eds., *Erection of the American Empire* (New York: Rand McNally, 1973) for a discussion of U.S. policy during this period; also see Williams, *Contours of American History*. For a list of interventions, see U.S. Senate, *Instances of the Use of United States Armed Forces Abroad, 1798–1945: Hearing before the Committee on Foreign Relations and the Committee on Armed Services,* 87th Cong., 2nd sess., September 17, 1962.

28. Pearce, ibid.

# CHAPTER 3

# Onto the World Stage

*By 1900 we were generally aware that our power had worldwide significance and that we could be affected by events far afield; from that time on our interests were constantly involved in important ways with such events.*

—George Kennan[1]

By entering World War I in April 1917, President Woodrow Wilson made a commitment that went far beyond excursions into Asia, Central America, and the Caribbean. U.S. entrance raised the question once again of the society's ability to control the state. The president and other advocates of entrance in the war had to create support for it with a three-year campaign, aided by provocative events such as the sinking of the *Lusitania* and the Zimmermann telegram, to achieve even a bare consensus among the public to pursue a war on another continent.[2]

President Wilson—whose narrow reelection margin in 1916 was based on his campaign slogan "He kept us out of the war"—had to resort to utopian phrases such as "the war to end all wars" as well as to economic incentives to break the historic pattern of nonintervention in European wars and wrest from a reluctant Congress a declaration of war. The president overcame the internal opposition, including his fundamentalist secretary of state, and, according to contemporary observers, a majority of the population, through the force of his advocacy and the efforts of an agile propaganda apparatus.[3]

The differences grew between the reality of U.S. foreign policy, especially with respect to Central America and the Caribbean, and the principles embodied in Wilson's statements on self-determination, which were repeated endlessly by political orators and read by grade

25

school students. On the eve of U.S. entry into World War I, as
President Wilson formulated his fabled ideology of the self-determination of nations and promised to make "the world safe for
democracy," he also ordered marines to occupy Haiti and the
Dominican Republic.[4]

Wilson maintained the Declaration of Independence as his ref-
erence point when he wrote in a March 1913 draft message for
Congress, "It shall not lie with the American people to dictate to
another people what their government shall be or what use they
shall have or what persons they shall encourage or favor." Secretary
of State Robert Lansing penned onto the draft's margin: "Haiti, S.
Domingo, Nicaragua, Panama."[5] President Wilson deleted the sen-
tence and a year later forged the first entangling military alliance
abroad as the United States entered World War I. During World War
I, the president sought and received vastly expanded powers, and
the first modern national security state was constructed. A crisis
mentality ruled, secrecy prevailed, and censorship and repression
were widespread.[6]

When he convinced Congress to declare war, the country went
along with the president, but profound disillusionment occurred
after the war, when Wilson's Fourteen Points (his goals for a just
peace and a democratic world) dissipated and the cause of democracy
suffered from the banalities and venalities of postwar European
leaders. Wilson's wartime consensus broke down. The Senate refused
to ratify the enforcement clause that would have given teeth to the
League of Nations Charter. The opposition to the League used George
Washington's warning against permanent alliances as an argument.
Massachusetts senator Henry Cabot Lodge said that the United States
had no interest in getting involved in Balkan squabbles. A handful
of opposition senators, led by William Borah of Idaho, took the
argument further and called for a hard evaluation of the policy of
expansionism per se. Their call went unheeded, as did Wilson's
desperate appeals for an imperial internationalism.

In 1919, as the French and British prime ministers haggled over
the amount of war reparations and the details of territorial boundaries,
a depression struck. The U.S. public, which had watched in dismay
as European leaders made a mockery of the democratic ideals for
which U.S. troops had fought, responded by crying "never again"
to involvement in European wars, and by 1920 this reaction to World
War I had set in. In place of Wilsonian globalism, a mood of so-
called isolationism developed. In practice, however, the policy was
more one of unilateralism. The United States did not abandon its
spheres in Latin America or Asia, but rather eschewed further

involvement in Balkan wars. Nevertheless, on one issue the U.S. government and its European allies found themselves in full agreement: the Russian Revolution.

## The Russian Revolution

*The events of the past months go to show that the central and most binding provision of the Treaty (and of the League) is an unrecorded clause by which the governments of the Great Powers are banded together for the suppression of Soviet Russia. . . . Apart from this unacknowledged compact there seems to be nothing in the Treaty that has any character of stability or binding force. Of course, this compact for the reduction of Soviet Russia was not written into the text of the Treaty; it may rather be said to have been the parchment upon which the treaty was written.*

—Thorstein Veblen[7]

When the Bolsheviks took power in Russia in the fall of 1917, the worst fears of capitalist leaders took on a concrete form. If the Bolsheviks remained in power, there would exist a permanent alternative model, and a source of encouragement, for the working classes of Europe, Asia, Africa, Latin America, and the United States. Having tried and failed to smash the communists through four years of intervention and support of counterrevolution, the capitalist powers did the next best thing: They stopped the spread of revolution. The formal colonial powers and the United States repressed nationalist revolutions in their own colonies and spheres of influence throughout the World War I period. By the 1920s, most of these revolutions had acquired some socialist tendencies, and some, such as China and Vietnam, had come under the influence of the Third International itself.

Inside the United States, the internal repression that began during World War I continued. The pattern for the post–World War II cold war was set by the infamous Palmer raids. Inspired and led by Attorney General A. Mitchell Palmer, these attacks and deportations concentrated on Bolsheviks and anarchists, many of them recently arrived immigrants. The anti-communist hysteria was spread through a propaganda apparatus similar to one used during World War I. The propagandists tried to convince the U.S. public that the communists were everywhere and that the Soviet Union was conspiring to overthrow the government of the United States.[8]

**Between the Wars**

The so-called isolationist years between the two world wars were misnamed. The term referred mainly to the refusal of the U.S. government to become involved in European conflicts, which, in part, was a reaction to the widespread public belief that national leaders had deceived the public about the reasons for entrance into the war and may have been manipulated by the financial interests that supported those leaders.[9] The world of 1919 was not safer for democracy, as Wilson had promised, and much of the U.S. populace suspected that the boys who died had done so in vain—or for the benefit of greedy bankers and weapons merchants.

Neither Congress nor President Franklin Delano Roosevelt changed basic policies during the "good neighbor" period. In Nicaragua, for example, the notorious National Guard was trained by occupying U.S. Marines to take over antirevolutionary duties, and in 1933 one of Roosevelt's first acts was to send an intimidating warship to Havana after the overthrow of the Machado dictatorship.

During the 1930s and 1940s, in fact, the United States encouraged dictatorial regimes in the Caribbean and Central America. The purpose was stability—for U.S. business interests. In this period, President Franklin Roosevelt reportedly said of Nicaraguan president Anastasio Somoza García, "He's a son of a bitch, but he's ours."[10]

A similar leader appeared in Cuba. Like Somoza, Fulgencio Batista was an army sergeant who moved into command when a "vacuum" arose during revolutionary activity in 1933. In Haiti, "Papa Doc" Duvalier ruled from the early 1940s with brutality toward his own people and servility toward Washington. In the Dominican Republic, "our son of a bitch" was General Leonidas Trujillo, who established a dictatorship rivaling the Somoza "kleptocracy" in Nicaragua.[11] In El Salvador, General Maximiliano Hernández Martínez slaughtered as many as thirty thousand peasants in 1932, but was duly recognized by Washington.

At home, the U.S. government had to use gentler means of managing dissent. As recessions came and went, the state alternately repressed and made concessions to militant publics. Thus, it maintained the republican form of government that had served so well as a base for the nation's miraculous growth and prosperity.[12] Farmers, workers, and small businesses became more vocal and expressive during critical times; these groups attacked big business and its connections with government and government as the servant of big business. Government, to maintain credibility, had to grant concessions or

attempt to coopt various populist, socialist, and progressive movements from the 1870s through the 1930s.

After World War I, this populist politics angrily reasserted itself
in a variety of movements related to both foreign and domestic
economic policies.[13] The populism of the 1920s, which Franklin
Roosevelt fashioned skillfully into the larger New Deal coalition of
the 1930s, could not be easily manipulated into foreign conflicts.
In the 1930s, class struggle emerged clearly; workers and union
leaders became militant about workshop issues as well as about
policies that again would allow callous capitalists to send men
overseas to fight "imperialist" wars. Press revelations and congressional investigations about the shenanigans of munitions manufac-
turers, bankers, and government officials prior to World War I, and
revelations by New Dealers that the large corporations were less
than mindful of the country's interests, bonded Roosevelt's public
foreign policy to an "isolationist" popular consensus. Behind the
scenes, however, Roosevelt, the Wilsonian internationalist, maneu-
vered the country into a tacit alliance with the nations that became
the Allies.[14]

While the cosmopolitans inside the cabinet and in policy circles
tried to prepare for the "inevitable" entry of the United States into
the European war in the late 1930s, the president continued to yield
in his speeches to the majoritarian "spirit that intimidates authority
and provides the popular energy to curb and resist it."[15] The
Depression of the 1930s—which was an almost total breakdown of
the economic system—had produced a surge in populism that in
turn threatened the myriad arrangements that the owners of the
productive system had reached with the officials of the state. The
rise of industrial unions, and their ability to wage massive strikes,
impressed itself at all levels of state authority, and the turbulence
of the 1930s in labor relations made a profound impression on the
circles that planned and executed policy.

### World War II

Once the Japanese succeeded in pulling the United States into
World War II, U.S. leaders began a debate over not only what war
policies to pursue, but what kind of peace to strive for as well. The
Allied alliance with the Soviet Union raised serious hackles among
one sector of the U.S. elite that saw the Soviets as an equally if not
more dangerous enemy than Adolf Hitler. Roosevelt occupied a center
position, arguing that the Soviets were bearing the brunt of Hitler's
fury and resources, which meant that the British would be able to

survive and that the United States could retake territories won by the Japanese in the Pacific.

In terms of war strategy, Roosevelt neither acceded to Joseph Stalin's plea to invade Nazi-occupied France and thereby relieve the German siege of the Soviet Union, nor did Roosevelt do nothing in hopes that the Nazis and the Soviets would exhaust each other. Instead, the United States supplied Stalin with war aid and launched a small invasion of North Africa, a precursor to a move into Italy. From 1942 until June 1944, U.S. forces in the Pacific fought Japanese troops on an island-by-island basis, while in North Africa outnumbered German forces stalled the Allied contingent. Meanwhile, the Soviets bore the brunt of the Nazi war machine, and with their almost miraculous victory over Hitler's best troops at the Battle of Stalingrad in 1942, Soviet troops put the Axis armies on the defensive.

The tide had been turned, as it had with Napoleon's invasion more than one hundred years earlier, by the severity of the Russian winter, but also by the incredible performance of the Red Army. It was not until June 1944, after the Nazis had suffered staggering losses and were in full retreat westward, that Roosevelt launched the second front with a massive invasion of German-occupied France. For Stalin and his staff, who had watched for two and one-half years as the Red Army had fought and lost millions of troops and the Soviet Union had lost millions of civilians, the United States was simply dallying on the margins of the main war, waiting for the Soviets and the Germans to weaken each other. Stalin brought this memory of the millions lost with him to the bargaining sessions with Roosevelt and Churchill in which postwar plans were made.

Some within the U.S. military and civilian command favored a continuation of the war through change in enemies. General George Patton, before he died, argued for an invasion of the Soviet Union by the Allied forces. However, Roosevelt and the majority of the command structure dismissed such an idea. The U.S. public was war-weary, and the Europeans were totally exhausted. The idea of attacking the Soviets intrigued some members of the ultraright but was dismissed by the very people who later emerged as the managers and planners of the U.S. national security state.

One fact was certain. Once the United States possessed nuclear weapons and no longer had to rely upon the Soviets as the only force that could neutralize Germany in the future, the notion of extending the wartime alliance became distasteful, if not downright unacceptable, to a majority of President Harry Truman's top aides.

## Notes

1. George Kennan, *American Diplomacy, 1900–1950* (New York: Mentor, 1951), Foreword.

2. See Barbara Tuchman, *The Zimmermann Telegram* (New York: Macmillan, 1966).

3. See George Creel, *How We Advertised America* (New York: Harper and Brothers, 1920), on the work of the Committee of Public Information at home and abroad.

4. On July 28, 1915, U.S. Marines went to Haiti, where they remained until 1934. In May 1916, Marines occupied the Dominican Republic, staying until 1924. Nicaragua of course was occupied throughout this period; marines held Cuba from 1917 until 1922, Panama from 1918 to 1920, and made a landing in Honduras in 1919. General John Joseph "Black Jack" Pershing also made several punitive raids into Mexico in 1918 and 1919.

5. Walter LaFeber, *Inevitable Revolutions* (New York: W. W. Norton, 1983), p. 54.

6. See Robert Justin Goldstein, *Political Repression in Modern America* (Boston: G. K. Hall, 1978), pp. 105–135; and Alan Wolfe, *The Seamy Side of Democracy* (New York: Longman, 1973), on such events as the violent suppression of antiwar socialists and trade unionists, the jailing of Eugene V. Debs, and the postwar deportations of thousands of radicals.

7. Thorstein Veblen, "The Economic Consequences of The Peace," in *Essays in Our Changing Order,* ed. by Leon Ardzrooni (New York: Kelley, 1934), p. 464.

8. See George Louis Joughn and Edward M. Morgan, *The Legacy of Sacco and Vanzetti* (New York: Harcourt Brace, 1948), on that most famous example of anticommunist hysteria during the 1920s. See also Saul Landau, "The Deportation of the IWW in 1917" (Master's thesis, University of Wisconsin, 1959).

9. See Helmuth C. Engelbrecht, *One Hell of a Business* (New York: Robert McBride, 1934); and Helmuth C. Engelbrecht and Frank Hanighen, *Merchants of Death: A Study of the International Armament Industry* (New York: Dodd, Mead, 1934). Also see Wayne S. Cole, *Senator Gerald P. Nye and American Foreign Relations* (Minneapolis: University of Minnesota Press, 1962).

10. Bernard Diederich, *Somoza: The Legacy of U.S. Involvement in Central America* (New York: E. P. Dutton, 1981).

11. National Bipartisan Commission on Central America, *Report of the National Bipartisan Commission on Central America* (Washington, D.C.: The Commission, 1984, 0-432-785), p. 22.

12. U.S. government policies toward farmers and urban workers historically have been a mixture of repression and concession. See Robert Justin Goldstein, *Political Repression in Modern America: From 1870 to the Present* (Cambridge, Mass.: Schenkman, 1978).

13. Irving Kristol called populism "a sentiment basic to any democracy—indispensable to its establishment but also ironically, inimical to its survival." From "Corporate Capitalism in America," *Public Interest* 41 (Fall 1975):127–128. Populism became anti-interventionist, in part, as revelations disclosed some of the nefarious activities of arms traders, bankers, and others who profited from the U.S. entry into World War I. See Horace C. Peterson, *Propaganda for War* (Norman: University of Oklahoma Press, 1939). Populism embodied sentiments ranging from antimonopolism to strong control of the arms industry, as well as antisemitism, racism against blacks, and a general hatred of what was thought of as the eastern Jewish banking establishment.

For a full treatment of populism as progressivism and as paranoia, see Richard Hofstadter, *The Progressive Movement, 1900–1915* (Englewood Cliffs, N.J.: Prentice-Hall, 1963); and Richard Hofstadter, *The Paranoid Style in American Politics, and Other Essays* (Chicago: University of Chicago Press, 1979).

14. Charles A. Beard, *President Roosevelt and the Coming of War: 1941* (New Haven, Conn.: Yale University Press, 1948), pp. 407–451; Charles A. Beard, *American Foreign Policy in the Making: 1932–1940* (New Haven, Conn.: Yale University Press, 1946), pp. 273–279; Robert A. Divine, *Roosevelt and World War II* (Baltimore, Md.: Johns Hopkins University Press, 1969), pp. 24–48. Also see Stephen E. Ambrose, *Rise to Globalism* (New York: Penguin, 1985), pp. 23–37.

15. Kristol, "Corporate Capitalism in America," p. 127.

# CHAPTER 4

# The Cold War

*It is an old picture . . . a picture of Western Europe and Western civilization threatened by hordes of invaders from the East.*

—William C. Bullitt,
former U.S. Ambassador to Moscow[1]

*We have about 50 percent of the world's wealth but only 3.6 percent of its population. . . . In this situation, we cannot fail to be the object of envy and resentment. Our real task in the coming period is to devise a pattern of relationships which will permit us to maintain this position of disparity. . . . We need not deceive ourselves that we can afford today the luxury of altruism and world-benefaction. . . . We should cease to talk about vague and unreal objectives such as human rights, the raising of living standards, and democratization. The day is not far off when we are going to have to deal in straight power concepts. The less we are hampered by idealistic slogans, the better. . . . The final answer might be an unpleasant one, but . . . we should not hesitate before police repression by the local government. This is not shameful since the Communists are essentially traitors. . . . It is better to have a strong regime in power than a liberal government if it is indulgent and relaxed and penetrated by Communists.*

—George Kennan,
Director of State Department Policy Planning, February 1948[2]

When the noncommunist Allies met at Bretton Woods in 1944 to shape the postwar world economy, they agreed that the United States would be the predominant economic force in the "free world."[3] By the summer of 1945, after U.S. Air Force planes had dropped two atomic bombs on Japanese cities, killing three-quarters as many people as the United States lost throughout the war, U.S. military superiority, if not invincibility, also was established.[4]

Unlike the rest of the war's major combatants, the United States emerged relatively unscathed; indeed, the war helped the country recover from the devastating Depression of the 1930s.[5] By 1945, the United States controlled three-fourths of the world's invested capital and two-thirds of the world's industrial capacity. The war also had brought full employment and a flexible economy that handled the conversion to peacetime production.

When the Japanese finally surrendered, the Allied leaders looked to Washington: What kind of order would U.S. leaders attempt to impose on the variety of social and economic systems around the world? In late 1945, the United States appeared as an economic Mecca and a political paradise to politicians and intellectuals in the war-ravaged capitals of Western Europe and the underdeveloped Third World. Nevertheless, U.S. leaders worried about how they could perpetuate their newly found preeminence. Recollections of militant workers', farmers', and citizens' movements of the 1930s remained alive in the memories of U.S. leaders as they attempted to plan a rational world order with Washington as the hub.

However, before the blood of World War II's more than 50 million victims had dried, revolutionary wars erupted around the globe—in Vietnam, Malaya, the Philippines, China, parts of Africa, and Greece. These nationalist struggles, which peaked after the war, actually had begun much earlier, often before the Russian Revolution and, as in Vietnam, even before the American Revolution. The military and administrative expenses of colonialism for the weakened imperial powers, the untenability of pre–World War II imperial rationales, and the newly gained strength of anticolonial movements all combined to spell the death of the old European empires.

But despite the high-sounding wartime rhetoric of freedom and self-determination, these wars of independence became submerged into the conflict between East and West. U.S. leaders shaded the world map into "free world" territories and those areas controlled by the communists. Congress backed the president as he forged military alliances, and like Truman, the members ignored George Washington's alliance warning that "nothing is more essential than that permanent inveterate antiparties against particular nations and passionate attachments for others, should be excluded; and that, in place of them, just and amiable feelings toward all should be cultivated." The U.S. government formed anti-Soviet pacts with the Western European nations as well as less overt antirevolutionary arrangements with underdeveloped states. The newly acquired partners would have junior, not equal, status.[6] Using its economic strength and nuclear monopoly, the United States dictated favorable terms for itself in the partnerships and, by providing Europe and Japan with generous aid with which to rebuild from the war, ensured that their recovery would follow the U.S. model.

The realities of world politics, economics, and military power put the United States in a unique position in 1945. U.S. leaders could have devised a postwar order based on the "grand alliance" of World War II, which would have included work with the Soviets, who still enjoyed a favorable image in the U.S. media. When Germany surrendered, a photograph appeared in the press of U.S. GIs and their Soviet counterparts embracing emotionally by the Elbe River as East met West in a victory over fascism. President Truman wrote to Stalin on May 8, 1945: "Now that the Nazi armies of aggression have been forced by the coordinated efforts of Soviet-Anglo-American forces to an unconditional surrender, I wish to express to you and through you to your heroic Army the appreciation and congratulations of the United States Government on its splendid contribution to the cause of civilization and liberty."[7] Instead of taking a conciliatory approach, however, U.S. leaders decided, after little public discussion or debate, to opt for exclusivity and polarization. In so doing, U.S. leaders had to convert the Soviet Union's image from that of heroic wartime friend to implacable postwar adversary.[8]

Led by Harry Truman and Winston Churchill, Western politicians and pundits erased recent history, when "Uncle Joe" Stalin was a close ally, and offered the public a stark choice: "freedom" or "totalitarianism." They declared that the moment had arrived when "nearly every nation must choose between alternative ways of life."[9] The postwar USSR, Truman and Churchill proclaimed, intended to dominate the world; the Soviets, both politicians warned, would use any and every tactic to do so. The global struggle for freedom during World War II became a postwar life-or-death situation.

The crisis premise of the cold war, and its corollary, that the burden of playing the lead role in the politics of free world "defense" and survival fell on the shoulders of the United States, made believers out of skeptics, fanatics out of sensible moderates. "This is not just a casual argument," Dwight Eisenhower declared, while still president of Columbia University in 1951. "This is a war of light against darkness, freedom against slavery, Godliness against atheism."[10] The successful transformation of this mammoth global conflict idea into policy was supposed to lead to what Henry Luce called the American Century, a phrase that indicated that any traditional tension between democracy and imperialism could be submerged under the universal

banners of freedom and free enterprise. The United States' historic
frontier would become the world itself. The Manifest Destiny of the
nineteenth century became the fate of the globe in the twentieth.
According to one of his biographers, Luce actually believed that
"God had founded America as a global beacon of freedom."[11]

### The Truman Doctrine: The World as Frontier

The American Century embodied the unstated implication that
the United States would become the arbiter of political and economic
systems in the rest of the world. Unlike most previous empires, the
United States had no worthy rivals. Indeed, its leaders presumed
that they could decide the world's fate. The problem was to figure
out a way simultaneously to control U.S. society without appearing
to make apparent alterations in its political and social forms.

The men who made global decisions based their world vision on
a concept of U.S. national security that Dean Acheson succinctly
summarized in 1947: "We are willing to help people who believe
the way we do, to continue to live the way they want to live."[12]
Domestically, national security required continuation of wartime
bipartisan consensus to eliminate debate on such basic issues as
budget allocations for "defense" and the means and ends of foreign
policy.

The Truman Doctrine, invoked to "save" Iran, Greece, and Turkey,
became the operating global national security policy in the cold
war era. The United States, the doctrine declared, had the right to
intervene in order to save entire regions from communist subversion.
From the Mediterranean in the late 1940s, to Southeast Asia in the
1960s, to Central America in the 1980s, the word "save," while used
in terms of combating Soviet influence, actually has meant preventing
indigenous independence movements from taking their countries out
of the U.S. orbit.

In March 1947, President Truman delivered a speech to Congress
that announced publicly what already had secretly become U.S.
policy.[13] In asking for aid to Greece, the president declared: "I
believe that it must be a policy of the United States to support free
peoples who are resisting attempted subjugation by armed minorities
or by outside pressures."[14] Ironically, some of the Greek recipients
of U.S. aid had collaborated with the Nazis just two years before,
and the foes of U.S. national security had composed the heart of
the Greek resistance to the Axis. The Soviets, supposedly intent on
world domination, became sufficiently intimidated by the very announcement of Truman's doctrine to abandon their Greek comrades

by cutting off their supplies.[15] With U.S. arms and advice, the Greek monarchy and right-wing military crushed the antifascist rebel movement and became one of the most repressive governments in Europe.

U.S. intervention in Greece marked a foreign policy turning point. When Britain informed Washington that it was ending its occupation in Greece, General George Marshall worried that this meant British withdrawal from the Middle East as well. As self-assumed heirs to Pax Britannica, U.S. leaders viewed a communist victory in the Greek civil war as unacceptable because such a victory would establish a trend away from capitalism in Europe. Strategically, Greece was seen by U.S. policymakers as the test of U.S. will and credibility with other Western European nations and as a launching pad for U.S. access to the great resources of the Middle East.[16] The stated justification for an emerging Pax Americana downplayed economic motivations. "The only way we can sell the public on our new policy," explained one government memorandum, "is by emphasizing . . . Communism vs. democracy" as a "major theme."[17]

Senator Arthur Vandenberg, a former Midwest isolationist won over to Truman's globalist posture, advised the president at the time of the Greek crisis to "make a personal appearance before Congress and scare hell out of the country."[18] By creating the specter of a new evil empire that threatened the postwar gains of the "free world," the Truman Doctrine served, in the words of Truman adviser Clark Clifford, as "the opening gun in a campaign to bring people up to [the] realization that the war isn't over by any means."[19]

To accomplish the American Century, the image of the heroic Soviets, who had contributed to "civilization and liberty," had to be undone. A rapid turnaround of public opinion required a rewriting of history, one that would deemphasize the "heroic" role of the Red Army and instead concentrate on events after the war, such as the Berlin crisis.[20]

## Creating a Permanent Enemy

In the postwar period, the most convincing case for Soviet perfidy arose out of the disposition of Eastern Europe; here, the Soviets broke promises to the West about assuring free elections in Poland and other Eastern European states and instead replaced the destroyed semifeudal order with Communist party–led governments.[21] The United States accused the USSR of having set up "satellite" states with puppet governments. To the large number of Polish and other Eastern European voters in the United States, who already shared anti-Soviet sentiments, and to other members of the public as well, the argument was immediately persuasive.[22]

Yet while Stalin was determined to retain the Eastern European states won from the Axis as a buffer zone, the objective realities of postwar Soviet life hardly were conducive to launching an aggressive campaign for world domination. "In no way did the Soviet Union appear, at that moment, as a military threat to this country," George Kennan wrote. "The Soviet Union was utterly exhausted by the exertions and sacrifices of the recent war."[23]

Soviet war losses were staggering, far beyond what any other nation had suffered: an absolute loss of between 25 and 30 million persons;[24] another 20 million wounded; 200 major cities destroyed. In German-occupied areas, two-thirds of all dwellings were demolished. In the face of such devastation, the Soviet state attempted to mobilize the population to the tasks of internal reconstruction.

The Soviets actually eschewed opportunities to advance communist causes in Italy and France and bowed quickly to U.S. military pressure, or outright threats, in Iran and Turkey. The Soviets lacked the economic and military capability needed for an aggressive policy that would have entailed operations on several fronts. The Soviet economy was destroyed, and the population was tired and war-ravaged—hardly the ingredients for a successful empire. The United States, on the other hand, had a monopoly on nuclear weapons for the first four years after the war and a booming economy. The U.S. cultural apparatus had acquired skills and sophisticated methods of selling, presenting, and fashioning images unsurpassed in the Western and certainly Eastern parts of the world. These techniques had become institutionalized on Madison Avenue and in Hollywood. The United States developed television technology for home use before the Soviets had cleared the rubble from their bombed-out cities.

The postwar world unquestionably offered U.S. leaders an opportunity for world shaping. U.S. ideals had triumphed. The U.S. version of democracy, its Declaration of Independence, its presidents' proclamation of the four freedoms[25] had inspired the forces of freedom in the war against fascism.[26] It should have appeared to U.S. leaders that, in FDR's words, they had "nothing to fear but fear itself." Instead, they feared independence for others, and they feared any loss of control abroad or at home.

### The Meaning of Freedom

Aside from its sensational, irrational side, fear of communism and the Soviet Union had a historically consistent and materially rational component. The onset of the cold war signaled the resumption of the hostility that the capitalist democracies traditionally had displayed toward the USSR.[27] That hostility was fundamentally based on a fear of and an objective antagonism toward the Soviets' organization of their society. They advocated socialism—public ownership of productive property. The Soviets placed severe limits on outside access to their labor force, markets, and raw materials. The Soviets were atheists and did not believe in the basic notions of free speech, press, and assembly as understood by U.S. and Western European populations. The Soviets were collectivists, eschewing the notion of individualism so basic to U.S. capitalism and consumerism.

Conflicts arising during the cold war years, whether in the First, Second, or Third World, were seen by men in Washington, as by the public at large, as part of a global struggle for hearts, minds, cultures, and ways of life. The cold war was a war between two antagonistic social, political, and economic systems. As President Eisenhower told Senator Styles Bridges in May 1957, after more than ten years of global struggle between the United States and Soviet Union, "I want to wage the Cold War in a militant but reasonable style whereby we appeal to the people of the world as a better group to hang with than the communists."[28]

By "the people of the world" Eisenhower meant Third World reformers and revolutionaries. The cold war U.S. mentality assumed that only two choices existed—"hanging with" the communists or siding with the United States. Such a stark and threatening option appeared unnecessary and even absurd to liberation leaders throughout the underdeveloped world, many of whom fought against the Axis and quoted the U.S. Declaration of Independence as a statement of their basic ideals. Vietnamese leader Ho Chi Minh used that document as the basis for writing the Vietnamese constitution.[29] Like all Third World communists in the postwar period, Ho Chi Minh was also a nationalist, whose primary political passion was national liberation.

The participants of a failed coup attempt in El Salvador in 1944 were similarly inspired by the notions of freedom espoused by U.S. leaders during the war. A *Time* reporter described their April action as follows:

> The people here drank their sedition directly from the slogans of the United Nations. It was possible for the Diario Latino to conduct an anti-Martinez campaign for a whole year merely by featuring phrases of Roosevelt and Churchill on the Four Freedoms. Perhaps naively, they believed them. They were convinced by its utterances the United

States would not look unkindly on their efforts to unfurl the Atlantic Charter on this bit of Pacific coast. Their leaders botched matters, and the first thing they knew, the embassy doors were slammed in their faces when they sought asylum from their hangmen. . . . The State Department responded to the *Time* correspondent that asylum might be extended to those threatened by mob violence, but never to anybody pursued by the constituted authorities. In less stuffy language, a dictator fleeing the retribution of his people would find embassy doors ajar, but for democrats hunted by the dictator's goons they would be bolted. It was an elucidation that could not fail to impress the Salvadoran public.[30]

Salvadorans who revolted in 1944—like their heirs of today—also were fighting for Franklin Roosevelt's four freedoms: freedom of speech, freedom of worship, freedom from want, and freedom from fear. The Salvadorans' fate, however, was inextricably determined by the unspoken but, for Washington policymakers, most important fifth freedom—the freedom for the United States to enjoy unimpeded access to labor, land, resources, and markets. As in earlier years, U.S. leaders judged less-developed nations not by their economic or political success or the openness of their political systems, but by their degree of affinity for U.S. policies.

It is difficult to find one case of a right-wing, repressive, or outright fascist regime in the postwar Third World that the United States did not ally with, arm, or support economically; it is equally difficult to discern a case of U.S. support for a genuine nationalist revolution since 1945. Right-wing governments invariably offered their labor forces, markets, and resources to U.S. companies, while genuinely nationalist ones tried to bring under some state control the key sectors of their economies.[31]

Noam Chomsky termed the fifth freedom the "freedom to rob and exploit," adding: "Infringement on the four official freedoms in enemy territory always evokes much agonized concern. Not, however, in our own domains. Here, as the historical record demonstrates with great clarity, it is only when the fifth and fundamental freedom is threatened that a sudden and short-lived concern for other forms of freedom manifests itself, to be sustained for as long as it is needed to justify the righteous use of force and violence to restore the Fifth Freedom, the one that really counts."[32]

For the United States to uphold the fifth freedom in a world stirring with movements intent on gaining the other four, U.S. leaders would have to commit vast resources on every continent to hold back—and even roll back—the rising tide of revolutionary nationalism. At a moment when U.S. leaders publicly espoused the wartime rhetoric of freedom and self-determination, a new structure and method for waging counterrevolution—secret, covert, and hidden from public and world scrutiny—had to be constructed: the national security state.

## Notes

1. Quoted in W. A. Swanberg, *Luce and His Empire* (New York: Charles Scribner's Sons, 1972), p. 306, from an article entitled, "The World From Rome," *Life* (December 1944).

2. Also see George Kennan, "Morality and Foreign Policy," *Foreign Affairs* 64, no. 2 (Winter 1985/86):205–218.

3. See Walter LaFeber, *America, Russia and the Cold War, 1945-1966* (New York: John Wiley, 1975); John L. Gaddis, *The United States and the Origins of the Cold War, 1941-1947* (New York: Columbia University Press, 1972); Michael Moffitt, *The World's Money* (New York: Simon and Schuster, 1983), pp. 13–25; and Adam Ulam, *The Rivals: America and Russia Since World War II* (New York: Viking, 1971).

4. On the use of atomic bombs to prevent Soviet entry into the Asian theater, see Gar Alperovitz, *Atomic Diplomacy* (New York: Penguin, 1985). Also see Lyuba Zarsky, Walden Bello, and Peter Hayes, *American Lake: Nuclear Peril in the Pacific* (Melbourne: Penguin Books, 1986), and Stephen E. Ambrose, *Rise to Globalism* (New York: Penguin, 1985), pp. 93–101.

5. Official unemployment figures showed 1.5 million unemployed in 1929, 12.8 million unemployed at the Depression's height in 1933, falling to 8.1 million in 1940. Wartime production and conscription brought the figure down to 1 million or less in 1943, 1944, and 1945, but it rose to only 3.6 million in 1949, falling back to 1.8 million in 1953, and reaching peaks of 3.5 million (1954) and 4.6 million (1958) with the Eisenhower recessions. The average unemployment rate during the 1930s was 18 percent; the 1950s average was 4 percent. Total Gross National Product for all of the 1950s was also more than double that of the 1930s, in constant dollars. See William Lerner, ed., *Historical Statistics of the United States* (Washington, D.C.: Bureau of the Census, 1976), part 1, pp. 135 and 224.

6. The key alliance was the North Atlantic Treaty Organization (NATO), undertaken in 1949; for a discussion of its international implications and the misleading way it was sold to the U.S. Congress, see Ambrose, *Rise to Globalism,* pp. 174–181. Also see Dean Acheson, *Present at the Creation* (New York: W. W. Norton, 1969), pp. 352–382; and Richard Barnet, *The Alliance—America, Europe, Japan* (New York: Simon and Schuster, 1983). The Australia–New Zealand–United States Alliance (ANZUS) was formed in 1952. Today, U.S. bases may be found in Australia, Belgium, Bermuda, Canada, Greece, Iceland, Italy, Japan, the Netherlands, Norway, Panama, the Philippines, Portugal, South Korea, Spain, Turkey, the United Kingdom, and West Germany. Facilities are maintained in the British-owned territories

of Bermuda and Diego Garcia, the Danish territory of Greenland, and the
U.S. territories of Ascension Island, Guam, Johnson Atoll, the Marshall
Islands, Midway Island, the Marianas Islands, and the U.S. Virgin Islands.
By 1956, the United States had defense pacts with forty-two nations, which
prompted Adlai Stevenson to comment that "the sun never sets on an
American commitment." The emerging national security apparatus did not
respond well to the notion of "neutralism" espoused by India's leaders as
they won independence from England, or by Yugoslavia, which broke away
from the Soviet camp. Such complexity would force the national security
elite to add a disturbing gray color to its black-and-white picture of the
world.

7. *Public Papers of the Presidents of the United States: Harry S Truman,
1945* (Washington, D.C.: U.S. Government Printing Office, 1961), p. 51.

8. One of the means used to turn the positive Soviet image into a
negative one was by equating Stalin with Hitler and Soviet communism
with German Nazism. On May 13, 1947, President Truman said, "There isn't
any difference in totalitarian states. I don't care what you call them, Nazi,
Communist or Fascist." *Public Papers of the Presidents of the United States:
Harry S Truman, Containing the Public Messages, Speeches and Statements
of the President, January 1, 1947–December 31, 1947* (Washington, D.C.:
U.S. Government Printing Office, 1963), p. 238. Also see Les K. Adler and
Thomas Paterson, "Red Fascism: The Merger of Nazi Germany and Soviet
Russia in the American Image of Totalitarisms, 1930's–1950's," *American
Historical Review* 75 (February-April 1970):1046–1064.

On Henry Wallace, Harold Ickes, Claude Pepper, and others who sought
a policy of cooperation, see Acheson, *Present at the Creation,* pp. 258–
260, 298–300; and Lloyd Gardner, *Architects of Illusion* (Chicago: Quadrangle
Books, 1970), pp. 200, 292–293.

9. *Public Papers of the Presidents of the United States: Harry S Truman,
1947* (Washington, D.C.: U.S. Government Printing Office, 1963), p. 178.

10. Dwight David Eisenhower, *Mandate for Change* (New York: Doubleday, 1963), p. 85.

11. Swanberg, *Luce and His Empire,* p. 217.

12. U.S. House of Representatives, Committee on Foreign Affairs, *Hearings: Assistance to Greece and Turkey: The Marshall Relief and Reconstruction Are Chiefly Matters of American Self-Interest,* 80th Cong., 1st sess.,
May 8, 1947, p. 43. Also see William Appleman Williams, *America Confronts
a Revolutionary World* (New York: William Morrow, 1976), p. 164.

13. Lawrence Wittner, *Cold War America* (New York: Holt, Rinehart, and
Winston, 1978), p. 31. Also see Lawrence Wittner, "The Truman Doctrine
and the Defense of Freedom," *Diplomatic History,* no. 4 (Spring 1980):161–
187; Lawrence Wittner, *American Intervention in Greece: 1943–1949* (New
York: Columbia University Press, 1982), and Acheson, *Present at the Creation,*
pp. 290–301.

14. Ambrose, *Rise to Globalism,* p. 132.

15. Stalin severely criticized even limited assistance given to the Greek
rebels by Marshal Tito. "What do you think," Stalin asked Yugoslavia's

vicepremier in early 1948, "that Great Britain and the United States—the United States, the most powerful state in the world—will permit you to break their lines of communication in the Mediterranean? Nonsense. . . . The uprising in Greece must be stopped, and as quickly as possible." Cited by Lawrence Wittner, *Cold War America*, p. 36.

16. See Wittner, *American Intervention in Greece;* Wittner, "The Truman Doctrine." Also see Ambrose, *Rise to Globalism,* pp. 79–80; Robert Dallek, "The Postwar World: Made in the USA," in Sanford Ungar, ed., *Estrangement* (New York: Oxford University Press, 1985), pp. 27–50; and Gabriel and Joyce Kolko, *The Limits of Power: The World and United States Foreign Policy, 1945–1954* (New York: Harper & Row, 1972), p. 72.

17. Wittner, *Cold War America*, p. 33.

18. Eric Goldman, *The Crucial Decade* (New York: Vintage Books, 1960), p. 59.

19. Cited in Noam Chomsky, *Turning the Tide* (Boston: South End Press, 1985), p. 45. Also see Wittner, *American Intervention in Greece.*

20. On the Berlin crisis, see Ambrose, *Rise to Globalism,* pp. 172–174; and Acheson, *Present at the Creation,* pp. 345–357.

21. On Stalin's interest in securing a "buffer zone," see Walter LaFeber, *America, Russia, and the Cold War* (New York: John Wiley and Sons, 1967), pp. 12–20, 29–34; and John Lewis Gaddis, *Russia, the Soviet Union, and the United States: An Interpretive History* (New York: John Wiley and Sons, 1978), pp. 175–193. On Soviet–Eastern European relations, see Joyce and Gabriel Kolko, *The Limits of Power* (New York: Harper and Row, 1972), pp. 176–217.

22. Ambrose, *Rise to Globalism,* p. 110. The Soviets could have made an equally strong case against U.S. control of most of Latin America. The United States dominated most of the hemisphere through puppet dictators, most of whom ruled through brutal repression. As historian Stephen E. Ambrose captured the paradox: "Free elections in East Europe would result in anti-Soviet governments but it was equally true that free elections in Latin America probably would bring power to anti-American governments" (p. 63).

23. George Kennan, "Containment: Then and Now," *Los Angeles Times,* December 29, 1985. For more on Kennan's views, see John Donovan, *The Cold Warriors: A Policy-Making Elite* (Lexington, Mass.: D. C. Heath, 1974), pp. 58–80; George Kennan, *Memoirs: 1925–1950* (Boston: Little, Brown, 1967); and Gardner, *Architects of Illusion.*

24. According to James Backett, *Demographic Trends and Population Policy in the Soviet Union* (Washington, D.C.: U.S. Government Printing Office, 1962), pp. 509–510, "Between 1941 and 1946 the Soviet Union experienced an absolute decline of between 25 and 30 million persons. Some indication of the military losses can be had by comparing prewar and postwar populations by sex. There were probably about 95 million males and 105 million females in mid-1941. At the beginning of 1950 the estimates show only 78 million males and 102 million females. The net

declines of 17 million males and 3 million females would suggest that male military losses may have approached 15 million."

25. The four freedoms were proclaimed by President Roosevelt on January 6, 1941, in his annual message to Congress; they were freedom of speech and expression, freedom of worship, freedom from want, and freedom from fear.

26. Unquestionably, the Red Army bore the brunt of actual fighting. Compare the figure on Soviet dead with the 405,400 U.S. soldiers killed in the war.

27. Beginning in 1918, when U.S., British, French, and Japanese troops invaded Siberia to support czarist forces against the Bolsheviks, Soviet relations with the West have been difficult. Washington did not recognize the Soviet government until 1933. At the Locarno Conference of 1925–1926, British and French diplomats sought to involve Germany in an anti-Soviet bloc; at Munich in September 1938, British prime minister Neville Chamberlain gave Germany a "free hand" to invade Russia. See Carl Marzani, *We Can Be Friends* (New York: Garland Publications, 1971), pp. 114–141; and Frederick Lewis Schuman, *American Policy Toward Russia Since 1917* (Westport, Conn.: Hyperion Press, 1977). On relations during World War II, see Robert Beitzell, *The Uneasy Alliance* (New York: Alfred A. Knopf, 1972). For a highly partisan but nonetheless interesting account, with an introduction by Senator Claude Pepper, see Michael Sayers and Albert E. Kahn, *The Great Conspiracy Against Russia* (New York: Boni and Gaer, 1946).

28. Cited in Stephen E. Ambrose, *Eisenhower, the President* (New York: Simon and Schuster, 1983–84), p. 380.

29. Even earlier, during the Versailles conference in 1919, Ho had approached President Wilson's residence hoping to gain his support for a permanent Vietnamese presence in the French Parliament. "The appeal went undelivered. United States Marines, guarding President Wilson in his quarters, chased the would-be petitioner away, 'like a pest.'" James Earys, *In Defence of Canada, Indochina: Roots of Complicity* (Toronto: University of Toronto press, 1983), p. 4.

30. Cited in Noam Chomsky, *Turning the Tide,* p. 43.

31. Examples include Iranian President Mohammed Mossadegh, elected in 1951, who sought to nationalize his country's oil fields and was overthrown by the CIA in 1953; the Arbenz presidency in Guatemala, ousted by a CIA coup in 1954; the Cuban Revolution, invaded in 1961; the Allende presidency in Chile, attacked from 1970 to 1973; and numerous instances in Africa and Asia during the 1950s and 1960s. A more recent, although more restrained, example is the Alan Garcia administration in Peru. Examples of rightist governments encouraging exploitation of their resources and labor force by foreign firms also are numerous, including the U.S.-backed regimes in Iran, Guatemala, and Chile, as well as the regimes of South Korea, Duvalier's Haiti, Marcos' Philippines, and Indonesia.

32. Chomsky, *Turning the Tide,* p. 47.

# CHAPTER 5

# The National
# Security State

*The task of a public officer seeking to explain and gain support for a major policy is not that of a writer of a doctoral thesis. Qualification must give way to simplicity of statement, nicety and nuance to bluntness, almost brutality, in carrying home a point. . . . In the State Department we used to discuss how much time that mythical "average American citizen" put in each day to listening, reading, and arguing about the world outside his own country. Assuming a man or woman with a fair education, a family, a job in or out of the house, it seemed to us that ten minutes a day would be a high average. If this were anywhere near right, points to be understandable had to be clear. If we made our points clearer than the truth, we did not differ from most other educators who could hardly do otherwise. So our analysis of the threat combined the ideology of communist doctrine and the power of the Russian state into an aggressive expansionist drive, which found its chief opponent and, therefore, target in the antithetic ideas and power in our own country.*

—Dean Acheson[1]

*It must be the policy of the United States to support free peoples who are resisting attempted subjugation by armed minorities or by outside pressures.*
—Harry Truman[2]

After World War II, U.S. citizens continued to believe that they lived under the same democracy as did their forefathers, with the durable republican government that the Founding Fathers had fashioned and that Abraham Lincoln had fought a civil war to preserve. But at the same time that the populace prepared to resume peacetime life, the United States became the center of the largest imperial system ever known in world history. The U.S. citizenry felt it had prevented Hitler from imposing his tyranny, and in the postwar period, U.S. power now was seen as the only means to stop the new tyranny—communism. The United States, its leaders told the world, was the only nation able to play the role of defender of freedom and keep the banner of liberty flying high.

However, as the 1950s began with the cold war threatening to become a hot war in Europe and in parts of the Third World, the U.S. population found itself living amid confusion and contradiction. The 1945 promises of world peace and cooperation apparently had evaporated, and most believed the communists were to blame. The war mentality continued, with a two-year hiatus, into the postwar period. Basic U.S. freedoms, such as speech, press, and assembly, were being limited by national security "needs."[3] The open government of law had turned into a secret government that disregarded the law behind the vague rubric of "national security." The leaders of the most powerful nation on earth declared that a clear and present danger—the international communist conspiracy—threatened "our" way of life.

The creation of a permanent enemy and the expansive commitments implied by the Truman Doctrine necessitated the development of a vast bureaucratic apparatus capable of waging both hot and cold wars around the globe. The national security state as it emerged legislatively and practically in the late 1940s was a new way of governing the United States in peacetime. Policymakers at the time saw this state as a necessary fusion of power and flexibility in the executive so as to allow the United States to secure its perceived global economic, political, and military interests.

By invoking national security, the president could claim wartime powers during peacetime. "Maximum flexibility" to deal with the communist enemy emerged as a policy need, one that required the U.S. public to accept that dealing with the Soviet devil required unusual and indeed unprecedented changes in the U.S. way of conducting peacetime political affairs both at home and abroad.

In the early postwar years, Washington created military alliances— the North Atlantic Treaty Organization (NATO), the Southeast Asia Treaty Organization (SEATO), the Central Treaty Organization (CENTO), and the Australia–New Zealand–United States Alliance (ANZUS)—the charters of which prohibited intervention by one state in the internal or external affairs of another for any reason. In addition, the United States signed the U.N. and Organization of American States (OAS) charters.[4] While the United States supported the birth of an elaborate system of international laws and institutions to prevent intervention, the government simultaneously erected national security agencies, such as the CIA, that would allow Washington policymakers to covertly intervene abroad—thereby permitting them to circumvent the new international legal order with impunity, or "plausible deniability."

The National Security Act of 1947 and a series of other measures established the CIA, the National Security Council, and related agencies. But these measures also provided for a parallel state structure—a state within the state—that would be inaccessible to the public and to Congress.[5] This structure had a large, separate, and partly hidden budget endowed with enormous powers for military activity without the constitutional scrutiny of Congress. "Classified," "eyes only," "top secret" became everyday terms within the national security apparatus and, before long, throughout the government.

The visible, accountable, and legal part of the government apparatus began to live in a strange cohabitation with the "lawless state."[6] The national security sector gained increasing power from this arrangement and with it the ability to withhold from the legal state ever larger areas of information about "security" activities.[7] The result was a bifurcated state, part of which was open and accessible to the U.S. public and part of which was a secret, suprastate entity whose agenda and inner workings had to be kept not only from the enemy, but from the state's own citizens as well. Indeed, the "enemy" knew far more about this secret state's activities than did the U.S. public. General George C. Marshall, secretary of state, sent a memo to President Truman in February 1947 that expressed concern about the scope of the CIA's mandate: "The powers of the proposed agency seem almost unlimited and need clarification."[8]

### The Domestic Cold War: Bipartisanship and Repression

To wage a cold war and construct a national security state required that U.S. leaders establish domestic consensus at home among elites and the mass public. In the postwar era, President Truman garnered consensus by convincing Congress of the advantages of bipartisanship and intimidation of those who disagreed.

Historian Stephen E. Ambrose called Truman's policy an "open-ended doctrine" that "broke sharply with America's past." In order to make the policy work politically, another new practice had to be established: bipartisanship among governing elites. The "isolationist" Republicans, the America Firsters,[9] the tight-fisted midwestern conservatives, and the public at large had to be convinced of the gravity

of the situation, the urgency of the need, and the relationship, for
example, of events in Greece, Turkey, or Iran to U.S. interests.
Truman successfully put the argument to conservative Republicans
as one based on the future of freedom, of U.S. obligations, of the
immediate threat posed by Soviet communist ambitions. Those in
Congress who raised objections were furiously Red-baited.[10]

Bipartisanship eliminated meaningful congressional debate about
the premises and day-to-day exercise of foreign policy. Beginning
with the day in 1947 when Senators Arthur Vandenberg and Robert
Taft listened to President Truman explain the nature of the communist
menace and decided to abandon their conservative, isolationist convictions, congressional bipartisanship regarding foreign affairs remained cemented well into U.S. involvement in the Vietnam War.[11]

Taft reluctantly acceded to Truman's funding requests for the
rebuilding of Western Europe, and Taft did not make public waves
about the expanded power of the executive to make foreign policy
through the use of national security prerogatives. National security
from its inception in 1947 as formal policy and language depended
upon the public's acceptance of the "clear and present danger" from
"the enemy" to U.S. security. At the congressional level, the acceptance of bipartisanship meant more than ceding unprecedented
peacetime powers to the president; bipartisanship signified that
congressional leaders agreed to play a junior role in managing or
controlling the economy, politics, and military structure of the "free
world."

Having established the demonic enemy as an ever-present threat,
a small national security elite could and did manipulate what C.
Wright Mills described as the "middle levels of power."[12] By this
Mills meant that power to control international affairs and the
important issues of domestic life became centered in a small circle
inside the executive branch. Congress still could obstruct, delay,
and cause problems, but it could not truly participate in the crucial
decisions of global power.[13] However, the top officials in the national
security bureaucracy were able to control discussion and debate on
key foreign policy questions through control of information. The
obsessive need for secrecy allowed the president, or those acting
in his name, to invoke national security not only in times of national
difficulties but whenever it became convenient.[14]

### The Great Repression

Now bearing the generic name McCarthyism, the 1947–1955 campaign to silence critics and skeptics of the new cold war policy

effectively stopped national debate not only about the means and ends of U.S. foreign policy, but also about what national security actually meant. The word "freedom" sufficed to explain the country's goals and ideals; national security became the catchall for preserving and extending the sphere. "Communism" became the convenient conversation stopper.

McCarthyism could have been labeled Trumanism. The postwar anticommunist crusade originated with the Democratic president from Missouri.[15] Only ten days after Truman announced his "doctrine" to roll back communists overseas (March 1947), he established the Federal Employee Loyalty Program, which by the end of 1952 had forced some 6.6 million people to undergo loyalty and security checks. Although the program dismissed 490 government employees and led 5,900 others to resign, "not a single spy or saboteur was discovered. The price of this fantastic operation was a steady erosion of political liberty."[16]

The wave of repression unleashed by Truman centered on people who resisted cold war policies at home and abroad, many of whom made up the left–liberal–labor alliance that fought for the New Deal programs of the 1930s. All those in actual or potential opposition to the American Century were targeted, particularly those working in opinion-forming institutions who might have access to communication and could reach the public with dissenting points of view. The media and Hollywood were purged by private vigilante organizations that worked closely with the Federal Bureau of Investigation (FBI). Universities forced professors to sign humiliating loyalty oaths, and loyalty tests were even submitted to grade school teachers, veterinarians, and librarians.[17]

The purges reached into the leadership and ranks of the trade unions. Seeking to roll back the progressive labor legislation and important alliances and organizations formed among workers in the 1930s, the "witch-hunters" mounted a fierce anticommunist campaign that touched the government, the media, the Congress, and the unions.[18] Congressional passage of the Taft-Hartley Act—which, among other things, forced union officials to disavow membership, affiliation, or belief in the Communist party—purged the most militant sectors of organized labor and helped force union leaders to fall into step with the state and business. The purging of left-wing elements inside the unions not only affected the status of U.S. workers, but forced union leaders to sign onto the premises and policies of the cold war abroad.

The leading intellectuals of the age celebrated Western freedom, yet paradoxically built the anticommunist ideology to a crescendo pitch. The very ideal of the free society, where speech, press, and assembly were fundamental rights, was compromised by the policy that supposedly was meant to preserve it. Dissent from this policy became dangerous. Those who did not buy into it soon became targets and then victims of one of the most lightning and devastating political purges in U.S. history.[19]

Although McCarthyism did not originate with the senator from Wisconsin, he and his followers, imitators, and sycophants elevated the purge of dissent to hysterical levels. Unlike the repression unleashed by Truman, which targeted all opposition to empire abroad and domestic consensus at home, the political thrust behind Joe McCarthy's drive was to remove from power the cold war corporate liberals, the very heart of the establishment itself. McCarthy challenged the cold war's authors to follow through on a brutal policy that he insisted was dictated by the very logic of their own position. If the United States were to wage cold war against communism, McCarthy in effect declared, then the current leaders of the government, and key related institutions, were too weak and tainted by compromises made with the enemy to carry the fight to victory. He at first implied, and later used, the word "treason." If, as those in the political consensus stated their premise, the international communist conspiracy was the world's most evil and menacing villain, then these moderates and liberals were guilty of lacking basic will and vigilance.[20]

McCarthyism worked, and it coincided with developing events. The Soviets had exploded their atomic bomb, thus ending the U.S. monopoly.[21] Indeed, the Soviets had defied U.S. power. That was the interpretation offered by the right wing for the 1949 Chinese Communist victory. President Truman, in the midst of the growing McCarthyite mood, responded by calling for a stronger national security strategy.

### NSC-68: Blueprint for Turning the Cold War Hot

In April 1950, a National Security Council directive tagged NSC-68 mandated a vast military mobilization for the United States as well as the Allies "with the intention of righting the power balance, and in the hope that through means other than all-out war we could induce change in the nature of the Soviet system."[22] This rearmament was to ensure that the communists would be contained everywhere in the world, that the territories, with their resources, labor supplies, and markets would not fall into the hands of a rival social and economic system. The assumption that the United States could and should unilaterally undertake this global task did not explicitly rule out rollback for China or Eastern Europe, nor did the assumption advocate direct military confrontation with the Soviets. But the assumption did define the Truman Doctrine. The United States would become the world enforcer.

As tough as the language in NSC-68 was, it did not go far enough to appease the extreme right wing. The same "coddlers," it contended, that lost China to communism and sold out the Poles, now lacked the guts to take them back. Backed by sensationalist press reports and considerable financial support from certain sectors of the business community, the rabid right-wingers successfully fashioned an interventionist public mood from the liberal framework, one that made possible the commitment of U.S. troops overseas.

In late June 1950, President Truman applied his doctrine to Korea, in response to an invasion by North Korean troops over the 38th parallel. National security, said the president, demanded that the United States prevent South Korea from falling into communist hands, thus stopping the dominoes from toppling throughout eastern Asia.

The Korean conflict, as well as upheavals in Indochina, Greece, and the Middle East, involved more than falling dominoes. The notion of preserving U.S. credibility abroad emerged as a key strategic factor in the minds of U.S. policymakers. If the United States did not prevail in one area, the lessons learned by enemies or potential enemies would allow for the undermining of freedom elsewhere and indeed everywhere. Dominoes and credibility, linked together, expressed the major guidelines of policy thinking about postwar revolutions, no matter how much language revolutionary leaders borrowed from the Declaration of Independence or how much they affirmed their love for the United States.[23]

## Testing the Bomb: National Security Secrecy at Home

The example of atomic testing illustrates the domestic side of national security operations. The urgency, the secrecy, and the deadly powerful nature of the material that the atomic bureaucracy controlled established the relationship between government and the citizenry under the national security state. Truman himself announced the policy of atomic bomb testing in a speech in 1946, thereby setting a precedent for such present-day national security slogans as "peace through strength." On November 30, 1950, Truman told a news conference that the United States would respond appropriately to meet the military situation caused by China's entrance into the Korean War.

"Will that include the atomic bomb?" a reporter asked.

"That does include every weapon we have."

"Does that mean that there is active consideration of use of the atom bomb?" asked the same reporter.

"There has always been active consideration of its use," Truman replied.[24]

For more than a decade, the Atomic Energy Commission (AEC) supervised atmospheric testing at the Nevada and Pacific test sites. The Soviet Union's successful explosion of a nuclear weapon in 1949 only made more urgent the national security apparatus' desire for its own destructive superiority. Alternatives to an A-bomb race were not considered at policy levels.

During the course of atomic testing in the 1950s," "unacceptable," indeed dangerous, levels of radioactive fallout dropped on both civilian populations and military personnel in the test areas, mostly Nevada, Utah, and Arizona. Rather than inform the public and the GIs, and risk the possibility of a national debate about the priorities of health versus nuclear-based national security, AEC officials decided to withhold the news about the hazardous levels of radiation and lied outright to the people living in the areas drenched by fallout from the tests.[25]

In the days of "dirty" bombs, the people of St. George, Utah, for example, received AEC pamphlets and lectures and were shown films to reassure them that no danger existed from the deadly material that was visibly falling upon them and making them nauseated, dizzy, and psychologically disoriented. The AEC officials' correspondence and internal discussion, some of which have now become accessible to the public, demonstrate that the AEC members feared that the outcome of a debate about nuclear testing might threaten the bipartisan consensus and that the public might force them to stop testing, thus thwarting their vision of obtaining scientific nuclear perfection and military omnipotence. So AEC officials invoked national security secrecy and continued to "dose" unsuspecting members of the population until President John Kennedy signed the Atmospheric Test Ban Treaty in 1963, which ended above-ground explosions.

Three decades passed, but the nuclear architects, both military and civilian, deliberately failed to inform the population of St. George, Utah, about the hazards to which they had been exposed. Nor did any of the nuclear elite recant or apologize to St. George cancer victims for not telling them at the time of the tests to take showers, dry clean their clothes, hose down their homes and cars, and get periodic medical checkups. Under the cover of national security, this group of nonelected and publicly obscure men opted instead to preserve their ability to carry out more tests, no matter what the ultimate health effects on the public.[26]

The testing example is just one of the uncounted instances in which national security officials either lied to, or withheld the truth from, the public when it was convenient to their goals to do so. Soviet leaders had little interest in learning about the results of fallout on human health in St. George, but the residents themselves had every right to know. National security bureaucrats could argue justifiably that the Soviets might well have an interest in learning facts and figures about the explosive yields, the destructive power, and the efficiency of trigger mechanisms of the bombs, but misinforming the affected townspeople had no relationship to national security, except in the most devious way. Soviet and U.S. scientists knew only too well from the bombs dropped on Hiroshima and Nagasaki about the "troublesome" aspect of nuclear weapons. Nevertheless, the justification for withholding the information was precisely that the enemy would learn vital U.S. national security secrets.

The nuclear bureaucrats used secrecy to prevent what should have been a public debate. They classified the health hazard data on the grounds that they would affect national security. In reality, the debate could have affected only the ability of the AEC elite to continue working on their nuclear obsession.

### Notes

1. Dean Acheson, *Present at the Creation* (New York: W. W. Norton, 1969), pp. 489–490. For one discussion of this famous passage, and Acheson's exaggeration of the "Soviet threat," see John Donovan, *The Cold Warriors: A Policy-Making Elite* (Lexington, Mass.: D. C. Heath, 1974), pp. 81–106.

2. Truman made this remark while announcing the Truman Doctrine in his joint address to Congress, March 1947.

3. These needs were like the "need to know," a rationale for restricting information. See Morton Halperin, Jerry Berman, Robert Borosage, and Christine Marwick, *The Lawless State* (New York: Penguin, 1978).

4. The Charter of the United Nations, Chapter I, Article 4: "All members shall refrain in their international relations from the threat or use of force against the territorial integrity or political independence of any state, or in any manner inconsistent with the Purpose of the United Nations."

The NATO Charter, Article 1: "The Parties undertake, as set forth in the Charter of the United Nations, to settle any international disputes in which they may be involved by peaceful means in such a manner that international peace and security, and justice, are not endangered, and to refrain in their international relations from the threat or use of force in any manner inconsistent with the purposes of the United Nations."

The Charter of the OAS, Chapter III, Article 15: "No State or group of States has the right to intervene, directly or indirectly, for any reason whatsoever, in the internal or external affairs of any other State. The foregoing principle prohibits not only armed force but also any other form of interference or attempted threat against the personality of the State or against its political, economic and cultural elements."

5. See Thomas Etzold and John Lewis Gaddis, *Containment: Documents on American Policy and Strategy, 1945–1950* (New York: Columbia University Press, 1978), pp. 1–23.

6. Halperin et al., *The Lawless State.*

7. On the decision to make atomic energy a matter of national security, rather than international knowledge, see Gar Alperovitz, *Atomic Diplomacy* (New York: Penguin, 1985), pp. 243–248; Lloyd Gardner, *Architects of Illusion* (Chicago: Quadrangle Books, 1970), pp. 176–201; Gabriel Kolko, *The Politics of War* (New York: Random House, 1968), pp. 540–543; and John Lewis Gaddis, *Russia, the Soviet Union, and the United States: An Interpretive History* (New York: John Wiley and Sons, 1978), p. 179.

8. President Truman, reflecting with hindsight on the decision to establish the CIA, told his biographer that he thought "it was a mistake." "[T]hose fellows in the CIA don't just report on wars and the like, they go out and make their own, and there's nobody to keep track of what they're up to. . . . It's become a government all of its own and secret. They don't have to account to anybody."

"That's a very dangerous thing in a democratic society, and it's got to be put a stop to. The people have got a right to know what those birds are up to. . . . Secrecy and a free, democratic government don't mix." Merle Miller, *Plain Speaking: An Oral Biography of Harry S Truman* (New York: Berkeley, 1974), p. 392.

9. The America Firsters called for strict obedience to the Neutrality Act of 1935. The group, which took its name from a 1936 book, *Save America First,* written by Jerome Frank, chairman of the Securities and Exchange Commission, included old fashioned antiwar populists, including Senator Burton Wheeler; pro-German figures, such as aviator Charles Lindbergh; and fascist demagogues, such as Father Coughlin, a Catholic political leader. There were even some Roosevelt liberals, such as Chester Bowles and Robert M. Hutchins, whose names appeared on the America First letterhead.

10. Senator Claude Pepper (D-Fla.) was among the victims; he had opposed the Truman administration's anti-Soviet policy, met in 1945 with Joseph Stalin, and made a number of speeches before groups such as the American Slav Congress that later were labeled subversive. Representative George Smathers defeated "Red Pepper" in the 1950 Democratic primary election in Florida, largely by calling him an "apologist for Stalin" and tying him to various alleged communist organizations. In the same year, Representative Richard M. Nixon took a California Senate seat from Helen

Gahagan Douglas, whose sins included voting against funds for the House Un-American Activities Committee and opposing aid to Greece and Turkey.

11. Stephen E. Ambrose, *Rise to Globalism* (New York: Penguin, 1985), p. 86.

12. C. Wright Mills, *The Power Elite* (New York: Oxford University Press, 1956).

13. The exceptions to this were the congressional leadership, or, as later developed, the heads of key oversight committees.

14. On wiretapping and breakins during the Nixon administration in the name of national security, see Seymour Hersh, *The Price of Power* (New York: Summit Books, 1983), pp. 87–88, 91–92; Carl Bernstein and Bob Woodward, *All the President's Men* (New York: Simon and Schuster, 1974); Philip Kurland, *Watergate and the Constitution* (Chicago: University of Chicago Press, 1978), pp. 69–70; and Richard Ben-Viniste and George Frampton, Jr., *Stonewall* (New York: Simon and Schuster, 1977), pp. 118–124.

15. For a useful overview, see the chapter on Truman-McCarthyism in Robert Justin Goldstein, *Political Repression in Modern America* (Boston: G. K. Hall, 1978), pp. 385–396.

16. Lawrence Wittner, *Cold War America* (New York: Holt, Rinehart, and Winston, 1978), pp. 38 and 96. Truman also authorized the attorney general to compile a list of "totalitarian, fascist, communist or subversive" organizations. The resulting roster of ninety-one groups was used by state and local governments, defense-related industries, and schools in a variety of discriminatory ways, mainly in the case of employment. The Subversive Activities Control Board was established by the attorney general to order certain organizations to register as communist action, communist front, or communist infiltrated. Such groups had to put the label "mailed by a communist organization" on anything they mailed. The attorney general had the power to deport suspected subversives. See David Caute, *The Great Fear* (New York: Simon and Schuster, 1978), p. 28.

17. Caute, ibid., p. 74.

18. Ibid., pp. 270, 355, 371.

19. Caute noted that "during the crucial years of the great fear the most influential, opinion-forming faction of the American intelligentsia largely (but not wholly) abandoned the critical function that all intellectuals in all countries ought to sustain toward government agencies and government actions." Ibid., p. 53. See pp. 422–424 on the University of California loyalty oath and pp. 466–479 on actions against scientists.

20. McCarthy's trajectory began with a speech in Wheeling, West Virginia, Feb. 9, 1950, where he announced he had a list of 205 communists "working and shaping the policy of the State Department." He held hearings against State Department personnel beginning in March 1950, against the Voice of America in February 1953, against the U.S. Army Signal Corps from April to July 1953, and against the U.S. Army beginning in April 1954. The latter proved to be his undoing. He was censured by the Senate on December

2, 1954. See David M. Oshinsky, *A Conspiracy So Immense: The World of Joe McCarthy* (New York: The Free Press, 1983).

21. The Soviet Union's successful explosion of an atomic bomb in 1949 was followed by a number of celebrated spy cases—Klaus Fuchs and Harry Gold in 1950 and Julius and Ethel Rosenberg in 1951—in which the defendants were prosecuted for leaking "atomic secrets" to the Russians. For descriptions of this period, see ibid., pp. 103–106; and Caute, *The Great Fear,* pp. 58–67.

22. "A Report to the National Security Council by the Executive Secretary on United States Objectives and Programs for National Security, April 14, 1950," NSC-68 was the result of President Truman's directive of January 30, 1950, for the construction of a hydrogen bomb, attached to which was a letter ordering the secretaries of state and defense to review U.S. foreign and defense policy (available in the U.S. National Archives or reprinted in Thomas Etzold and John Lewis Gaddis, eds., *Containment: Documents on American Policy and Strategy, 1945–1950* [New York: Columbia University Press, 1978], pp. 385–442). Paul Nitze, chairman of the State Department's policy planning staff, led a small study group composed of officials from the two departments and the Joint Chiefs of Staff. The document was produced six weeks later and was adopted by the National Security Council on April 14. Within the State Department, the document represented the victory of Dean Acheson's and Paul Nitze's hard-line views over those of Soviet specialists Charles Bohlen and George Kennan, who did not see the Soviets as a military threat.

NSC-68 first defined the general aims of the United States and the Soviet Union, arguing that "the fundamental purpose" of U.S. policy was "to assure the integrity and vitality of our free society, which is founded upon the dignity and the worth of the individual." Conversely, according to the document, the Soviets wanted to "retain and solidify their absolute power, first in the Soviet Union and second in the areas under their control. . . . Achievement of this design requires the dynamic extension of their authority and ultimate elimination of any effective opposition to their authority" (pp. 5–6).

The document backed containment: "As for the policy of 'containment,' it is the one which seeks by all means short of war to (1) block further expansion of Soviet power; (2) expose the falsities of Soviet pretensions; (3) induce a retraction of the Kremlin's control and influence; and (4) in general, so foster the seeds of destruction within the Soviet system that the Kremlin is brought at least to the point of modifying its behavior to conform to generally-accepted international standards" (p. 21).

"Containment militarism," which called for a massive buildup of both nuclear and conventional forces, was essential to guarantee U.S. national security, the document concluded. Guidelines for this policy included (1) no negotiations because conditions were not conducive to convincing the Kremlin to change its policies; (2) the development of a hydrogen bomb to counter the Soviet atomic arsenal; (3) a rapid buildup of the conventional military; (4) an increase in taxes to pay for this; (5) strong alliances under U.S. leadership; and (6) action to undermine the Soviet regime.

23. The United States shipped tens of thousands of arms to the French to prevent the "loss" of Indochina, which "would have critical psychological, political and economic consequences." *The Pentagon Papers* memo went on to say that "the loss of any single country would probably lead to the relatively swift submission to or an alignment with communism by the remaining countries of this group." "Furthermore," the domino parade of horrors continued, "an alignment with communism of the rest of Southeast Asia and India, and in the longer term, of the Middle East (with the probable exceptions of at least Pakistan and Turkey) would in all probability progressively follow. Such widespread alignment would endanger the stability and security of Europe." The writer's nightmare projection ended with the loss of control of vital raw materials and food and the loss of Japan to communism. Senator Mike Gravel edition of *Pentagon Papers I* (Boston: Beacon Press, 1971-72), pp. 83–84.

24. The dialogue is cited in David Wise, *The Politics of Lying: Government Deception, Secrecy, and Power* (New York: Random House, 1973), p. 316.

25. *Paul Jacobs and the Nuclear Gang.* (Transcript, New Time Films, 1979).

26. "I think national security demanded what was done. I think the Army did the proper thing. Now, I will also say that as the years went on, we got more and more careful and we knew more." (Peter Haas, deputy director, science and technology, Defense Nuclear Agency, in ibid.)

# CHAPTER 6

# The CIA and the
# New Interventionism

*No State or group of States has the right to intervene, directly or indirectly, in the internal or external affairs of any other State.*

—Charter of the Organization of American States, Article 15e

During the course of World War II, Latin American nations, especially those in the Caribbean and Central America, delivered the food and raw materials that the United States had requested for its war effort. Latin American presidents, parliaments, and dictators all accepted the artificially low prices that Washington set for their commodities. Regional governments cut special deals ensuring that the United States, and not the Axis powers, had access to products such as coffee, fruit, and sugar as well as to special materials needed for war production.[1] Latin governments, however, believed that after the war they would enjoy greater access to the U.S. market and more advantageous trade. The motives of these government leaders varied from subservience and expectations of future rewards to genuine antifascism.

Cubans and other Latin Americans fought as volunteers alongside the U.S. armed forces. Inside Cuba, moderates, liberals, and leftists banded together in an antifascist effort and in 1940 drafted a strong democratic constitution. They cooperated politically with the United States by taking strong measures against representatives of the Axis operating on Cuban territory.[2] The language of Cuban politics in

59

the year preceding U.S. entry into World War II and during the war resembled the democratic and antifascist idiom used by Roosevelt and Churchill to mobilize their home fronts; democracy also became a source of inspiration among nationalist and liberationist forces in the Third World.[3] The Allies used democratic and antifascist rhetoric to popularize the war effort, which encouraged leaders of independence movements to think that the defeat of the Axis also would result in the liberation of the colonies. In Vietnam, India, and other parts of Asia and Africa as well as in the Caribbean and Central America, World War II appeared not only as the battle between Western democracy and German-Japanese totalitarianism, but also as the instrument for freeing territories and peoples from imperial and colonial bondage.

After the war, it appeared to middle-class patriots in Central America that there could be no progress as long as the United States continued to keep the region a virtual protectorate. Many of the young men and women who became doctors, lawyers, accountants, architects, and university professors in the era of the Good Neighbor policy accepted the fact of U.S. dominance over their region, but assumed that within such a framework a more equitable arrangement could be charted. They joined or formed social democratic or Christian democratic political organizations to challenge local oligarchies and, ultimately, U.S. hegemony. Nevertheless, such members of the professional class, like those of their social class who opted for revolution, believed in the letter and spirit of the U.S. Declaration of Independence and after World War II took seriously the clauses in the U.N. and OAS charters that prohibited intervention.

Although few middle-class politicians expected the United States to abandon its dominant role in the region, many did believe that the pattern of military intervention that prevailed from the 1890s on had to cease and that the United States would have to make serious concessions to the democratic promises its leaders had made during World War II.[4] How, asked founding social democrats such as Jose "Pepe" Figueres of Costa Rica, Luis Muñoz Marin of Puerto Rico, Romulo Betancourt of Venezuela, and young patriots such as José Napoleon Duarte and Guillermo Ungo of El Salvador, could the United States continue to back right-wing oligarchs and military cliques after having committed itself to antifascist and democratic principles?

Instead of addressing the issue of Central American development, U.S. leaders concentrated on rebuilding Europe. As the Soviets assumed that they would prevail in Eastern Europe, so did U.S. leaders believe unquestioningly in U.S. predominance over the political and economic life of Latin America. The U.S. elite assumed that it would control the destinies of the tiny banana republics. Some U.S. figures even protested the inclusion of these nations in the United Nations, and, when that became inevitable, the Organization of American States was seen as a legalized regional means of control.[5]

The United States virtually ignored Central America until its internal political development came into conflict with U.S. "national security." That collision first occurred in Guatemala regarding the issue of the right to independence. The result of this conflict defined the future political possibilities for Central America and again locked the United States into its prewar pattern of tight control of the region.

Guatemala's peculiar political process, as compared to most of Latin America, made it a test case for the use of the new national security agencies to hold onto an area that previously had been subject to blunt gunboat and dollar diplomacy. President Truman already had established a tough posture, which allowed his successor to move more subtly, if not covertly.

## The Ascendance of the CIA

Following President Truman's threat to use force in the Mediterranean in 1946 and 1947 and his use of troops in Korea between 1950 and 1953, the national security apparatus, and President Eisenhower in particular, turned to the CIA as a more efficient, and lower profile, enforcer of U.S. interests than was the military.

Although the Berlin blockade may have been the opening shot of the cold war, the Korean War marked the ascendance of national security as the core of U.S. policy. But the war also illustrated many of the dilemmas inherent in that policy. Truman had to finesse the constitutional issues raised by his ordering troops to Korea by calling it a U.N. police action.[6] The U.N. force was put under the command of General Douglas MacArthur and committed to battle on June 30, 1950, five days after the North Korean invasion.[7] After being almost driven into the sea, MacArthur's forces launched a counteroffensive on September 15, 1950, making an amphibious landing at Inchon near the city of Seoul, and marched north, nearing the Yalu River, Korea's border with China. Chinese forces joined the fray on November 26, forcing U.N. forces back below the 38th parallel.

MacArthur wanted to carry the war north of the Yalu and regain not just Korea, but all of China, for the "free world." But the consensus among the national security elite, and indeed among most of the citizenry, was that taking on China, then allied with the Soviet Union, was much too risky. Over the vociferous objections of the right wing and the "China lobby," Truman sacked MacArthur on April 11, 1951, after the general had threatened to attack China.[8]

The war, now confined to more limited objectives (restoring the postwar boundary), still ground on for two more years while U.S. bombers devastated North Korean lands and cities. Total U.S. casualties were 33,000, and more than one hundred thousand were wounded; total Korean and Chinese dead and wounded exceeded 2 million. The war left the line of demarcation between North and South Korea intact, with repressive communist and capitalist governments above and below it.

The Korean War emerged logically as a key issue in the 1952 election campaign. Dwight Eisenhower accurately read the public mind and, using his military status and prestige artfully, made a solemn promise, if elected, to end the war. As with other overseas wars that did not result in quick U.S. victories, the Korean War produced its own syndrome, a surly public mood that would make it difficult for the next president to commit U.S. troops to faraway conflicts.

Nevertheless, U.S. policymakers had no intention of renouncing plans to intervene in Asian affairs. Indeed, the national security elite had ordered the bombing of North Korea, with a tonnage that exceeded the amount dropped on Germany in World War II. North Korean cities were devastated; civilian dead, wounded, and homeless totaled more than 1 million.

The Korean War's demonstration of U.S. will, determination, and ruthlessness did little, however, to inhibit revolutionary nationalism in Vietnam, where the French were engaged in their own counter-revolutionary war with the forces of Ho Chi Minh. As Eisenhower took office and made plans to quickly end the Korean War, some inside his cabinet already were calculating ways to aid the French— including the use of U.S. forces. Eisenhower, however, sensitively gauged what was politically possible in light of the popular distaste for violent overseas adventures with U.S. soldiers. Given that he also was unwilling to abandon U.S. control and influence abroad, Eisenhower felt compelled to turn away from the use of overt military force and toward the covert violence of the CIA.

### Iran and Guatemala

When Iranian leader Mohammed Mossadegh, an Islamic nationalist, nationalized Iranian oil in 1953, Eisenhower ordered the CIA to topple him and replace his government with one friendly to U.S. interests. The Agency successfully arranged a coup in 1953, installing the pro-U.S. shah.[9] Inside the national security apparatus, the Iranian coup was viewed as a successfully managed crisis. There is little evidence that policymakers thought seriously about what this intervention would do to the course of Iranian history or, indeed, to the future of U.S.-Iranian relations. Time, in the world of the covert activists, became a frozen entity, as if the world of the moment would somehow infinitely project itself.

In the mid-1950s, the clandestine military operation in Iran was one of two subsequently publicized CIA-directed interventions. In Guatemala, a democratic reform process had begun in 1944 under President Juan Jose Arevalo. When Arevalo's successor, President Jacobo Arbenz Guzmán, moved to take some control of land use, railroads, and labor relations inside his own country, he ran up against the U.S.-owned United Fruit Company (UFCO) and set in motion an example of U.S. national security in action. As in Iran, the CIA organized a coup to overthrow an elected government and replaced it with a servile but brutal military regime, which, in turn, ensured U.S. access to labor, markets, and raw materials—the fifth, and unspoken, freedom.[10]

The Guatemala coup taught nationalists throughout the Third World, and especially in Latin America, that the United States would continue to use force in order to preserve economic and political control in the U.S. "sphere." Seven years later, in 1961, Fidel Castro correctly assumed that his nationalization of U.S.-owned enterprises would inspire, at minimum, CIA efforts to destabilize his regime and, more likely, would result in full-scale military action by the United States. The CIA-orchestrated coup in Guatemala gave notice to reformists and revolutionaries throughout Latin America that any attempts to create more equity in the social order, particularly those that threatened the low overhead of U.S. businesses in the Latin countries, would incur the immediate wrath of Washington's covert enforcer: the CIA.

The Guatemala case also demonstrated that the historic marriage between business and government policymaking circles in Washington remained firm, that the "old boy network" was in good working order. The overthrow of democracy in Guatemala in 1954 was carried out in the interest of the United Fruit Company—and, presumably, future U.S. investors—and was paid for by U.S. tax dollars.

In 1954, the United Fruit Company was the largest landowner in Guatemala and controlled an estimated 70 percent of the country's total acreage. UFCO was also the nation's largest employer and exporter, thereby monopolizing Guatemala's main cash crop, bananas. UFCO was a "state within a state, owning Guatemala's telephone and telegraph facilities, administering its only important Atlantic harbor," and owning nearly every mile of railroad track in the country.[11] By virtue of its ownership of the harbor and railroads alone, United Fruit literally controlled the nation's international commerce.

When President Jacobo Arbenz Guzmán took office in March 1951, he dedicated himself to continuing the goals of his predecessor: agrarian reform, labor protection, an improved educational system, and tax reform. One year later, the Guatemalan Congress passed an agrarian reform bill that empowered the government to expropriate uncultivated portions of plantations greater than 223 acres. The owners of lands expropriated—the value of which would be determined by their declared taxable worth—would receive twenty-five-year government bonds that would accrue with a 3 percent interest rate. Under Arbenz, the Congress also approved moderate labor reforms, including minimum wage standards, and initiated tax reform.

These long-overdue reforms threatened the United Fruit Company's control. For decades, UFCO had enjoyed "total exemption from internal taxation, duty-free importation of all necessary goods, and a guarantee of low wages."[12] In addition, UFCO had consistently undervalued its land holdings in order to reduce its already minimal tax liability. United Fruit's subsidiary railway company, International Railways of Central America, had never paid taxes to the Guatemalan government until the Arbenz presidency. In addition, UFCO had only 15 percent of its vast land holdings in production; this left the other 85 percent legal target for expropriation and redistribution to landless peasants.[13]

The development of UFCO's operation in Guatemala had not contributed to the social, economic, and political development of the country as a whole. Quite to the contrary, not only had UFCO reaped enormous profits without any significant contribution to the nation's welfare; its corrupt business practices had thwarted efforts to attain economic and political independence. The minister of labor and economy under Arbenz, Alfonso Bauer Paiz, said:

> All the achievements of the Company were made at the expense of the impoverishment of the country and by acquisitive practices. To protect its authority it had recourse to every method: political intervention, economic compulsion, contractual imposition, bribery, [and] tendentious propaganda, as suited its purposes of domination. The

United Fruit Company is the principal enemy of the progress of Guatemala, of its democracy and of every effort directed at its economic liberation.[14]

A former twenty-year employee of United Fruit shared this view of the giant multinational:

"Guatemala was chosen as the site for the company's earliest development activities at the turn of the century," wrote Thomas McCann, "because a good portion of the country contained prime banana land and because at the time we entered Central America, Guatemala's government was the region's weakest, most corrupt and most pliable. In short, the country offered an 'ideal investment climate,' and United Fruit's profits there flourished for fifty years. Then something went wrong: a man named Jacobo Arbenz became President."[15]

In March 1953, the Guatemalan government expropriated 209,842 acres of UFCO's uncultivated land. The U.S. State Department issued a formal complaint to Guatemalan officials. Secretary of State John Foster Dulles himself had close ties with United Fruit. As a young attorney, Dulles had negotiated United Fruit's takeover of the railway system with the Guatemalan government. His brother, Allen Dulles, director of the CIA, had done legal work for the J. Henry Schroder Banking Corporation, the president of which "was himself on the board of the railroad company, even while it was controlled by United Fruit."[16] General Walter Bedell Smith, former chief of the CIA and in 1954 John Foster Dulles' undersecretary of state, was put in charge of the CIA Guatemala operation; one year after the successful coup, UFCO appointed Smith to its board of directors. The assistant secretary of state for inter-American affairs, John Moors Cabot, had family-owned stock in United Fruit, as did U.N. ambassador Henry Cabot Lodge. Eisenhower's personal secretary, Anne Whitman, was married to UFCO's public relations director.[17]

Smith and the Dulles brothers convinced Eisenhower that Arbenz was a communist. Two years earlier, in 1952, United Fruit had circulated a report to members of the U.S. Congress about the infiltration of international communism in Guatemala, and by 1954 some of the "information" contained in the report had found its way into official State Department reports and public statements on Guatemala.

Under the rubric of national security, Eisenhower gave the "go ahead" for the CIA plan to overthrow the elected government and impose the rule of then-exiled Guatemalan general Castillo Armas.

With arms and planes purchased by the CIA, Castillo Armas "liberated" Guatemala on June 27, 1954, and two weeks later the nation "celebrated" the junta's declaration of Anticommunism Day. On July 13, 1954, the U.S. government granted official recognition to the government of Castillo Armas.[18]

Just a few months earlier, President Arbenz had predicted the intervention in a speech to the Guatemalan Congress:

> The essential character of the international situation with relation to Guatemala is that, as a consequence of the agrarian reform and the economic and social development of the country, we face a growing threat of foreign intervention in the internal affairs of Guatemala, placing in danger the stability of our constitutional life and the integrity of our national independence.[19]

Was the CIA's role in the "liberation" of Guatemala consistent with the Agency's charter, which in 1947 authorized the CIA to "perform such other functions and duties related to intelligence affecting the national security as the National Security Council may from time to time direct"? Was the overthrow of Guatemalan democracy—the country that was ruled for the next thirty years by a series of brutal military dictatorships—part of the "other functions" originally intended by the CIA's creators? Moreover, were covert operations carried out against the integrity of sovereign nations in keeping with the letter and spirit of the U.S. Constitution?

By converting nationalist activities in Iran and Guatemala into global events, U.S. national security officials found a universal formula that could be applied against revolutions anywhere, and with the CIA as the agency, these same officials could invoke "plausible deniability" so as to stave off embarrassing questions and charges of illegal behavior.[20] From the CIA's actions in overthrowing the legitimate governments of Iran in 1953 and Guatemala in 1954 through the beginning of the Vietnam War, national security doctrine and practice developed a counterrevolutionary strategy to answer revolution throughout the Third World.

### Notes

1. The dollars that did flow into the region, however, did not translate into increased purchasing power to buy U.S. products because such goods were going to the war effort. Instead, the accumulated dollars fed inflation in Latin America.

2. Cuba expelled German, Japanese, and Italian consular officials. Ironically, one of these officials, Amadeo Barletta, the Italian consul-general, was also the General Motors distributor in Havana. He moved to Argentina in 1940 and then returned to Cuba after World War II and resumed his GM distributorship.

3. Communists formally joined the 1940 Cuban cabinet as part of the antifascist front. One of them, Carlos Rafael Rodriguez, is today a member of the Cuban Politburo.

4. In his message to Congress January 6, 1941, President Roosevelt set forth the "four freedoms:" freedom of speech and expression, freedom of worship, freedom from want, and freedom from fear. In the Atlantic Charter, concluded August 14, 1941, Roosevelt and Churchill pledged to "respect the right of peoples to choose the form of government under which they will live, and they wish to see sovereign rights and self-government restored to those who have been forcibly deprived of them. . . . They will endeavor, with due respect for the existing obligations, to further the enjoyment by all states, great or small, victor or vanquished, of access, on equal terms, to the trade and to the raw materials of the world which are needed for their economic prosperity."

5. Walter LaFeber, *Inevitable Revolutions* (New York: W. W. Norton, 1983), p. 97.

6. Because the Soviet Union had undertaken a boycott of the U.N. Security Council in January 1950 in response to the presence on it of Nationalist China, the USSR did not veto the U.S. resolution in June of that year calling for joint U.N. military action against the North Korean invasion of the South. Some fifteen countries joined the United States in the war, but the majority of troops were from the United States. See Robert Leckie, *The Wars of America* (New York: Harper and Row, 1981), pp. 835–925; and I. F. Stone, *The Hidden History of the Korean War* (New York: Monthly Review Press, 1952).

7. There is no question that North Korean forces attacked the South. However, some perspective is necessary to understand the origins of the Korean War. First, the attack hardly was unprovoked. South Korean president Syngman Rhee in early 1950 had declared that South Korea was determined "to unify our territory by ourselves," even if that entailed "bloodshed." Both sides had been staging attacks and border raids since 1947. Philip C. Jessup, a U.S. diplomat assigned by Washington to report on the area around the 38th parallel, described the situation in April 1950: "There is constant fighting between the South Korean Army and bands that infiltrate the country from the North. There are very real battles, involving perhaps one or two thousand men. When you go to this boundary as I did . . . you see troop movements, fortifications, and prisoners of war." Cited in William Blum, ed., *The CIA: A Forgotten History* (London: Zed, 1986), p. 85.

The South Korean Army had been placed on the alert near the 38th parallel several weeks before the North Korean hit, and President Rhee threatened in a radio address just two months before the invasion that he was about to liberate the North. See ibid., Chapter 7.

It also is doubtful that the Soviets controlled North Korean actions, especially after the invasion was launched. Nikita Khrushchev wrote that Joseph Stalin told him that North Korean premier Kim Il-sung launched the invasion of the South without Stalin's initiation. According to Khrushchev, "Stalin called back all our advisers who were with the North Korea divisions and regiments." Khrushchev recalled Stalin's explanation: "'It's too dangerous to keep our advisers there. They might be taken prisoner. We don't want there to be evidence for accusing us of taking part in this business. It's Kim Il-sung's affair.'" Edward Crankshaw, *Khrushchev Remembers* (Boston: Houghton Mifflin, 1970), pp. 367–370.

8. See John Spanier, *The Truman-MacArthur Controversy* (Cambridge, Mass.: Harvard University Press, 1959); and Dean Acheson, *Present at the Creation* (New York: W. W. Norton, 1969), pp. 671–680.

9. See Barry Rubin, *Paved with Good Intentions: The American Experience and Iran* (New York: Penguin Books, 1981), pp. 29–90; and Yonah Alexander and Allan Nanes, eds., *The United States and Iran: A Documentary History* (Frederick, Md.: Avetheia Books, 1980), pp. 213–258, on the Anglo-Iranian oil dispute and events leading up to the overthrow of Mossadegh. On the coup's execution, see, especially, Kermit Roosevelt, *Countercoup: The Struggle for Control of Iran* (New York: McGraw Hill, 1979).

10. See the discussion of FDR's four freedoms in Chapter 3.

11. Stephen Schlesinger and Stephen Kinzer, *Bitter Fruit* (Garden City, N.Y.: Doubleday, 1982), pp. 12, 78. Also see Richard H. Immerman, *The CIA in Guatemala: The Foreign Policy of Intervention* (Austin: University of Texas Press, 1982).

12. Schlesinger and Kinzer, ibid., p. 70.

13. Ibid., pp. 50–75. Also see Immerman, ibid.

14. Schlesinger and Kinzer, ibid., p. 73; and Immerman, ibid.

15. Thomas McCann, *An American Company: The Tragedy of United Fruit* (New York: Crown, 1976), p. 45.

16. Schlesinger and Kinzer, *Bitter Fruit,* p. 106.

17. Ibid., p. 93, 106.

18. For a useful account of the coup, see Blanche Wiesen Cooke, *The Declassified Eisenhower* (Garden City, N.Y.: Doubleday, 1981), pp. 218–292. Also see Philip C. Roettinger, "The Company, Then and Now" *The Progressive* (July 1986):50.

19. Schlesinger and Kinzer, *Bitter Fruit,* p. 77.

20. See Marcus Raskin, "Democracy and the National Security State," *Law and Contemporary Problems* 40, no. 3 (Summer 1976):206. Also see David Wise, *The Invisible Government* (New York: Vintage Books, 1964).

# CHAPTER 7

# Cuba:
# National Security Fiasco

*Oh what a tangled web we weave,*
*When first we practice to deceive!*

— Sir Walter Scott, *Marion*

After the United States intervened in 1898 to "help" Cuba gain
independence from Spain, Cubans enjoyed the trappings of democracy
without the substance. Although regular elections took place, some
were so fraudulent that they provoked violent revolts. Washington
routinely suppressed these revolts because the Platt Amendment
gave it the "right" to intervene in Cuban affairs.[1] Although by the
1950s well-educated North Americans did not automatically associate
Cuba with the periodic landing of U.S. Marines or think of Cubans
having to live under the thumb of a brutal, U.S.-controlled dictator,
Cubans, on the other hand, were all too aware of U.S. intervention.
Cubans knew the slogan "Yankee go home!" before Fidel Castro's
revolutionaries broadcast it to the world.[2]

Cubans also were linked in multiple ways to North American
culture and commerce. Baseball was a Cuban passion, and Havana
was one of the franchises in the AAA International League. Cubans
labored in U.S.-owned sugar mills, in copper and nickel mines, on
cattle ranches, and in a variety of other enterprises. "Both mother
and daughter," as songwriter Morey Amsterdam wrote, were "drinking
rum and Coca Cola" and "working for the Yankee dollar" in the
U.S.-owned hotel and gambling industry. On the eve of the Cuban
Revolution, U.S. corporations and individuals owned the best Cuban

lands and much of the country's major industry, means of communication, and mass media. U.S. companies controlled the utilities and telephone company, the oil refineries and mines, and considerable urban and rural real estate. The United States had a large economic stake in Cuba.

Educated Cubans also shared the ideals of the Declaration of Independence and sought inspiration from the great U.S. poets and presidents. The Cuban "apostle," José Martí, wrote extensively on Walt Whitman, Herman Melville, and other democratic theorists in U.S. letters.[3] It was precisely the anguish of living in a society that appeared to be so close to a living U.S. democracy, yet was so far from realizing these ideals, that helped drive Cubans to revolutionary activity. The freedom extolled by the great U.S. writers could not flourish amid the gross class inequalities of Cuba. The priorities of prerevolutionary Cuba illustrated the dramatic disparity between rich and poor. While Cuba imported more Cadillacs than did any other Latin American country, one-third of Cuba's population was illiterate. The Havana and Santiago de Cuba slums were among the worst in Latin America.

After World War II, in which Cubans volunteered and fought alongside U.S. troops against the Nazis, the same old patterns continued. Roosevelt's promises about democracy never materialized in Cuba. Following the 1948 elections, the victorious party engaged in large-scale corruption.[4] In 1952, former president Fulgencio Batista, who had helped the United States by channeling the 1933 revolution into a benign, and indeed corrupt, reformism, seized the presidency with the barest pretense of a democratic election. Washington immediately recognized the Batista government, to the outrage of the Cuban public.

In 1953, one year before the CIA organized the coup that overthrew the Arbenz government in Guatemala, a young Cuban attorney organized a bold assault on the island's second largest military base. Fidel Castro and a band of some one hundred fifty nationalists failed to take Fort Moncada in Santiago de Cuba or to produce a spontaneous uprising against Batista, but they did gain vast public recognition and sympathy for their bravery and patriotism. Castro argued that insurrection against governments that do not have consent of the governed was not only justified but obligatory.

Castro was imprisoned and released two years later. In December 1956, he returned to the island with a force of less than one hundred men to start an insurgency in the Sierra Maestra range. On January 2, 1959, his bearded rebel army marched into Havana and declared the triumph of the Cuban Revolution. U.S. national security officials had secretly tried to organize a last-minute coup to save the armed forces and prevent a revolutionary victory.[5] Anti-Yankeeism burst out of the Cuban populace and was fueled by facts that the revolutionary government revealed about the extent of U.S. domination of Cuba.[6]

In 1959 and 1960, militant Cubans held street celebrations whenever the government announced that it had "intervened" in a U.S.-owned enterprise. "Intervention" was the legal name given to the transition stage between private ownership and nationalization and was used to justify state intervention while proceedings took place to determine whether or not the targeted company had violated revolutionary laws. Most of them, of course, had.[7] Havaneros danced, holding coffins with the telephone emblem on them or with oil company names, to celebrate the takeover of U.S. property. U.S. officials did not find this behavior the least bit amusing. In fact, Cuba emerged as a growing national security issue.

## The Cuban Revolution and the U.S. Response

The rapid unfolding of the Cuban Revolution after January 1959 brought a sense of rising panic to national security officials in Washington.[8] Revolution—which fundamentally meant economic reorganization, a change in basic property relations—was their anathema as well as their raison d'être. In just the first few months after taking power, Castro made it clear that the revolution would be run for the majority of poor Cubans, not for U.S. interests or, for that matter, to please U.S. public opinion.[9] By 1960, Castro brought Cuba's labor force, resources, and markets under state control and some under state ownership. With each diplomatic protest from the State Department, the Cuban leader intensified his anti-Yankee rhetoric and action. "Cubans," he announced, "shall own Cuba, and Cubans shall dictate what becomes of the resources and wealth on the island."[10]

The state "intervened" in those U.S.- and Cuban-owned enterprises that reportedly were violating the new revolutionary rules on labor relations, resource utilization, and marketing. Some firms and lands were nationalized outright, with agrarian reform bonds offered as partial compensation. The U.S. ambassador no longer could consider himself the most important man on the island.

Throughout 1959 and 1960, Castro pushed rapid reforms. He slashed rents, nationalized utilities, and carried out a massive agrarian reform that resulted in the expropriation of more than 6 million hectares by mid-1963. These moves violated a rule that Secretary of State John Foster Dulles enunciated to an oil company executive in 1956: "The United States would not acquiesce in the rights of nationalization" because of an "international interest [that] goes far beyond composition of shareholders alone, and should call for international intervention."[11]

Despite a rapid deterioration in relations, U.S. investors in Cuba still clung to the notion of U.S. invincibility. Dr. René Vallejo, a Cuban gynecologist who in 1958 had joined Castro's guerrilla force in the mountains, subsequently was appointed to direct the Agrarian Reform Institute in Oriente Province. In this capacity, in 1960, one of his tasks was to deliver the order nationalizing the King Ranch, whose thousands of acres were located in eastern Cuba. The Cuban government offered agrarian reform bonds in compensation. The United States had a choice: honor the bonds and thereby offer the Cuban government credit or refuse to honor them and thereby render them worthless.[12]

Vallejo described the attitude of disbelief on the part of the ranch manager, whom Vallejo had known and whose wife had been Vallejo's patient. At first, the U.S. manager thought the Cuban doctor was playing a practical joke, but when the manager realized the seriousness of the mission he told Vallejo: "You can't do this, you know. You are taking away property of U.S. citizens and every time that has happened the U.S. Marines come in and get it back. And that's the way it's going to be again."[13]

The expectation of the King Ranch manager was shared by other corporate directors, bankers, and major shareholders. In Iran in 1953, just the threat of nationalizing oil had provoked a CIA-led coup. In 1954, President Jacobo Arbenz of Guatemala was ousted by the CIA merely for trying to tax the United Fruit Company. From late 1959 on, Castro's policies went beyond measures even contemplated by Mossadegh or Arbenz and therefore became an area of national security "crisis." Because there was insufficient public support for direct intervention, Cuba became the concern of a secret task force set up under Vice President Richard Nixon, whose job was to destroy the revolution and replace it with a pro-U.S. government.[14]

But unlike Arbenz and other social democrats who thought they could bargain with the United States, Castro assumed that Washington would meet the Cuban Revolution with implacable hostility. He armed the populace, formed civilian militias, and quickly carried out the basic reforms in education and housing that gave millions of Cubans a material and moral stake in their revolution.

As the United States cut off its trade, commercial, and military relations, Castro reforged those links with the Soviet Union. By early 1960, it appeared clear to U.S. political leaders that Castro was trying to prove not only that revolution could succeed on the U.S. doorstep, but that revolution could be accomplished with Soviet aid.[15] In July 1960, Washington threw down the gauntlet by encouraging U.S.-owned oil refineries in Cuba to refuse to process Soviet oil and by cutting off the Cuban sugar quota.[16]

No one who had followed the unfolding conflict was surprised by the invasion of the island in April 1961. The strike force was composed of Cuban exiles trained, financed, and controlled by the CIA and was launched from the east coast of Nicaragua with the full support of President Luís Somoza. But after less than seventy-two hours, the Cuban exiles that had landed in the Bay of Pigs on the south coast of Cuba either had been killed or captured by the country's volunteer militia and army. "Victory," said John F. Kennedy, with a trace of sadness in his voice, "has a thousand fathers; defeat is an orphan." The president took the blame for what became known as "the Bay of Pigs fiasco." The blame should have fallen on the shoulders of those who first designed a CIA whose operations would include overthrow of governments.

The decision to organize a clandestine operation to overthrow the Cuban government was made by Eisenhower in April 1959, two years before the invasion actually was launched. As Castro told the story, he went to Washington to explain Cuba's needs and his policies to meet them.[17] Eisenhower, Castro was told, could not see him, but Vice President Nixon would.

> Nixon shook hands and smiled when we met in an office. I sat down and for about an hour I explained very carefully and precisely the nature of our economic and social problems and some of the solutions we had in mind to resolve them. He seemed to pay attention, but made no comments at all. At the end of the meeting we shook hands and I presume that he went straight into President Eisenhower's office and told him, "The man is a communist. Let's get rid of him."[18]

Eisenhower agreed with Nixon that Castro was an immediate threat to U.S. national security. However, Eisenhower was reluctant to commit troops in light of the fact that the cold war was thawing, and he also felt pressure from business sectors to reduce military spending. Neither the U.S. people nor the president had an appetite for another Korea, a long and bloody war with little prospect of a clear-cut victory. Eisenhower, Nixon, and the CIA instead chose the Guatemala model: They organized an invasion force, in this case composed of anti-Castro Cuban exiles, and simultaneously applied economic and political pressure in an effort to weaken the Cuban government.

As with all such "national security" operations, the CIA violated existing laws and international agreements. The Agency launched a campaign of orchestrated deception designed not only to trick Castro but also to convince the U.S. public that its own government was not violating the law—until the day that the government could pull the victory rabbit out of the hat and render moot the issue of lawbreaking.[19]

The CIA made lying into a routine way of life in order to mislead the press, Congress, and those members of the government not involved in the plot.[20] The attorney general was not allowed to enforce the law; the FBI could not investigate prima facie violations of innumerable federal statutes. State and local authorities had to collaborate as well, without any debate, public discussion, or serious analysis of the possible consequences of the operation on the future of the United States.

President Kennedy, however, discovered that an operation that entailed systematic lying to the public institutionalized prevarication at all levels. The president himself received distorted information as the intelligence and covert operational arms of the CIA hopelessly confused their roles. The very people whose responsibility it was to plan a successful invasion self-servingly distorted information about internal conditions in Cuba, about the ability of the revolutionaries to resist the invasion, about the unity of the exile forces, and, finally, about the possibilities for military success.[21]

The operation also took on a bureaucratic life of its own. Shortly after the president was inaugurated, CIA director Allen Dulles told Kennedy that he would face a "disposal problem" should he not go ahead with the invasion of Cuba. What would the president do with the thousands of Cuban exiles that had been promised his support for the liberation of their island? They had been well trained in the arts of death and destruction. Would the exiles be easily assimilable into the United States? It would be unlikely that President Somoza would accept thousands of trained and armed Cubans in Nicaragua; Miguel Ydígoras, the Guatemalan dictator, also would be reluctant to take them. So, the CIA chief concluded, Kennedy either had to launch them or try to deal with the political consequences of what would appear to be cowardice and betrayal.[22]

Kennedy was not the only victim of the CIA's lying. After B-25s, painted with Cuban Air Force insignia and piloted by Cuban exiles, bombed several military airports in Cuba, the dignified U.S. ambassador to the United Nations, two-time presidential candidate Adlai Stevenson, swore that the United States had not been involved in these preinvasion bombings. Formidable figures in the White House had told him this, and he had conveyed their lies to the world in a widely publicized speech before the U.N. General Assembly. In fact, the air raids, as the press discovered, originated in Florida; the Cuban exile pilots were trained and paid by the CIA.

Stevenson's humiliation was shared by top White House adviser Arthur M. Schlesinger, Jr., a distinguished historian. Schlesinger, who was designated the front man for the CIA's hand-picked replacement Cuban government and had to speak in its name (the members of this government remained virtual prisoners of the Agency in the Florida Everglades), uttered falsehoods about the nature of the invasion as well as of the exile attack force.[23]

The White House influenced powerful publishers not to pursue stories that might have led to discoveries about the nature of the Bay of Pigs operation. *New York Times* reporter Tad Szulc discovered the important facts about the Bay of Pigs landing, including its date, place of embarkation, and number of troops.[24] Given that Congress had not declared war, there were no legal limits on his writing the story. Nevertheless, the *Times* publisher phoned the White House and asked President Kennedy if the *Times* should run the story. Kennedy purportedly said that publication would adversely affect national security. The *Times* then censored key facts in the Szulc story: the date of the invasion and the place of disembarkation. Kennedy later said that he had erred and that had the *Times* published the facts, he might have had to cancel the operation. But the *Times* publisher assumed that U.S. interests required the nation's leading newspaper to obey the secrecy rules of the national security apparatus.

The CIA added to its payroll thousands of Cuban exiles who were expected to participate in the invasion and non-Cubans who served as case officers, supply coordinators, and payroll masters. Accountants, lawyers, and public relations experts became CIA personnel. More ominously, the Agency assembled an elite squadron known as Section 40—a kind of SS unit, also made up of Cuban exiles—to "mop up" after the invaders secured the island.[25]

This vast illegal bureaucracy began operating in 1959, endured well beyond the 1961 invasion, and involved criminal elements, such as Mafia specialists for assassination plots.[26] When their specific assignments ended, however, these criminals had a hold upon the White House.[27] They were witnesses to government illegality. Men such as Adlai Stevenson and Arthur Schlesinger could not long ignore the obvious question: How could such a government then be expected to apply the very law of which it was so contemptuous?

The Bay of Pigs operation opened a new chapter in national security history. Thousands of people, coordinated in secret, operated in the United States and several other countries. National security managers not only planned the overthrow of a foreign government; they also selected the future officeholders in the new government. It was one of the largest conspiracies history had ever known.

For all of President Kennedy's talk about freedom and democracy, he did not force the CIA to replace the former Batista officers who remained the military commanders of the invasion. Or was Kennedy unaware of the composition of the counterrevolutionary force's military leaders—had he been deliberately misled by the CIA? Did he know of the Section 40 operation? Did he authorize the numerous assassination plots against Castro?[28]

Castro told of one assassination plot. He was fond of chocolate milkshakes and frequented the Havana Libre Hotel (formerly the Havana Hilton), which had the best shakes. The CIA, according to Castro, had delivered a "pernicious poison" to its agent, the bartender who routinely prepared the milkshakes. The bartender had hidden the venom in the freezer, next to the chocolate ice cream container. On the following night, when Castro showed up for his milkshake, the poison luckily stuck to the side of the freezer and the bartender did not want to risk attracting the attention of Castro's bodyguards by trying to pry the container loose. The man was caught soon after, as the result of an informer, and he confessed the plot. Castro's chemists subsequently analyzed the poison and discovered that had Castro swallowed it, he would have died without the toxin leaving a trace in his bloodstream.

Kennedy's refusal to allow U.S. aircraft to participate directly in the bombing of Cuba, which originally was planned as part of the Bay of Pigs operation, indicated that he foresaw outraged international reaction. Key friends and allies did not share the view that the Cuban Revolution posed a grave threat to U.S. national security. Kennedy knew that the operation to bring about Castro's demise and install a "friendly" government had to be kept covert in order to avoid blatantly flying in the face of international law, custom, and opinion. At best, the covert operation offered a flimsy "plausible deniability" excuse.

Western European leaders understood the dynamics of revolutionary nationalism. Given U.S. power, the allies believed that the U.S. government was overreacting to what they viewed as fundamentally a neocolonial independence struggle. The Europeans had more experience and therefore were more sophisticated at managing colonial and neocolonial unrest.

General Charles de Gaulle, a conservative, had seen the inevitability of the revolutionary process. After becoming president in

1958, he withdrew French forces from Algeria, and France subsequently reforged amicable relations with its ex-colony. But the national security elite in Washington did not even consider the possibility that the United States could "lose control" of territory located within the nation's historic sphere. De Gaulle understood that attempts to maintain hegemony by force produced horrific consequences for the people of both nations.[29] Had Kennedy considered these consequences and understood the lessons the French learned in Algeria and Indochina, the United States might have avoided not only the fiasco of the Bay of Pigs but the catastrophe of Vietnam.

Unlike the French president, national security intellectuals did not see political developments in the Third World as part of a historical process, a process that often replicated the United States' own struggle against British colonial domination in the eighteenth century. Nor were policymakers willing to settle for diplomatic relations on an equal footing, however amicable, with independent, geographically proximate nations that previously had been subordinate to the United States. Any loss of control was viewed as a grave threat to U.S. national security.

## The Alliance for Progress and Counterinsurgency

The Cuban Revolution forced national security planners out of their complacency. The world scene had changed, and the old formulas for preventing revolution no longer worked. Castroism had emerged as a spreading political virus threatening U.S. hegemony throughout the Third World. Just five years after the successful Iran and Guatemala coups, the national security elite had to return to the covert drawing board to devise a new policy to stem the tide of Third World revolution. The urgency of the situation was heightened by a sense of growing competition between the United States and the Soviet Union, whose influence in the Third World seemed to be expanding rapidly.

What emerged from the policy circles in the aftermath of the April 1961 failure was the Alliance for Progress, a positive challenge to Castro and to revolutionaries throughout the Third World. The Alliance called for a development competition and promised that Washington would help Latin America arise from poverty and leap onto the road to modernization. At the same time, the CIA continued its efforts to harass and, if possible, destroy the Cuban economy.

The national security elite turned to a formula used effectively by Woodrow Wilson and Franklin Roosevelt—the elite turned on the rhetoric of democracy and let it flow from the mouths of the president and his key associates and allies. Their words were matched by an impressive economic offering to all the countries of the hemisphere, save Cuba. "Let us once again transform the American continent into a vast crucible of revolutionary ideas and efforts," said President Kennedy, "a tribute to the power of the creative energies of free men and women—an example to all the world that liberty and progress walk hand in hand."[30]

The Alliance for Progress did not spring from a newfound zeal to better the lot of Latin Americans. This policy to promote development and democracy was based on the fear that if Washington did not offer a progressive model for social change, someone else would, and the United States could "lose" Latin America. This was not altogether a new idea in Washington policy circles. The notion of a modern infrastructure as the foundation for development below the Rio Grande was introduced by Secretary of State William Jennings Bryan in 1913. Infrastructure existed as an idea in academic and policy circles even in the somnolent councils of the Eisenhower administration. Secretary of State John Foster Dulles, terrified that the United States would lose pieces of territory, even suggested the developmental carrot along with the military stick for Guatemala in 1953. "If we don't look out," he warned Congress, "we will wake up one morning and read in the newspapers that there happened in South America the same kind of thing that happened in China in 1949."[31]

The idea that the United States should make a massive contribution toward Latin American development had been raised by Fidel Castro in early May 1959, when he addressed a meeting of twenty-one Latin American nations. "Latin America's economic development requires a financing of thirty thousand million dollars over a period of ten years," Castro told the assembled Latin leaders. "Only from the United States can we get such a sum and only through government financing." Castro proceeded to raise the political counterpart to economic development that Kennedy also used later. "Political instability—tyranny—is not the result of underdevelopment but the cause of underdevelopment."[32]

President Kennedy made the Alliance for Progress and the Latin American Peace Corps program the centerpieces of his hemispheric policies.[33] Kennedy opened the U.S. checkbook to promote development, claiming that democracy and stability would follow modernization. With this bold and humanitarian approach, the Kennedy administration captured the imagination of progressive Latin Americans. Such a model presumed that the middle classes, both professional and business, would lead an economic offensive to displace the oligarchies that stultified the political and economic life of most countries in the region. A kind of foreign New Deal, a Latin American Marshall Plan, the Alliance for Progress tied economic reform to political democracy on the grounds that sane growth not only required the consent of the governed, but that without it the Castro model would be equally or more appealing.[34]

In fact, the Alliance did take some of the steam out of the revolutionary locomotive that the Cuban Revolution had fueled. In the early, heady days of Alliance talk, big spending plans, and progressive rhetoric, the media paid less attention to the other, the unattractive side of the Kennedy policy coin: counterinsurgency. But the liberal activism of the Alliance and the national security rigidity of counterinsurgency could not, it turned out, become successfully wed in one happy policy. Instead, the military side first eroded and then destroyed the progressive developmental side. Counterinsurgency not only reinforced the repressive mechanisms of traditional power and control—state police, national guard, and elite army units—it also consolidated the hold of the national security planners and froze out the innovators who sought to reform the old system through structural development.

The national security bureaucracy, while uneasy about talk of democracy and development, felt very comfortable with the military side of the Kennedy program. The national security policymakers placed little trust in reform; their bottom line was keeping territory under U.S. control. To accomplish that, they trusted the generals, not the reformers, the secret police officials, not the development economists. The U.S. tradition with Latin America was built on the notion that U.S. security depended on the native military and the oligarchs and ultimately on the willingness of the president to send troops and gunboats.[35] The inherent conflict in the Alliance was mirrored in the young president himself, who combined progressive rhetoric with fierce anticommunism. He greatly admired tough generals in his own army such as Maxwell Taylor, "Kennedy's general," and Edward Lansdale, the counterinsurgency expert, who tried to convince the national security elite that reform and counterinsurgency were necessary marriage partners in the modern world.

Counterinsurgency, however, meant that the U.S. government would have to support the same repressive organs that for decades had maintained the oligarchies and their privileges. While Alliance for Progress officials proposed a vigorous campaign to demonstrate the superiority of capitalist democracy over revolutionary socialism, counterinsurgency operators who sought to wipe out revolutionaries used antidemocratic methods and trained local security forces in them.

The enlightenment language that inspired progressive Latin Americans also obscured for them the inevitable return to the dark ages of repression that would follow logically from the counterinsurgency programs. The Kennedy leaders were taking no chances. The Cuban experiment had electrified Latin America, not only because of Cuba's reforms in such areas as literacy, health, employment, and education, but also because Cuba claimed that its revolution proved that dedicated guerrillas could overthrow tyrants and their U.S.-backed armies.[36] The national security planners' failure to destroy Castro and the Cuban Revolution only increased the planners' determination to prevail elsewhere.

In Southeast Asia, the twin policies of development and counterinsurgency also appeared, and as in Latin America, the military side prevailed. Vietnam became the supreme test of U.S. will and determination as well as a test of the U.S. ability to adapt its national security policy to the lessons of three years of bloody war in Korea and the successful Cuban Revolution. Should U.S. power prevail in Vietnam, national security planners thought, the lesson will be crystal clear for the rest of the Third World: No more revolutions will be permitted.

### Notes

1. After the Spanish-American War, with Cuba under U.S. military administration, Cubans were allowed to hold a constitutional convention. They were informed by the U.S. Secretary of War, Elihu Root, that the withdrawal of U.S. forces depended on the inclusion in the new Cuban constitution of a set of provisions sponsored by U.S. senator Orville Platt, of which Article III read: "The government of Cuba consents that the United States may exercise the right to intervene for the preservation of Cuban independence, the maintenance of a government adequate for the protection of life, property, and individual liberty, and for discharging obligations with respect to Cuba imposed by the treaty of Paris on the United States, now to be assumed and undertaken by the government of Cuba."

A letter from General Leonard Wood, military governor of Cuba, to President Theodore Roosevelt demonstrated the importance of the Platt Amendment to the United States: "There is little or no real independence left to Cuba under the Platt Amendment. . . . She is absolutely in our hands, and I believe no European government for a moment believes that she is otherwise than a practical dependency of the United States. With the control we have over Cuba, a control that will soon undoubtedly become a possession, we shall soon practically control the world sugar market. . . . I believe

Cuba to be a most desirable acquisition for the United States" (cited in Peter Bourne, *Fidel: A Biography of Fidel Castro* [New York: Dodd-Mead, 1986], pp. 8–9).

The Cubans complied on June 12, 1902, U.S. forces withdrew May 20 of that year, and, for good measure, the Platt Amendment was incorporated subsequently in a U.S.-Cuban treaty on May 22, 1903. U.S. forces subsequently occupied Cuba from 1906 to 1909 and 1917 to 1922 and intervened briefly in 1912. In 1934, U.S. emissary Sumner Welles negotiated a treaty with the government of Carlos Mendieta, thereby abrogating the Platt Amendment. See Louis A. Perez, Jr., *Intervention, Revolution, and Politics in Cuba, 1913–1921* (Pittsburgh: University of Pittsburgh Press, 1978), and Ambrosio V. López Hidalgo, *Cuba y la Enmienda Platt* (Havana: Siglo XX, 1921).

The amendment prefigured the Roosevelt corollary to the Monroe Doctrine, proclaimed in 1904; see Alexander DeConde, *A History of American Foreign Policy* (New York: Charles Scribner's Sons, 1978), pp. 351–353; and the *Congressional Record*, 58th Cong., 3rd Session, vol. 39 (Washington, D.C.: U.S. Government Printing Office, 1905), p. 19.

2. See C. Wright Mills, *Listen Yankee* (New York: Ballantine Books, 1960); Jean Paul Sartre, *Sartre on Cuba* (New York: Ballantine Books, 1960).

3. Jose Martí, *On Art and Literature* (New York: Monthly Review Press, 1982).

4. See Jorge Dominguez, *Cuba* (Cambridge, Mass.: Belknap Press, 1978), pp. 93–129.

5. Hugh Thomas, *Cuba: The Pursuit of Freedom* (New York: Harper and Row), 1971, pp. 1015–1019.

6. Robert Smith, *The United States and Cuba* (New York: Bookman Associates, 1960).

7. See James O'Connor, *The Origins of Socialism in Cuba* (Ithaca, N.Y.: Cornell University Press, 1970), pp. 155–168.

8. For Castro's version of events, see Martin Kenner and James Petras, eds., *Fidel Castro Speaks* (New York: Grove Press, 1969), pp. 4–16.

9. After trials, some seventy-one Batista-era officials were shot on January 21, 1959; several hundred more may have been killed that year. Herbert L. Matthews, *Revolution in Cuba* (New York: Charles Scribner's Sons, 1975), pp. 131–135; and R. Hart Phillips, *The Cuban Dilemma* (New York: Charles Scribner's Sons, 1962), pp. 96–97.

10. Reprinted in *La Revolución,* September 1960.

11. Gabriel Kolko, *The Roots of American Foreign Policy* (Boston: Beacon Press, 1969), pp. 81–82.

12. O'Connor, *The Origins of Socialism in Cuba,* p. 322.

13. Told to the author by René Vallejo, July 1968.

14. Peter Wyden, *Bay of Pigs: The Untold Story* (New York: Simon and Schuster, 1979), pp. 29–31.

15. The Soviet Union, through its willingness to provide arms, economic aid, and infrastructural investment, has acted as an insurance company to those Third World revolutions, such as Cuba or Vietnam, that established

hegemonic political rule by communist parties. Cuba, for example, is a partner in the Soviet commercial and economic system. Countries such as Nicaragua that are revolutionary but not communist are eligible for aid, but not the size and scope given to those that have a consolidated Marxist-Leninist government in power.

16. See O'Connor, *The Origins of Socialism in Cuba*, pp. 161–165, and Maurice Zeitlin and Robert Scheer, *Cuba: Tragedy in Our Hemisphere* (New York: Grove Press, 1963), p. 175. On sugar, see Robert F. Smith, *What Happened in Cuba* (New York: Twayne Publishers, 1963), pp. 277–278.

17. On the same trip, Castro spoke before the Council on Foreign Relations and encountered a barrage of hostile questions. For an account, see Laurence Shoup and William Minter, *Imperial Brain Trust* (New York: Monthly Review Press, 1977), pp. 42–43.

18. Conversation between Castro, author, Frank Mankiewicz, and Kirby Jones, July 1974, in Havana.

19. In practice, however, the CIA found that its Cuban operation was more difficult to organize than had been previous clandestine coups. For one thing, it was difficult to maintain secrecy with such a large operation; thousands of Cuban exiles living in the United States had to be recruited, trained, financed, and sent to Guatemala for final preparations before the actual invasion from Nicaragua. Moreover, the plan had to span two administrations, endure endless bickering among the Cuban factions, and survive the predictable jealousies and rivalries inside the national security management circles as well.

One of the Miami conspirators, David Attlee Philips, had belonged to the CIA's station in Cuba in 1959. Philips, who had a passion for theater and real-life deception, formed a bogus public relations outfit to issue optimistic statements about the course of the invasion itself. Under Philips' direction, not a word of truth emerged about the actual progress of the landing and the ensuing battles. Philips called himself one of the world's greatest liars in his book *The Night Watch* (New York: Atheneum, 1977).

20. David Attlee Philips' phony PR firm issued press releases on the Bay of Pigs landing and the ensuing battles, claiming that the invaders were on the verge of victory even as they faced total defeat. See ibid.

21. "The CIA men . . . were in the enviable position of both organizing a clandestine operation and preparing the intelligence data through which the validity of the venture could be judged." Karl E. Meyer and Tad Szulc, *The Cuban Invasion* (New York: Praeger, 1962), pp. 79–80.

22. Wyden, *Bay of Pigs,* pp. 99–101; and Schlesinger, Jr., *A Thousand Days* (Boston: Houghton Mifflin, 1965), p. 242.

23. Schlesinger, ibid., p. 277.

24. Wyden, *Bay of Pigs,* pp. 153–155; and Schlesinger, ibid., p. 261.

25. Author's conversations with members of the "mop-up" squad and with some of their CIA commanders, 1977–1981.

26. See U.S. Senate, Select Committee to Study Governmental Operations with Respect to Intelligence Activities, *Alleged Assassination Plots Involving*

*Foreign Leaders* (Washington, D.C.: U.S. Government Printing Office, 1975), pp. 79–180. Some of the Cuban exiles trained by the CIA later turned to drug trafficking and other sorts of crime, with a proclivity for extreme violence. See Penny Lernoux, "The Miami Connection," *The Nation,* February 18, 1984, pp. 186–198.

27. Among those working inside the CIA's Miami station, known as JMWAVE, was E. Howard Hunt, an Agency "cowboy," or clandestine operator, who brought together key Cuban exiles with military and intelligence experience. One of them was Bernard Barker, a former Batista security official. The two men, and others involved in the Bay of Pigs conspiracy, emerged later in relation to the infamous Watergate affair under President Nixon. Their names also appeared in the Warren Commission report on the Kennedy assassination. Others would later be linked to criminal activities or clandestine operations in Chile and Nicaragua.

28. White House personnel allegedly came up with plots ranging from giving Castro an exploding cigar to poisoning his wetsuit.

29. For example, de Gaulle warned Kennedy on Indochina: "You will find that intervention in this area will be an endless entanglement. Once a nation has been aroused, no foreign power, however strong, can impose its will upon it. . . . The ideology which you invoke will make no difference. Indeed, in the eyes of the masses it will become identified with your will to power. That is why the more you become involved out there against Communism, the more the Communists will appear as the champions of national independence." Charles de Gaulle, *Memoirs of Hope: Renewal and Endeavor* (New York: Simon and Schuster, 1970), p. 256.

30. John F. Kennedy, at Punta del Este, March 13, 1961.

31. Cited in Walter LaFeber, *Inevitable Revolutions* (New York: W. W. Norton, 1983), p. 328. Unlike the liberal Kennedys, Dulles and his advisers did not want to spend money on development. His notion, closer to the Reagan view, was to push private investment in the region, thereby ensuring U.S. control by tying the local military establishments even closer to the United States. Dulles had reason to feel optimistic about this policy after the successful CIA coup in Guatemala.

32. *La Revolución,* May 6, 1959. Peter Bourne cited the real origin of the Alliance for Progress: "In his speech in Buenos Aires, Fidel proposed the creation of a Latin American Common Market . . . and that the United States launch a ten-year, $30 billion economic aid program for Latin America. The United States' representative rejected the latter plan as ridiculous. Three years later, President Kennedy would unveil essentially the same proposal as the Alliance for Progress. Ernesto Betancourt, who accompanied Fidel to the conference but who shortly thereafter went into exile in the United States, was responsible for coining the term, 'Alliance for Progress,' and provided it to Kennedy's staff." Bourne, *Fidel,* p. 177.

33. The Peace Corps promoted the notion of U.S. idealists going abroad to dispel the growing accusation about U.S. cultural imperialism. Peace Corps volunteers were supposed to "help the natives to help themselves."

However, in Kennedy's mind, the Peace Corps was very much a weapon
in the competitive struggle against communism. Each trainee received and
was tested on a pamphlet entitled "What You Must Know About Communism."
Peace Corps director R. Sargent Shriver emphasized to Congress that the
Peace Corps was an important anticommunist instrument. "Either we do
those jobs," Shriver said, referring to "helping" the natives, "or the Communists will." Gerard T. Rice, *The Bold Experiment: JFK's Peace Corps*
(Notre Dame, Ind.: University of Notre Dame, 1985), p. 257.

34. Robert F. Kennedy wrote that immediately after World War II, "we
were content to accept and even support whatever governments were in
power, asking only that they not disturb the surface calm of the hemisphere.
We gave medals to dictators, praised backward regimes, and became steadily
identified with institutions and men who held their land in poverty and
fear. . . . In the late 1950's the failure of this policy or lack of policy,
erupted into anti-Americanism and the growth of Communism. Vice President
Nixon was mobbed and stoned in Caracas. Communist revolution—a product
less of Castro and his band in the Sierra Maestra than of the bloody and
corrupt tyranny of Batista, which we supported to the moment of its collapse—
took power in Cuba; and Castro's defiance of the United States aroused the
secret admiration of many who hated communism, but rejoiced to see the
discomfort of the huge and seemingly callous giant to the north." Robert
F. Kennedy, *To Seek a Newer World* (Garden City, N.Y.: Doubleday, 1967),
pp. 65–66.

35. On the Alliance's support for military governments, particularly in
the case of Brazil, see Jerome Levinson and Juan de Onis, *The Alliance
that Lost Its Way* (Chicago: Quadrangle Books, 1970).

36. Revolutionaries before Castro had accepted the dictum "You can
make revolution with the army or without the army, but never against the
army." The Cuban guerrillas claimed that they had proved the old maxim
wrong. Revolution, of course, proved far less exportable than U.S. policymakers feared or revolutionaries hoped. French theorist Regis Debray contended that small groups of guerrillas could insinuate themselves into the
countryside in elusive *focos* (centers of guerrilla operations) and create
revolution virtually through force of will. But Ernesto "Che" Guevara's
spectacular failure in Bolivia, and the collapse of numerous other *foco*-type
insurgencies, demonstrated that local peculiarities and close ties between
the combatants and the local population were the determining factors in
the success of a guerrilla war.

# CHAPTER 8

# Kennedy, Johnson, and Counterinsurgency: The Institutionalization of Distortion

 *There are three billion people in the world and we have only 200 million of them. We are outnumbered 15 to 1. If might made right, they would sweep over the United States and take what we have. We have what they want.*
—Lyndon Johnson, November 1966

## Vietnam: The Early Years

At the end of World War II, the Allies returned Vietnam to the French, who fought a bloody war from 1946 to 1954 to retain their Indochinese colony. U.S. wartime policymakers had supplied Ho Chi Minh with arms, with which Ho's forces had fought courageously against the Japanese. Although his communism was no secret, Ho actively sought good relations with the United States, and President Roosevelt resisted French efforts to hold onto their old empire.[1] But the onset of the cold war and the "fall" of China in 1949 hardened attitudes. In 1950, determined to avert "Chinese expansionism," President Truman began to bankroll the French fight against Ho and the Viet Minh.[2]

Ironically, Ho Chi Minh had been one of the foremost opponents of Vietnamese reliance on China. Indeed, he voiced a deep-seated

Vietnamese fear of their neighbor. When some members of his party were arguing in 1946 that the Chinese would serve as a buffer force against the French, Ho protested:

> You fools. Don't you realize what it means if the Chinese stay? Don't you remember our history? The last time the Chinese came they stayed one thousand years! The French are foreigners. They are weak. Colonialism is dying out. Nothing will be able to withstand world pressure for independence. They may stay for a while, but they will have to go because the white man is finished in Asia. But if the Chinese stay now, they will never leave. As for me, I prefer to smell French shit for five years, rather than Chinese shit for the rest of my life.[3]

In early 1954, the U.S. military proposed direct intervention, including nuclear strikes, to save the French forces at the siege of Dien Bien Phu, but cooler heads prevailed. The painful experience of the costly yet inconclusive Korean War stopped Washington from intervening during the 1950s and, indeed, the French preferred to handle matters themselves.[4]

Under the Geneva Accords that brought the French effort to a close, Ho, apparently under pressure from the Chinese and Soviets, ceded the southern half of Vietnam to French administration for two years, on the promise that free elections would be held throughout the country on July 20, 1956. Ho was confident that he could win elections, as were Western observers.

Eisenhower himself wrote in his memoirs that if elections had been held, Ho would have won 80 percent of the vote, but Ho apparently had not reckoned with U.S. determination. Eisenhower, working with key Democrats and high Catholic church figures, ordered the CIA and select military units to build up the South Vietnamese army and police. Ngo Dinh Diem, a Catholic aristocrat, was chosen as the potential strongman; his supporters in the United States included such unlikely bedfellows as William O. Douglas, Cardinal Francis Spellman, and Senators Mike Mansfield and John F. Kennedy.[5]

When Diem refused to hold elections as promised in 1956, Eisenhower backed him. Dulles argued that because "free" elections—that is, elections in which a U.S.-backed candidate would win—were "impossible," they should not be held. This statement was echoed in Henry Kissinger's statement after the 1970 election of socialist Dr. Salvador Allende to the presidency of Chile that a country should not be allowed "to go communist because of the irresponsibility of its own people" and George Shultz's denunciation of Nicaragua's 1984 election almost a year before it occurred. (For several decades, the national security elite has defined "free elections" in the Third World as those contests in which the U.S.-backed candidate wins.[6]) For the rest of the 1950s, a U.S. bureaucracy— virtually a colonial administration—grew up in South Vietnam and bolstered Diem's capricious rule.

## Kennedy and Vietnam

By 1960, the notion of an American Century was less viable. The tide of Third World revolution, Western European recovery, and unexpected Soviet military and scientific breakthroughs had diluted the U.S. postwar supremacy. The memory of the stalemate in Korea had lessened the fervor for fighting wars "anywhere at any time." But the forward thrust for empire had not died; rather, it had mellowed during the Eisenhower years.

The forceful Kennedy brothers sought to revitalize the national security bureaucracy, which had grown cautious under the budgetary restraints and conservative attitudes that Eisenhower had imposed after the costly Korean War. John F. Kennedy assumed power as revolutions appeared to be spreading through the Third World. The questions he posed to his policy team were "where" and "how," not "whether," to meet this perceived mortal threat to the U.S. system.[7]

In his less than three years in office, President Kennedy did not make a reputation for his progressive programs at home, but he did initiate, in the words of his chief speechwriter, Theodore Sorenson, the "build-up of the most powerful military force in human history— the largest and swiftest build-up in this country's peacetime history."[8] Under Kennedy, national security meant Polaris and Minuteman missiles, increased reliance on the infantry and the navy, and massive escalation on the intelligence, covert action, and counterinsurgency fronts.

The national security forces felt tough by the time Kennedy died; they had fleshed out and matured from Eisenhower's more niggardly approach. The stage was set, even before Kennedy died in Dallas, for the United States to make Vietnam the "center of our concerns."

Kennedy's virile rhetoric called upon the U.S. public to make sacrifices for the country and, in turn, for other people struggling for freedom. Kennedy meant by "freedom" the same thing as Truman: Those nations that proclaimed anticommunism belonged to the "free world." No matter how vicious the dictator in power, as long as he was anticommunist, his nation belonged to the "free world." Freedom meant anticommunism, but Kennedy made it sound attractive, even positive. His handsome face showed will and determination as he told the world that the nation's citizens would "pay any price" and "bear any burden" in order "to get things moving again."

On the domestic front, Kennedy's pro–civil rights rhetoric seemed to give a meaning to the word "freedom" that obscured the realities of his foreign policy course. Liberals, long awaiting a charismatic leader after Franklin Roosevelt's death, flocked to Kennedy, although he delivered little in the way of civil rights or civil liberties initiatives. Few of the "best and the brightest" who joined the Kennedy team anticipated that Kennedy's course would steer the country into its most difficult conflict since the Civil War.[9]

### The Empire Takes a Stand in Asia

Some 10,000 miles from Washington, in what had become known only eight years before as the Republic of South Vietnam, Ngo Dinh Diem was having difficulty keeping the lid on a revolt that appeared by March 1960 to be developing into an insurgency. President Kennedy was determined to meet the challenge. Vietnam and Laos together seemed to be headed toward the Asian version of the Cuban revolutionary road, one that would seriously impede U.S. access to a strategic region.

Throughout 1961 and 1962, as the Kennedy team debated whether or not to send U.S. troops to Cuba, they also had begun to send over thousands of military "advisers" into Southeast Asia. The use of the word "adviser," however, misled Congress, the press, and the public. The men who advised were Green Berets, elite shock troops, specially trained for counterinsurgency warfare. They fought in rural Vietnam using the U.S. Embassy as headquarters and South Vietnamese Army installations as bases. With President Diem's blessing and with the cooperation of the client Thai government, the Green Berets and the air force coordinated a secret war in Laos to prevent the procommunist nationalist forces led by Souvanna Phouma from winning power there.[10]

Attorney General Robert Kennedy and national security adviser McGeorge Bundy worked with Generals Maxwell Taylor and Edward Lansdale and shunned some of the veteran CIA bureaucrats, whom Kennedy held in contempt because of their failure in the Bay of Pigs. The stodgy national security bureaucracy led by Allen Dulles at CIA and J. Edgar Hoover at FBI did not offer the "maximum flexibility" that Kennedy and his cohorts deemed necessary for proper imperial management in an era of rising revolutions.

## Eyeball to Eyeball

The first two years of Kennedy's administration were some of the most trying times since the national security apparatus had come to dominate the U.S. government. This period included the Bay of Pigs fiasco, the dramatic building of the Berlin Wall, rising tensions with the European allies, the erosion of the Diem regime in Vietnam, and, perhaps most important, the placement in September and October 1962 of Soviet medium-range missiles and bombers in Cuba.

As a result of Kennedy's less-than-secret intention to destroy the Cuban Revolution, the Soviets had agreed to Castro's request and did what the United States had done to them: They moved nuclear weapons close to U.S. territory. Washington had ringed Soviet territory with U.S. bases and had flown around-the-clock missions of Strategic Air Command bombers with live nuclear payloads to the Soviet border and then had turned back.

For the first time in its history, the United States faced—only 90 miles from its coastline—the reality of an enemy with the capability of delivering nuclear weapons. Kennedy answered the Soviet installation of intermediate-range missiles and bombers in Cuba with a naval blockade that stopped Soviet ships from reaching Cuba.

The anxious world waited as the superpowers went "eyeball to eyeball," as Secretary of State Dean Rusk phrased it. To the relief of most of the world someone "blinked"—the Soviets—and the missile crisis faded into the Kennedy-Khrushchev accords, which guaranteed Cuba's territorial integrity in exchange for the Soviets' removal of their nuclear weapons. Kennedy was prepared to remove U.S. nuclear missiles from Turkey, on the Soviet border, but Khrushchev began to dismantle the Cuban missiles before the Turkey deal was offered.[11]

Although Kennedy may well have learned lessons about dealing with the Soviets and the risks of nuclear war as a result of the missile crisis, it did not deter him sufficiently from moving further into Southeast Asia. By the time of his death in November 1963, the national security apparatus had become invested in Vietnam and was tied deeply to its politics by virtue of the crucial U.S. role in deposing the highly unpopular Ngo Dinh Diem, the very man the policymakers had imposed as president.[12]

U.S. involvement was especially important in conducting the war because U.S. advisers ran the counterinsurgency effort. The national security bureaucracy had made a policy investment in Vietnam, and the bureaucracy's primary focus turned from Cuba to Vietnam. Nevertheless, the CIA maintained a massive Miami-based operation in the early 1960s. Using acronyms such as JMWAVE, MONGOOSE, and MKULTRA for deadly exercises, the CIA set up programs designed to destabilize and sabotage the Cuban government and assassinate Castro. Harvard Ph.D.s designed plans to poison Fidel Castro's scuba diving suit and ordered CIA chemists to prepare potions that would make his beard fall out.[13]

Despite the CIA's continuing focus on Castro, revolution in Southeast Asia appeared as a far greater challenge to U.S. hegemony, one, that if met successfully, surely would lead to a surge of will and support for counterrevolution elsewhere. Vietnam and Laos then became the theaters in which Kennedy sought to reestablish U.S. might.[14]

### The Transition: From Advisers to Troops

By mid-1964, Lyndon Johnson's advisers had convinced him that the current level of counterinsurgency could not defeat the Viet Cong nor could increased advisers and aid to the South Vietnamese military accomplish the task. In order to protect himself politically during the coming presidential election and lay the groundwork for dispatching higher levels of U.S. troops to Southeast Asia, Johnson resorted to a national security ruse: the Gulf of Tonkin incident, which led to the Tonkin Gulf resolution.

Johnson presented a fabricated report to Congress that North Vietnamese warships had attacked a U.S. vessel in international waters, in the Gulf of Tonkin.[15] Congress responded to Johnson's impassioned request for emergency war powers by ceding its constitutional warmaking powers and granting the president the power to send U.S. troops onto the Asian mainland.

The Tonkin Gulf lie, with which direct troop involvement in Vietnam began, became institutionalized. The national security bureaucracy lied to Congress and the public, and one branch of the bureaucracy told lies to others. Lying became endemic if not organic to the national security apparatus during the course of the Vietnam War.[16] The Tonkin Gulf resolution, however, provided the administration with almost four years of bipartisan backing for its Vietnam policy, but that would not be enough.

Lyndon Johnson was elected in November 1964, and by an impressive margin. He ran as a peace candidate, depicting his opponent, Barry Goldwater, as dangerous and ideologically impulsive. Johnson's campaigners portrayed the president as a moderate man. In fact, Johnson had a guns-and-butter solution for bringing together domestic and foreign policy. With the social programs of the Great Society he wanted to finish what FDR had begun in the New Deal, while also realizing Henry Luce's American Century dream.

## The Dominican Intervention

On April 28, 1965, Johnson dispatched marines to the Dominican Republic to ensure that there would be no Cuban-style revolution there. The impact of the move was immense, especially on those whom Kennedy had convinced that the Alliance for Progress meant the end of the old interventionist U.S. policies. No Latin American could maintain illusions that the Alliance for Progress somehow meant that the United States had changed its interventionist ways. Some 23,000 U.S. troops squelched a popular Dominican movement and lent their support to an unpopular rightist military government that with U.S. acquiescence had ousted the elected president, Juan Bosch, in 1963.

No one can say what would have happened had Johnson not interfered in the internal affairs of the Dominicans. Some have argued that the move was both foolish and unnecessary, while others saw it as essential in stopping the spread of Fidelismo in the U.S. sphere of influence.

Like Batista of Cuba and Somoza of Nicaragua, Rafael Leonidas Trujillo, the Dominican *caudillo,* had appropriated or stolen a good share of his country's wealth. At the time of his assassination in 1961, Trujillo or members of his family owned almost half of the country's resources. Upon his death, that wealth fell into the hands of the state, and whoever controlled the state would either return the wealth to the private sector or use it as a base on which to build a different kind of economy. Shortly before gunmen ambushed Trujillo's car in 1961, the CIA had participated in an unsuccessful assassination attempt against him. Although the Agency's motive was never made clear, Trujillo was obstructing the Alliance for Progress.[17]

Kennedy had stated that given a choice between "a decent democratic regime, a continuation of the Trujillo regime, or a Castro regime, we ought to aim at the first, but we really can't renounce the second until we are sure we can avoid the third." Kennedy did try for the first, but the specter of Castroism drove him reluctantly, and Johnson enthusiastically, to support the second option.[18]

After Trujillo was killed, the majority of Dominicans participated in a free election, won in 1962 by Juan Bosch, a progressive nationalist but a far cry from being a Fidelista or communist. Bosch had spent some twenty years living in exile in the United States, and his older followers tended to be traditional nationalists but quite social democratic in their politics. The younger Bosch backers, however, were definitely influenced by Castro and the Cuban Revolution.

Determined to make the Dominican Republic a showcase of the Alliance for Progress, Kennedy backed the Bosch government, but as the Dominican president sought economic reforms and enthusiastic young politicos made anti-Yankee speeches, U.S. investors began lobbying for intervention. The air thickened with military plots, and Kennedy's early enthusiasm for Bosch waned. On September 22, 1963, as the State Department stood by, the Pentagon and CIA gave their Dominican military allies the go-ahead for Bosch's ouster. After Kennedy's death two months later, Johnson established formal relations with the new military regime, and U.S. aid, bank loans, and private investment poured into the country. When a revolt threatened to topple this military government, the national security intellectuals decided that they did not want Bosch reelected.

In violation of the OAS Charter, Johnson went ahead with an intervention that succeeded in restoring a pro-U.S. order.[19] Johnson weathered the initial domestic and international criticism; like Theodore Roosevelt in Panama before him and Ronald Reagan in Grenada after him, Johnson had learned the value of the fait accompli.

The U.S. Embassy in Santo Domingo issued reams of disinformation about the alleged communist proclivities of the defeated rebels, and preparations began for new U.S.-supervised elections, which were won in June 1966 by the rightist, pro-U.S. candidate Juan Balaguer.[20] The OAS came around and agreed to supply a peacekeeping force. Although thousands of Dominicans died, and, during the remainder of the 1960s, hundreds more would be killed or "disappeared" by the military, the Dominican intervention was a clear victory for Johnson and may explain his confidence that victory in Vietnam was simply a matter of willpower.[21]

### Escalation in Vietnam

Following substantial insurgent gains in 1964 and 1965—removing Diem did not make the South Vietnamese government popular— the Johnson administration began a process of deeper involvement in the Vietnam War. Each step was taken in the hope that it would tip the scales, that the Viet Cong and North Vietnam forces' threshold of pain finally would be exceeded.

Thus, napalming Viet Cong strongholds and bombing the North was considered a way to increase the costs to Hanoi and to bolster morale for the South Vietnamese forces. But when one level of bombing failed to work, more bombing was ordered, along with the dispatch of hundreds of thousands of U.S. troops. "Once the decision to bomb [the Democratic Republic of Vietnam] had been made," Gabriel Kolko explained, "the whole paralytic, dangerous logic of credibility extended to it as well. Once initiated, the escalatory process cannot be terminated until it delivers success, lest it, too, appear an implausible and ineffective instrument—thereby depriving military power of its ultimate menace and role as a deterrent."[22]

U.S. spokesmen offered justifications for the escalations that had worked in Greece, Korea, and Cuba and that would be used twenty years later in Central America. South Vietnam was being subverted by "arms shipments" from the North and was in turn an object of international communism. The fall of South Vietnam would lead to the "loss" of surrounding nations (dominoes), and finally, the United States simply could not afford to back down (credibility).

The purported reason for beginning to bomb North Vietnam and insurgent-controlled areas of the South was to respond to attacks against U.S. personnel and U.S. equipment at Pleiku and Qui Nhon in early 1965. Johnson's punishment for these attacks was labeled Rolling Thunder, which became a nine-year air war against the Vietnamese people, which resulted in the dropping of a greater tonnage of bombs than was dropped by all participants in World War II.

As U.S. troops grew from the 2 battalions landed in Da Nang in 1965 to 500,000 troops in 1968, the Vietnam War became an all-consuming venture. The Great Society faltered as budget deficits soared, and, finally, the domestic consensus came unglued by 1968 as opposition to the war became widespread.

The Vietnam intervention was characterized from the beginning by wholesale, systematic lying. As with the Bay of Pigs operation, national security officials lied to each other, just as government spokesmen lied to the public. Because no bureaucrat would be rewarded for expressing pessimism, tremendous pressure was exerted from above to show that U.S. policy was "working." But in Vietnam, because the war went on for so many years and received such wide media coverage, the government's mendacity became evident to the public, and the internal "credibility gap" led to a breakdown in consensus.

*The Pentagon Papers* exposed some of the institutionalized lying, but some of it was not revealed until a decade later. In 1982, CBS aired a documentary on the curious reporting about enemy troop strength by the commander of U.S. forces in Vietnam, General William Westmoreland. One of the program's consultants, Samuel Adams, a former CIA analyst, had watched his superiors distort the figures he had carefully deduced about Viet Cong strength. CBS suggested that General Westmoreland had misled President Johnson about the rebels' strength because "Westy" knew that Johnson did not want to hear the higher, or more accurate, numbers.

Indeed, as testimony revealed in the subsequent libel trial that Westmoreland brought against CBS, the general himself might well have been misled, before he in turn misled the president. What emerged from the trial and from the documents in *The Pentagon Papers* went beyond institutionalized lying in the name of national security. Lying, it turned out, was necessary to maintain a fragile consensus for a Vietnam policy that would have withered and died had the public and the policy elite itself known the truth.

"Policy" lying to maintain consensus cost the lives of Americans and Vietnamese. Fearing the withering rays of public exposure, national security spokesmen stated countless times that "the light is at the end of the tunnel," that it was only a matter of "six months," or that "with the next troop escalation, the enemy will be finished." Civilians and generals offered to the public a series of illusions that the United States could "win" the war in Vietnam.

In addition, the national security managers altered Vietnamese society in an effort to make it fit the illusion. They had forced changes in the South Vietnamese presidency, removed South Vietnam's military commanders, taught the army to fight "the American way," the air force to bomb, and the police and intelligence services sophisticated methods of repression. U.S. economic and social policies intruded on Vietnamese ways, and tens of billions of dollars poured into the Vietnamese economy and war machine. By 1969, U.S. officials ran South Vietnam. The national security objective—to build a U.S.-styled nation—had become a reality, as long as U.S. personnel remained to manage and direct it.

The purpose of bipartisan consensus, begun twenty years earlier on an appearance of "necessity" to contain the USSR, had worked for a short time to retain a U.S.-dominated world order. But U.S. power had ebbed, or it had not grown coincidentally as the Western European and Japanese allies, the Soviet Union, and Third World revolutionaries grew stronger. The bipartisan consensus of the 1940s and 1950s suffered severe reality blows. By 1970, only fading anti-communism provided the brittle intellectual glue to hold together diverging views inside Congress and among the policy elite.

To maintain the consensus for the Vietnam policy, the Johnson war team had to match the lies about day-to-day reality with new cleverness in stating the policy goals themselves, in demonizing anew the communist enemy, and, finally, in inventing catchy phrases that the media could use and then repeat to the public. The war in Vietnam was, from its outset, a war to stop a communist-led independence movement that had taken state power in the summer of 1945 on the heels of the Japanese defeat before the French could reassert colonial domination. Without understanding or caring about the depths and legitimacy of this movement, the national security elite undertook to win the "hearts and minds" of the people of South Vietnam. The national security trajectory under Kennedy and Johnson led the U.S. people to believe that the United States could somehow "win" a cultural war without knowing the language, customs, or history of the people and nation U.S. troops sought to liberate.

However, when the democracy-spreading rhetoric is compared to U.S. military tactics, to the lies and deceptions that national security officials used to obfuscate Vietnamese reality, a more base layer of motives is revealed. Phrases such as "get things moving again" or "assume any burden" and "pay any price" invariably meant that presidents had decided to destroy yet another liberation or independence movement by using horrible weapons on villages and rice paddies. The use of "freedom" language became particularly dramatic during the Vietnam War. Those who used the strongest rhetoric also told the biggest lies.

Secretary of Defense Robert McNamara and President Lyndon Johnson told the public and Congress countless times that the end was near, when both men knew it was not; that the enemy was on the run, when they knew it was not; and that they were fighting for freedom in South Vietnam. These men knew that the South Vietnamese leadership had no interest in freedom as the U.S. public understood it, but that if U.S. troops defeated the communist-led insurgency for independence, the labor, resources, and markets of Southeast Asia again would open for future development, exploitation, and design. This vast and populous region, inhabited by many millions of potentially cheap laborers, located in a strategic position with respect to China and the Soviet Union, held vast potential for the U.S. economic future. The "loss" of South Vietnam would cut off this rich resource. The national security elite never debated whether or not an area (nation-state or states) had to be controlled in order to be suitable for future development; it was assumed.

Just as Cuba's revolution could not be reversed by the CIA's army at the Bay of Pigs, so, too, the Vietnamese proved that their will, determination, and, in the end, military and political strategy could defeat the most powerful armed force with the most sophisticated technology available. None of this know-how could build a viable nation out of a Western creation; South Vietnam was not a durable concept. As a result of the Vietnam experience, the national security apparatus was weakened, limited, and circumscribed, at least for a decade.

A full-scale national debate never took place about why the United States had intervened in Vietnam. Recriminations abounded, and sorrow and mistrust spread, as did excuses, alibis, and sour-grapes analyses of how the United States could have "won." By putting the national security stamp on the war and not opening the debate on the premise of the policy itself, the basic cold war myths and dogmas remained intact.

## Notes

1. Richard Barnet, *Intervention and Revolution* (New York: World Publishing, 1968), pp. 181–184.

2. Archimedes Patti, *Why Vietnam?* (Berkeley: University of California Press, 1980), pp. 377–449.

3. Bernard Fall, *Last Reflections on a War: Last Comments on Vietnam* (New York: Doubleday, 1967), p. 85.

4. For more on Operation Vulture, the plan to "rescue" the French, see Barnet, *Intervention and Revolution,* p. 191; Gabriel Kolko, *Anatomy of a War* (New York: Pantheon, 1985), p. 82; and Peter Hayes, Lyuba Zarsky, and Walden Bello, *An American Lake: Nuclear Peril in the Pacific* (New York: Penguin, 1986), p. 55.

5. See Frances Fitzgerald, *Fire in the Lake* (Boston: The Atlantic Monthly Press, 1972), pp. 82–86.

6. For an account of the various stage-managed South Vietnamese elections in the 1960s, as well as ballots in the Dominican Republic, El Salvador, and elsewhere, see Frank Brodhead and Edward Herman, *Demonstration Elections* (Boston: South End Press, 1984), pp. 55–91.

7. President Kennedy's treasury secretary, Douglas Dillon, captured the essence of Kennedy's liberalism in a speech at the Harvard Business School on June 6, 1964, in which Dillon noted that the rate of increase in arms and space spending and interest on the national debt was double that of the Eisenhower administration, while spending on all other categories rose by "one third less than the comparable increase during the earlier four-year period." Quoted by Leo Huberman and Paul Sweezy, "The Kennedy-Johnson Boom," in Marvin Gettleman and David Mermelstein, eds., *The Great Society Reader* (New York: Vintage Books, 1967), p. 102.

8. "The Kennedy Administration's obsession with this hairy-chested form of warfare contributed to a fatal over-estimate of what the United States could hope to achieve in Southeast Asia." Godfrey Hodgson, "Disorder Within, Disorder Without," in Sanford Ungar, ed., *Estrangement: America and the World* (New York: Oxford University Press, 1985), p. 142.

9. Principled liberals in foreign policy, such as Chester Bowles, were dismissed when they raised questions about the prudence of aggressive policies in the Third World. Those who believed that the principles offered to support the just struggle of blacks at home also should have some application abroad and that Third World people merited treatment in contexts other than East versus West had no place in the Kennedy foreign policy scheme.

10. See Barnet, *Intervention and Revolution,* pp. 209–210; and chapters by Jonathan Mirsky and Stephen Stonefield, Gareth Porter, Fred Branfman, and Wilfred Burchett in Nina S. Adams and Alfred W. McCoy, eds., *Laos: War and Revolution* (New York: Harper and Row, 1970).

11. There is some indication that Castro may not have agreed with Khrushchev's method of bargaining directly with Kennedy, which excluded Cuba, the very subject of the affair.

12. On Kennedy's role in deposing Diem, see David Halberstam, *The Best and the Brightest;* and U.S. Senate, *Alleged Assassination Plots Involving Foreign Leaders, Interim Report of the Select Committee to Study Governmental Operations with Respect to Intelligence Activities,* 94th Cong., 1st sess., November 20, 1975, pp. 217–224.

13. See Warren Hinckle and William W. Turner, *The Fish Is Red: The Story of the Secret War Against Castro* (New York: Harper and Row, 1981).

14. In November 1963, John F. Kennedy was assassinated in Dallas, Texas. To this day, there has been no definitive work on who plotted and committed the murder. Almost all who have studied the affair have discovered irregularities in the behavior of members of the national security elite, especially those related to the variety of covert schemes against Cuba. Whether the proverbial chickens came home to roost may never be known. See Gaeton Fonzi, "Who Killed John F. Kennedy?" *The Washingtonian* 16, no. 2 (November 1980):157–237; and Anthony Summers, *Conspiracy* (New York: McGraw-Hill, 1981).

15. Kolko, *Anatomy of a War,* pp. 122–125, fn. 23 on p. 257; and U.S. Senate, *Hearings: Gulf of Tonkin: The 1964 Incident,* 90th Cong., 2d sess., February 20, 1968. See James Stockdale and Sybil Stockdale, *In Love and War* (New York: Harper and Row, 1984), part of which was excerpted by the *Washington Post,* October 7, 1984, p. D1, as "I Saw Us Invent the Pretext for Our Vietnam War." James Stockdale was a pilot on the aircraft carrier *USS Ticonderoga,* and on the night of August 4, 1964, he flew for three hours above the *USS Joy* and *USS Maddox,* which claimed they were being attacked by North Vietnamese vessels, and saw nothing.

16. The White House and its military allies imposed their own brands of secrecy on the already overladen "classification" complex. Secrecy no longer meant that information collected by intelligence agencies could not be shared with other government officials, elected or appointed, but that the intelligence bosses themselves had the power, indeed the obligation, to lie, if they deemed it essential to "national security."

17. U.S. Senate, *Alleged Assassination Plots,* pp. 191–215. The CIA informed staff investigators that the Agency had delivered weapons to a group of anti-

Trujillo assassins in the Dominican Republic, but not the weapons that actually were used in the Trujillo ambush.

18. Arthur M. Schlesinger, Jr., *A Thousand Days* (Boston: Houghton Mifflin, 1965), p. 660.

19. See Theodore Draper, *The Dominican Revolt: A Case Study in American Policy* (New York: Commentary, 1968); and Piero Gleijeses, *The Dominican Crisis* (Baltimore, Md.: Johns Hopkins University Press, 1977).

20. Herman, *Demonstration Elections,* pp. 17–53.

21. Normen Gall, "Santo Domingo: The Politics of Terror," *The New York Review of Books,* July 22, 1971, p. 15; Halberstam, *The Best and the Brightest.*

22. Kolko, *Anatomy of a War,* p. 149.

# CHAPTER 9

# The Nixon Doctrine

 *I've come to the conclusion that there's no way to win the war. But we can't say that of course. In fact, we have to say the opposite, just to keep some degree of bargaining leverage.*
—Richard M. Nixon, 1968[1]

*It is not our power, but our will and character, which are being tested tonight.*

—Richard M. Nixon, April 1970,
just before he ordered the secret invasion of Cambodia[2]

During the early days of World War II, the very mention of the words "security" or "national defense" could create a climate of emergency at home during a crisis abroad, enough to destroy rational and legal arguments and circumvent the Constitution. Tens of thousands of Japanese-Americans, for example, mostly from California, were placed in concentration camps for "security" reasons. President Roosevelt, by invoking emergency language, broke strikes, jailed union leaders, censored the media, and mobilized popular sympathy for these acts. War created an ideal climate for political manipulation, but if there were no war, the threat of an enemy attack was the next best thing.

The transition from war to peace in 1945–1948 did not alter the magical status of defense. Indeed, those who had run the vast wartime military apparatus had no intention of allowing their power to dissipate. They reorganized the military; the Departments of War and the Navy were collapsed into the Department of Defense, as was the newly created air force. By 1946, the usefulness of the newly emerging concept of national security in politics was widely understood. It was the wave of the future. The language and the atmosphere created around national security would be converted by a business-government partnership into public opinion and legislation, instruments with which to cripple leftist labor unions, limit New Deal regulatory drives, and stifle the ever-threatening impulses of populist and citizen-based opposition. National security could become the base for U.S. commercial culture insofar as it touched on politics.

As Richard Nixon emerged from the war, he and his campaign manager, Murray Chotiner, found their formula for success in this emerging culture. By focusing on the diabolical nature of the United States' "totalitarian" enemy, an aspiring politician did not have to be too specific about his actual programs. "Americanism" became a sufficient platform in postwar U.S. politics. It became Nixon's ticket to political office.

Nixon's congressional campaigns in 1946, 1948, and 1950 succeeded in part because he was able to cast his opponent as less patriotic than he, if not outright procommunist. Advised by Chotiner and various southern California business and public relations figures, Nixon turned campaigns into attacks. His staff spread rumors that his opponents were soft on communism. As he won his 1946 and 1948 House races and became a senator in 1950, Richard Nixon used campaign language that embodied a sense of crisis and emergency, both of which derived from the immediacy of the international communist threat.[3]

Nixon's initial campaign funding came from wealthy California businessmen who wanted a congressman more friendly to their interests than was the incumbent Democrat. Although Richard Nixon thrived in a culture of cold war suspicion and tension, he never allowed ideology to obstruct his debt to those who had funded and backed him.[4] In office, he stuck with the tactics that got him elected. As a member of the House Committee on Un-American Activities, Nixon became nationally known as the prime accuser of Alger Hiss. Nixon also became vociferously involved in the China (Taiwan) lobby. Through such activities, Nixon rose in six years from obscurity to the vice presidency in 1952.

Almost two decades later, President Richard Milhous Nixon had to figure out how to begin paying the bill for six years of war in Southeast Asia (the longest conflict in U.S. history), for the maintenance of a military force throughout large parts of the Third World and Europe, and for a national security bureaucracy of 4 million people.

Because of a half decade of public protest in the mid- and late 1960s and early 1970s, the mere mention of national security no longer automatically shielded government officials from public scrutiny. Indeed, Nixon would never forget that demonstrators had driven his predecessor, Lyndon Johnson, to take refuge in the White House and dissuaded him from seeking a second term.

The antiwar movement changed the political climate of the nation. Thousands of draft evaders fled abroad; thousands of others resisted, some by going to prison, while others went underground. Children of corporate officials and government leaders attacked their parents. By 1969, Congress also began to reflect the growing opposition to the Vietnam War. In 1965, only two senators, Wayne Morse of Oregon and Ernest Gruening of Alaska, opposed U.S. entry into the war. By 1969, a substantial minority felt deeply uneasy about the situation. The U.S. national security consensus appeared to be coming apart. World conditions had changed since the 1940s.

By 1970, the U.S. allies had recovered. They had used the Marshall Plan and the U.S.-financed defense umbrella to help free their governments from that burden, which in turn allowed them to subsidize industry. NATO had been built on national security grounds, but by the late 1960s West Germany and Japan had begun to emerge as serious economic rivals of the United States. In 1971, the dollar no longer could operate on the fiction that it was backed by gold, and President Nixon had to announce that the dollar no longer corresponded to gold supply. Balance-of-payments difficulties, trade deficits, and the ever-rising cost of maintaining the New Deal programs and Lyndon Johnson's Great Society package, along with the warfare state that had been its partner since 1947, were the issues facing Nixon; he had been but one of many political actors that had helped to create them. The facts of economic life were grim by 1969, when Nixon took office.

The United States faced a fiscal crisis, which also meant a decline in power and limits on spending compared to its immediate postwar stature, as well as a crisis of confidence. The public no longer accepted uncritically the postwar anticommunist dogmas. The growing public skepticism during the Nixon White House years threatened the very notion of national security as the guiding principle for the U.S. state. Neither Nixon nor his closest business friends and associates—nor indeed any members of the corporate and political establilshments—wanted to withdraw from the commitments that tied U.S. government and business to global wealth and power. The question was how to redefine a policy of interventionism so as to rebuild a strong consensus.

## Another Doctrine

The Nixon Doctrine, a variation on traditional U.S. interventionism, was designed to allow the United States to continue its globalist policies while accepting some of the revolutionary changes in the world since 1945. The communists of course would remain the perennial villains, and liberation and independence in the Third World would continue to be defined as communist and, therefore, as threats to U.S. national security. The Soviets and Chinese could be dealt with at the levels of trade and arms control, which were in U.S. interests, at the same time that both nations were being ideologically attacked. Appearances were crucial to Nixon's doctrine. The decline of real U.S. power could be masked with appropriate theatrics.

Nixon announced that there would be a "transition in foreign policy." In a February 25, 1971, report to Congress, Nixon declared that "we are at the end of an era. The postwar order of international relations, the configuration of power that emerged from the Second World War, is gone. With it are gone the conditions which have determined the assumptions and practice of United States foreign policy since 1945."[5] By this statement Nixon was admitting that there were limits on U.S. power and that he would be trying to salvage what he could of the empire.

Nixon and his national security adviser, Henry Kissinger, believed that a U.S. withdrawal from Vietnam would have a devastating effect on U.S. credibility and would encourage widespread revolution elsewhere. If the United States were seen as a "paper tiger," the "stable balance" that Kissinger sought would elude him, and the Soviets and Chinese might gain the upper hand. Therefore, Nixon stepped up the bombing of Vietnam and Cambodia in order to demonstrate the appearance of U.S. will and determination to the Vietnamese, the Soviets, potential Third World revolutionaries, and U.S. allies as well. Ironically, after Nixon and Kissinger had ordered massive B-52 bombing raids on Hanoi and Haiphong, North Vietnam's most populous cities, during Christmas 1972, neither man extracted any extra concessions from the Vietnamese communists. The peace treaty that was signed a little more than a month later, after immense loss of civilian life, was nearly identical to the one the two sides had agreed on before the bombings. However, the raids did create an image of Nixon as ruthless and even a bit maniacal.

A politician who was born of, and helped create, the cold war climate presided over its demise. One of the most prominent anticommunists of the 1950s signed a treaty with China and established detente with the Soviet Union. His negotiations took place in secret, which meant that Congress, the public, and even the vast national security bureaucracy were kept ignorant, lest they use Nixon's old dogmas against his new policies. Nixon and Kissinger lied to Congress at background briefings and on national television, just as Kennedy and Johnson had done about U.S. policies in Vietnam and Cambodia. Subsequently, Nixon and Kissinger offered national security as the reason for trying to cover up the White House role in Watergate and wiretapping. Under Nixon, national security became more than ever a personal way of looking at the world. Indeed, Nixon had some valid arguments. Given the identification of the U.S. president with "credibility" to allies and enemies alike and his core position in the informal imperial apparatus, national security and the person of the president had become hard to separate. As a result of the breakdown in the postwar consensus during the Vietnam War, Nixon resorted to nefarious schemes in order to stop the growing opposition without simply scrapping the Constitution.[6]

In order to deal with the levels of opposition that the Johnson years had fostered and that he anticipated his own policies would provoke, Nixon turned to dirty tricks, the kinds of tactics that had worked for him for decades. But now from his position as chief executive, he could invoke national security in order to cover routine criminal operations against his enemies. In addition to pursuing ongoing programs like COINTELPRO,[7] Nixon created a "plumbers" unit to spy on enemies, carry out "black bag jobs," and generally operate as a White House special operations unit. The IRS began auditing his "enemies list." Paranoid about leaks to the press, Nixon and Kissinger went after journalists and some of their own staff with wiretaps, which both men authorized under a national security mandate.[8]

Nixon created a special finance committee with its own funds, the Finance Committee to Reelect the President, headed by commerce secretary Maurice Stans,[9] a White House–controlled political grouping independent of the Republican party (Committee to Reelect the President), and, finally, a secret foreign policy apparatus headed by Kissinger and designed to circumvent the clumsy and stagnant national security bureaucracy. Nixon created a private national security apparatus over and above the institutionalized national security state.

Nixon and Kissinger realized during their first term in office that a bureaucracy built on myths of permanent international communist enemies and unstated needs to control other nations' economies could not easily adjust itself to a policy that demanded flexibility.[10]

In power, Nixon had to mediate between the myriad agency heads who bickered and fought about budgets, perks, and status. In such an atmosphere, where a policy could conceivably benefit one agency over another, leaks became a weapon. The media, by airing a sensational "inside" story, could help to defeat a policy that would benefit another rival group inside the apparatus. A move toward detente with the Soviets and Chinese, for example, threatened sacred ideological pillars supporting an inflated military budget and the variety of "security" agencies that allegedly protected the U.S. public from its mortal enemies.

Nixon and Kissinger never considered abandoning anticommunist rhetoric. Indeed, Nixon tried to create the appearance of an anticommunist madman in the White House, for enemies and friends alike to fear, while carrying on secret negotiations with the head demons themselves, so as to bring U.S. policy into line with changing realities. Nixon understood that the U.S. defense budget was not the flexible, and elastic, instrument it had been when the cold war began. If the United States could not indefinitely keep the Soviets on the defensive by expanding its military budget, then a tense but real detente would have to be worked out. Under Nixon's plan, however, the Soviets would have to be convinced that the United States was ready to assume an arms race or even launch a nuclear strike at the slightest provocation. In fact, detente with the Soviets, and with the Chinese, was meant as a bargaining chip that would convince Soviet leaders not to undertake or back Third World revolutions.

Kissinger believed that an arms control agreement would act as sufficient leverage on the Soviets—who deeply desired it—so that they would stop instigating and supporting independence movements in the Third World. Nixon and Kissinger mistakenly assumed that the Soviets could issue a statement or decree and Third World liberation movements would simply dry up. On the home front, Nixon and Kissinger feared that any changes in national security dogma would create serious problems. Nixon's intentions toward China and the Soviet Union, and his desire to change the Atlantic relationships and Middle East policies, would come into conflict with the shibboleths on which the national security apparatus was founded as well as contradict Nixon's own oft-repeated commandments about dealing with communists.

So, in the early 1970s, Nixon continued to maintain his traditional anticommunist rhetoric in public while undertaking secret negotiations with the Chinese and Soviets, acts that the old Nixon would have branded "treasonous." In 1974, Kissinger even opened a secret dialogue with Fidel Castro.[11] These initiatives, like the bombing of Cambodia, took place without the knowledge of Congress and even large parts of the national security bureaucracy and its established leaders.

But for the Third World, there was no detente. Not only did Nixon and Kissinger work strenuously to keep the remaining empire intact; they also allowed the expensive and idealistic Alliance for Progress to expire. Dictators suited the Nixon-Kissinger national security notion far better than did weak democracies and naive reformers. In any event, the Third World would not be allowed by the United States to assume center stage as a major actor in world policy. Henry Kissinger told Chilean chancellor Gabriel Valdes very frankly that "the axis of history starts in Moscow, goes to Bonn, crosses over to Washington, and then goes to Tokyo. What happens in the South is of no importance."[12]

Nixon's doctrine implicitly understood that the president could not rally the nation behind the use of U.S. troops abroad, short of another Pearl Harbor. Surrogate regional powers would have to maintain their land, labor, and markets inside the U.S. orbit, with the help of U.S. trainers, equippers, and advisers. On paper, the plan looked feasible. Before the local powers could do these jobs, however—as was proved by the failure of the South Vietnamese to sustain their government—these leaders required a solid military and civilian infrastructure, which was not easily attainable with the kinds of Third World rulers that Nixon and Kissinger found compatible with U.S. interests.

In lieu of old alliances and the ability to use U.S. troops, Nixon looked for platform countries, junior partners in the Third World that could help smash insurgencies or afford the United States air and intelligence bases. Israel, South Africa, Iran, South Vietnam, the Philippines, Turkey, and Pakistan became potential staging areas from which the United States launched counterrevolution. When crises arose in other pro-U.S. dictatorships, the Nixon White House responded as if a 911 call had been received, shipping whatever deadly aid was needed to keep nations from gaining independence.

### The Chilean Plot: "Spare No Expense"

On September 4, 1970, Salvador Allende, leader of a unified left electoral slate, unexpectedly won a plurality in the Chilean national elections. Unbeknownst to most Chileans and Americans, the CIA had been interfering in the campaign on the side of the right-wing candidate, Jorge Alessandri.[13] Despite the fact that the CIA outspent the Allende forces by 10 to 1, some 36.4 percent of the Chilean electorate opted for the left coalition. The Christian democratic candidate, Radomiro Tomic, who was much closer to Allende on key issues than to the right, polled more than 25 percent. The Chilean people had spoken.

On September 15, 1970, Pepsi Cola president Donald Kendall brought two of his close friends together for a meeting at the White House. Richard Nixon listened carefully and with alarm to the words of Don Agustin "Duney" Edwards, a leading Chilean banker and publisher of *El Mercurio,* the country's leading newspaper. Edwards told Nixon that an Allende presidency would transfer the control of Chile's wealth from private to public hands and that aside from the devastation such a move would cause in his own country, a transfer would provide a very compelling model for other socialists who could then use the electoral route to power.[14]

Nixon already had authorized covert action to try preventing Allende's electoral victory, but Nixon's conversation with Edwards convinced the president that the "national security threat" from Allende was even more urgent than he thought. In a meeting that lasted less than fifteen minutes, Nixon told the CIA director, Richard Helms, according to Kissinger, "that he [Nixon] wanted a major effort to see what could be done to prevent Allende's accession to power." Kissinger, who was present at the meeting, quoted Nixon as saying that "if there were one chance in ten of getting rid of Allende we should try it; if Helms needed $10 million he would approve it. . . . Aid programs should be cut; [Chile's] economy should be squeezed until it 'screamed.'"[15]

Helms later told a Senate committee about the session with the president. "If ever I carried the marshall's baton out of the Oval Office, it was that day." Helms had taken these notes when the president spoke:

One in ten chance perhaps, but save Chile
- worth spending
- not concerned risks involved
- no involvement of embassy
- $10,000,000 available; more if necessary
- full-time job—best men we have
- game plan
- make the economy scream
- forty-eight hours for plan of action[16]

To "save Chile," the CIA participated directly in murder, incited violence, and manipulated the press, political parties, Congress, labor unions, and professional and women's groups. The Agency worked with fascist elements as well as established figures. During three years, the length of Allende's presidency, the CIA spent tens of millions of dollars to destabilize his government.

The Agency funded fascist groups to instigate violence and middle class unions and professional organizations to organize strikes and work stoppages; the CIA also financed leading opposition newspapers, magazines, and political parties. CIA agents assassinated General Rene Schneider, head of Chile's armed forces, and tried to bribe members of the country's legislature to block Allende's ascension to the presidency. In coordination with the CIA's "dirty tricks," the Treasury Department cut off loans to Chile and worked successfully to deprive Allende's government of access to multilateral lending as well.

After three years of "destabilization," Allende was overthrown and killed in a bloody military coup that destroyed thousands of lives and the country's political and cultural institutions as well. With Allende's downfall went Chile's Congress, political parties, free press, educational system, and those aspects of the open society that Chileans had constructed and kept alive for more than one hundred thirty years.

For the national security managers, the Chile operation was an unqualified success. Washington recognized the new junta led by General Augusto Pinochet, and within a short time funds were again flowing from the United States and multilateral lending agencies. The CIA continued its role, this time by aiding the newly emerging repressive apparatus whose job was to organize scientific terror. The Chilean National Intelligence Directorate (DINA), which developed a capacity to assassinate its opponents overseas as well as in Chile, developed a "sweetheart" relationship with the CIA. The secret operation in Chile helped to produce the most enduring fascist government in South American history. By 1986, Pinochet had endured longer than Hitler.

### Nixon and the "Loss" of Southeast Asia

In Asia, the national security apparatus wreaked equally deadly results. Direct U.S. interference in Cambodia, in which the CIA helped to organize the removal of Prince Norodam Sihanouk, was justified on the grounds that the United States needed Cambodia in order to win in Vietnam and that Sihanouk was not sufficiently compliant to suit U.S. military objectives.

National security intellectuals continued to talk about freedom and credibility. Kissinger's accented basso profundo reiterated the need for "rapid response" to "national security" threats. The predicted "bloodbath" did not take place in Vietnam, but it did in Cambodia. U.S. national security interests had dictated the ouster of Prince Sihanouk, the one compromise politician that could hold together a fragile peace. Pro-U.S. Cambodian president Lon Nol permitted the U.S. Embassy to govern Cambodia, while the U.S. Air Force rained bombs on suspected Khmer Rouge targets.

When the U.S. Congress reflected in a vote the public's refusal to continue fighting the Southeast Asian war and U.S. forces withdrew in 1975, Lon Nol could not endure. The Cambodian Khmer Rouge did carry out a bloodbath far worse than the one U.S. officials had predicted for Vietnam.[17] U.S. officials, who had ordered the invasion and the bombing and had engineered the ouster of Sihanouk, took no responsibility for the aftermath of their stay in Cambodia. What did it have to do, after all, with U.S. policy or, indeed, with national security?

In presenting his version of the Vietnam War, Nixon adopted a tone of righteousness instead of generosity, as if the enemy had tricked "us" out of what was rightfully "ours." He reneged on important parts of the peace treaty. The Vietnamese began to assess their losses—in people killed, maimed, and psychologically destroyed; in land ruined by Agent Orange and other poisons and chemicals; in the unity of the Vietnamese as a people, part of whom had lived with a dynamic, absorbing, accumulative capitalism that came with U.S. troops, advisers, and their support system. These long-term reminders, along with wreckage of U.S. warplanes, unexploded bombs, and napalm canisters strewn about the countryside, had little meaning for most of the U.S. populace, who never did receive an adequate explanation of why U.S. troops were sent to Vietnam.

As a bankrupt and crippled nation began the uphill struggle toward rebuilding and reconciliation, Richard Nixon ordered a policy designed to inflict as cruel and horrible a punishment on Vietnam as could be managed without the recommitment of U.S. troops. Vietnam would receive no loans from multilateral agencies or private investment. Diplomatically, Nixon and subsequent presidents mandated a policy of hostility. The Vietnamese would become pariahs for what "they" had done to "us". As angry right-wingers muttered "self-inflicted defeat" and liberals wrung their hands, most members of the U.S. public reacted, as they had after every war, to the kind of political rhetoric that had advocated the commitment of U.S. troops to vague causes overseas.

Nixon, with ample aid from Kissinger, brought the concept of national security to the banality of personal whim. National security meant what he said it meant. An insecure man who entered politics hoping to become rich and famous, Nixon remained uncertain about his personal security even as he ruled the most powerful empire in the history of the world.

When Richard Nixon left office, not only the presidency but the national security agencies were in disarray. Nixon's activities had left a stain of doubt on what had been for more than twenty years the assumed if inexact meaning of those two words. The establishment figures who had helped to design and develop national security as a concept with which to govern an informal empire and informally mold domestic consensus had watched in dismay as the Nixon White House behavior became public. As Nixon waved goodbye from his helicopter after he was forced to resign, there were few in Washington who could offer any clarity about what national security actually would come to mean in the future.

The alliances that had been formed presumably to stop communist expansion had formed the basis of Luce's American Century, the outposts of U.S. empire abroad. They had fallen into disarray with the movements of history in the Third World, as 1974 seemed to kick off a literal volley of revolutions in Southeast Asia and Africa. Nixon, at one time the quintessential cold warrior, the anticommunist personified, had been forced to come to terms with the events of his time, with his own and his nation's limits, as he discovered them. During his presidency, the Bretton Woods agreements disintegrated and the United States lost its economic hegemony over the Western world. Nixon discovered that he could not afford to maintain his predecessors' levels of national security expenses. He tried instead to forge cheaper, more sustainable bilateral arrangements. He tried to emerge from the shadow of Vietnam by fostering "images" and "appearances" of the kind of power the U.S. once had possessed. He fostered U.S. ethnocentricity as he presided over an increasingly internationalized economy.

In college classrooms professors ask their students, "How many died in the Vietnam War?" and often the first student who answers offers the figure 58,000—the approximate number of U.S. dead. However, there is silence in the classroom when the professor informs the students that some 2 million Vietnamese died, not including the

Laotians and Cambodians. "I don't understand," a student blurts out. "What was it all for!"[18]

## Notes

1. Richard J. Whalen, *Catch The Falling Flag* (Boston: Houghton Mifflin, 1972), p. 137.

2. Seymour Hersh, *The Price of Power* (New York: Summit Books, 1983), p. 191.

3. Frank Mankiewicz, *Perfectly Clear: Nixon from Whittier to Watergate* (New York: Quandrangle/New York Times Books Company, 1973), pp. 31–57. On the 1950 campaign, see David Oshinsky, *A Conspiracy So Immense: The World of Joe McCarthy* (New York: The Free Press, 1983), p. 177. Also see Horace Jeremiah Voorjis, *The Strange Case of Richard Milhous Nixon [by] Jerry Voorhis* (New York: Eriksson, 1972), and William A. Reuben, *The Honorable Mr. Nixon* (New York: Action Books, 1956).

4. Robert Scheer, *America After Nixon* (New York: McGraw-Hill, 1974), pp. 51–56.

5. Richard Nixon, *U.S. Foreign Policy for the 1970s: Building For Peace. A Report to the Congress* (Washington, D.C.: U.S. Government Printing Office, 1971), p. 10.

6. See David Wise, *The Politics of Lying* (New York: Random House, 1973), pp. 14–15, 49–52, 342–347.

7. See Nelson Blackstock, *COINTELPRO: The FBI's Secret War on Political Freedom* (New York: Vintage Books, 1975).

8. Morton Halperin, Jerry Berman, Robert Borosage, and Christine Marwick, *The Lawless State* (New York: Penguin, 1976), pp. 123, 225–226. See John Erhlichman, *Witness to Power* (New York: Simon and Schuster, 1982), pp. 165–166.

9. See Maurice H. Stans, *The Terrors of Justice* (Chicago: Regnery Books, 1984), pp. 129–163.

10. On Nixon's and Kissinger's relationship to the bureaucracy, see Roger Morris, *Uncertain Greatness* (New York: Harper and Row, 1977). One good example Morris cited was the "back channel" set up by Kissinger between the White House and the Kremlin through the Soviet ambassador. Also see Seymour Hersh, *The Price of Power* (New York: Summit Books, 1983), pp. 37–45.

11. Kissinger delivered a handwritten note to Frank Mankiewiecz, a member of his foreign policy advisory board who was traveling to Cuba to make a film with the Cuban leader. The letter, which Castro read in Mankiewiecz' and the author's presence, asked that Castro send an envoy to New York under U.N. cover for secret discussions aimed at opening some form of relationship. Ultimately, the idea of establishing "interest sections"—embassies without formal accreditation—emerged from this diplomatic effort. Kissinger cut off the dialogue when the Cuban leader dispatched troops to Angola in support of the guerrillas. Personal communication, June 1974.

12. Hersh, *The Price of Power,* p. 263.

13. On Alessandri and subsequent U.S. plotting, see U.S. Senate, Staff Report of the Select Committee to Study Governmental Operations with Respect to Intelligence Activities, *Covert Action in Chile, 1963–1973* (Washington, D.C.: U.S. Government Printing Office, 1975); and ibid., pp. 258–276.

14. For a thorough account of how Allende's economic policies affected U.S. concerns in a key sector, copper, and the relationship between business concerns and U.S. foreign policy, see Norman Girvan, *Corporate Imperialism: Conflict and Expropriation* (New York: Monthly Review Press, 1976), pp. 52–97.

15. U.S. Senate, Select Committee to Study Governmental Operations with Respect to Intelligence Activities, *Interim Report: Alleged Assassination Plots Involving Foreign Leaders* (Washington, D.C.: U.S. Government Printing Office, 1975). Also see U.S. Senate, *Hearings before the Senate Select Committee to Study Government Operations with Regard to Intelligence Activities,* 94th Cong., 1st sess., 1975, chaired by Senator Frank Church. The Church Committee published a staff report entitled *Covert Action in Chile, 1963–1973.*

16. U.S. Senate, *Interim Report,* pp. 227–228.

17. However, Vietnam, a crippled nation in 1975, soon disgorged "boat people" and thousands of other refugees who became victims of a war in which the United States was no longer engaged and for which it took no responsibility. In the peace agreements Kissinger had promised $3 billion in U.S. aid to Vietnam, but he quickly slipped out of that promise. Like the entry into Vietnam, the U.S. exit from that land showed little concern for the Vietnamese people. A secret U.S. national security apparatus had dictated the need to fight the war in Southeast Asia in order to stop Chinese expansionism, and when the reasons for entering proved to be nonexistent if not downright silly, the national security managers simply forgot the original motives for the war and found new reasons to pursue it.

18. These questions and answers came from the author's experiences teaching at the University of California at the Santa Cruz and Davis campuses, 1983–1987.

# CHAPTER 10

# Ford, Trilateralism, and the Export of National Security

 *We live in an age of undeclared war, which has meant Presidential war. Prolonged engagement in undeclared Presidential war has created a most dangerous imbalance in our Constitutional system of checks and balances.*

—Senator Jacob Javits[1]

*Every American president since John Kennedy has been sacrificed as one of the costs of empire (and perhaps Kennedy too). . . . Vietnam defeated Lyndon Johnson. Richard Nixon's deployment against the Democrats of the agencies and techniques that Johnson mobilized against the antiwar movement terminated his presidency. Gerald Ford's interregnum ended when the Republican right decided that, in foreign policy, he and the 'traitor' Kissinger were indistinguishable from the Democrats. The Ayatollah Khomeini, in the end, defeated Jimmy Carter.*

—Norman Birnbaum[2]

*The international order created after World War II is no longer adequate to new conditions and needs.*

—Richard Cooper, Karl Keiser, and Mastake Kosaka[3]

Historians may remember President Gerald Ford for two dubious actions: pardoning Richard M. Nixon and causing the senseless death of forty-one Americans and the wounding of fifty others in the "rescue" of the ship *Mayaguez*, which had been captured by Cambodian government forces. Both acts occurred in the shambles in which Nixon had left the White House, which now was directed by an unelected president[4] who was forced to withdraw U.S. forces from Southeast Asia because Congress refused to vote funds to continue the war.

Ford also fought in vain against the lessening of national security commitments in Angola. But he failed to convince Congress of the need to continue a CIA covert operation there. Instead, legislators imposed the Clark Amendment, which forbade further CIA clandestine activities in Angola, thereby cutting short a CIA operation designed to impede the victory of the pro-Soviet Popular Movement for the Liberation of Angola (MPLA).[5]

Ford, continuing Nixon's detente policy, negotiated the Vladivostok Test Ban Treaty with the Soviet premier, Leonid Brezhnev. Gerald Ford was also the first president to preside over a U.S. public suffering from an acute "Vietnam syndrome," a reaction to the trauma of ten years of costly and fruitless war fought 10,000 miles away (the "Vietnam syndrome" also derived from the nation's historic noninterventionist inclination). After Nixon departed, Secretary of State Henry Kissinger, despite his Nobel Peace Prize, lost his magical touch. The mention of his name no longer conjured up the wizard image that he had created in media and political circles; he had suffered from his association with the Nixon shenanigans. By 1974, Henry Kissinger, the intellectual architect of national-security-as-appearance during the Nixon years, had lost his power to persuade, cajole, or even deceive Congress into ceding power to the executive. Indeed, national security as a doctrine itself was in a mess.

Congress passed the War Powers Act in 1974 over Nixon's veto as a reaction to the "discovery" that the members had been tricked, lied to, and manipulated by three presidents. Feeling its power for the first time in decades—although it neither possessed nor desired the ability to posit real alternatives to the national security structure—Congress forbade the president to commit U.S. forces without direct congressional approval.[6] Even though the act did not limit the executive's legal powers, which Lincoln had established during the Civil War, the no-confidence vote sharply limited overseas adventures.

Revolutions did spread throughout Africa and Asia in the wake of the U.S. defeat in Vietnam. But it was not U.S. weakness that spurred liberation forces in Africa. The collapse of Portuguese colonialism and the feudal regime of Ethiopia were not the results of the demise of U.S. power in Indochina. Similarly, revolutions in South Yemen and later in Afghanistan had little to do with the long and bitter war in Vietnam. In Southeast Asia, only Laos, Cambodia, and Vietnam broke from the "free world." The dominoes did not fall in the rest of the region.[7]

But the elite was worried that the system that it had constructed after World War II might be breaking down. The men who had accumulated immense power and privilege in and out of government perceived with some alarm the new limits that had been placed on the power of the U.S. state. Some of the more astute intellectuals and business leaders recognized that nationalist or even socialist revolutions could not be blocked or even seriously impeded without great consequences. These leaders began to look askance at the inflexible national security order and to perceive it as anachronistic.[8] Some liberal Democrats even fostered doubts that the "excesses" were all due to Nixon's madness and corruption and not the inherent operations of a national security system that operated above, beside, and around the law and Constitution. The establishment's answer was to set up a dialogue about the nature of the world and how it should be ordered.

The Trilateral Commission, sometimes confused with ruling class conspiracies and mysterious cabals, in reality was a discussion club composed of key U.S., Western European, and Japanese decision-makers from the world of politics, business, and academia. When the Rockefeller family offered to sponsor such a society, few in positions of power or aspiring to it turned down such a membership.

The Trilateral Commission addressed economic questions and the issue of national security. The commission's purpose in discussing changes was to maintain the status quo, which was a peculiar contradiction. The trilateralists admitted that world conditions had altered since 1945–1950, which in turn required structural reforms. At the same time, the trilateralists wanted to maintain the basic features of the structure they had created. Gerald Ford was the first trilateral president.

## Trilateralism and National Security

Trilateralism tacitly acknowledged that the marriage of national security and advanced capitalism required serious counseling if it were to remain an amicable relationship. None of the Trilateral Commission members questioned the premise of modern capitalism in its multinational corporate and banking forms. Rather, the members engaged in a common search for ways to ensure the survival of the Western way of life without fighting nuclear or even Vietnam-style wars. The commission staff was to produce ideas, methods, and formulas for the reproduction of the economic system that did not cause serious domestic ruptures or international conflagrations. Given the Rockefeller sponsorship of the commission, few doubted that the discussions would carry weight.

U.S. power as leader of NATO, the trilateralists agreed, had to remain as the foundation (security) for capitalist world trade and commerce. Without U.S. military power, the rising tide of revolutionary nationalism would quickly gain sufficient leverage so as to set different terms for labor, land, and markets, which would make capitalism's reproduction more difficult. Nationalism was considered anathema to the efficient functioning of the economic system.

Ironically, the very corporate executives who applauded the repression of Third World nationalism and resented those aspects of U.S., European, and Japanese nationalism that could produce barriers to trade assumed the permanence of the national security state. To keep that vast apparatus intact required the propagation of U.S. nationalist ideology so as to justify the expense involved in the maintenance of the very state power needed by the great corporations to ensure their future.

The multinational corporations and banks placed enormous burdens upon the U.S. national security state at the very moment it appeared least able to shoulder them. The world of capital could ill afford an avalanche of Third World countries breaking out of capitalism's dominion. U.S. power since the end of World War II had been the reliable guarantor of the multinationals' "stability."

By 1975, the cold war had encumbered the U.S. people with numerous alliances meant to carve out a substantial portion of the globe's real estate for current or future exploitation by U.S.—and to a lesser extent Western European and Japanese—entrepreneurs. Or, put another way, by forging the NATO alliance, the United States was at least blocking the path toward communist control of Western Europe. U.S. businesspeople understood the direct relationship of the military pact to economic and political goals.

The business community responded with avid support for the military buildups and the long-term political and economic relationships that obviously would accompany them. (Those involved directly in defense-related industries, of course, had special reasons to support such steps.) By the early 1970s, however, post–World War II conditions no longer existed. The Soviet threat to Western Europe—if indeed it ever existed—no longer could be described as imminent, nor could the Western Communist parties be said to pose any political threat to the continuation of capitalism.

Ironically, the Soviets, after decades of having been accused by aspiring presidential candidates and defense intellectuals of having surpassed the United States, reached some form of military parity in the late 1960s and early 1970s. The Soviet buildup had begun after the 1962 missile crisis and reached its acme just as Washington no longer possessed the overwhelming economic power to control its junior capitalist partners. The United States was visibly weaker even before President Nixon was forced to take the United States off the gold standard and abandon the Bretton Woods economic arrangements under which the capitalist world had functioned since 1945. Defeat in Vietnam, in this sense, symbolized more than the inability of the United States to control Third World revolutions. Defeat indicated that the U.S. desire for control had overreached its ability to do so.

Gerald Ford's cabinet and key advisers reflected establishment thinking. Detente, a modus vivendi with the Soviets and Chinese, would enliven trade, bring down the defense budget costs, and at the same time allow the United States to hold the line against Third World revolutions. Europeans wanted a thaw in relations with the East, partly for economic reasons and partly to keep the arms race carefully controlled. Europeans also pushed for more relaxed attitudes toward changes in the Third World, ones that European social democrats saw both as inevitable and controllable. The words "Marxist" and even "Leninist" did not throw the former colonial rulers into the kind of tizzy that the words provoked in U.S. national security circles.

## The New Right and National Security

Inside the national security elite, within circles of retired intelligence officers, defense and space contractors, ultraright businesspeople, and right-wing ideologues, a response began to develop to the erosion of U.S. power. These men and women formed associations and organizations dedicated to "restoring" U.S. power, building ever stronger the military, and recharging U.S. energies for a second round of the cold war. Right-wing attacks on Kissinger's sale of "the family jewels to the Soviets" at SALT I began to appear.[9] The emerging new right wing fought for the old ideology, indeed for the strengthening of anti-Sovietism in the face of detente.

By 1975, a coalition of cold warriors and new rightists sought to regain ideological dominance in U.S. politics. While they did so, President Ford and Secretary of State Kissinger continued to pursue detente in practice and anticommunism in ideology as basic U.S. national security policy. At the same time that Ford and Kissinger parleyed with the Soviets and Chinese, they continued to foster dictatorship throughout the Third World.

## The Export of the National Security Model

Ford inherited the Nixon Doctrine. When Nixon ordered Richard Helms and the CIA to eliminate Salvador Allende's socialist government in Chile, Nixon's policy reflected the continuing refusal of U.S. leaders to accept alternative economic models. Ford continued the policy and indeed presided over its worst abuses toward Third World peoples. During his tenure, most of the countries of Latin America were run by military dictatorships; nor did democracy flourish in the Pacific, Washington's other traditional region of influence.[10]

Washington exported the national security model to Third World countries and sent advisers to teach the native militaries scientific methods of repression. Washington also opened up a market for weapons, some quite exotic,[11] and sent U.S. military teachers to provide instruction in the use of these weapons. In short, the national security apparatus arranged a marriage, or in some cases tightened an existing one, between the U.S. military and those of friendly Third World nations.

Fiercely anticommunist military regimes with strong loyalty to the United States would reduce the threat of communist or nationalist insurrections and thereby the need to use U.S. forces to suppress them. It sounded simple enough. The Inter-American Defense Board, the military schools and academies in Texas and Panama, the close liaison among U.S. military missions in countries such as Chile, Argentina, Pakistan, and South Korea all would combine to show the intimate relationship of interests among real anticommunists.

Problems did arise because the military rulers of nations such as Chile, Taiwan, and the Philippines did not understand the rules governing appropriate national security behavior outside their own countries. Pinochet, for example, did not understand that one ought not carry violence to U.S. or Western European territory. For General Augusto Pinochet or President Ferdinand Marcos, an enemy was an enemy, and enemies were defined as communists and had to be eliminated no matter where or under what circumstances. Both men had learned this moral imperative, they claimed with some justification, from their U.S. teachers and advisers.

On the morning of September 21, 1976, a car bomb detonated by a remote control apparatus killed Orlando Letelier, former Chilean ambassador to the United States and defense minister under President Salvador Allende, and Ronni Moffitt, his colleague at the Institute for Policy Studies. Within a week, the FBI discovered evidence that pointed not only to the Chilean government as the culprit in the crime, but to a national security conspiracy that spanned six countries, all ruled by pro-U.S., fanatically anticommunist military juntas.

A special agent of the FBI investigating the Letelier assassination, who was stationed in Buenos Aires and operating as legate in the embassy, met an Argentine military intelligence officer, who after several drinks began to complain about the "stupidity" of the Letelier "hit." As the FBI agent listened, trying to conceal his amazement, a story emerged about a secret organization, named Operation Condor, of national security agencies that spanned the Southern Cone and reached into the middle of Latin America as well. The CIA knew about Operation Condor, the Argentine explained, and indeed had played a key part in setting up the computerized links between the intelligence and operational units of the six military regimes: Chile, Argentina, Uruguay, Brazil, Paraguay, and Bolivia.

The FBI special agent pretended to remain calm as his Argentine counterpart recounted the chilling details of an international murder organization. In the agent's classified "CHILBOM" cable to the FBI director on September 28, 1976, he wrote, "Operation Condor . . . was recently established between cooperating intelligence services in South America in order to eliminate Marxist terrorist activities in the area." The classified cable reported that "Chile is the center for Operation Condor." In addition to carrying out joint intelligence and surveillance activities against "leftists, communists and Marxists," the cable continued:

> A third and most secret phase of Operation Condor involves the formation of special teams from member countries who are to travel anywhere in the world to non-member countries to carry out sanctions up to assassination against terrorists or supporters of terrorist organizations from Operation Condor member countries. For example, should a terrorist or a supporter of a terrorist organization from a member country of Operation Condor be located in a European country, a special team from Operation Condor would be dispatched to carry out the actual sanction against the target.[12]

During the Nixon-Ford administration, and with the administration's approval, the Southern Cone became one great national security operation. The CIA helped construct, advise, and support the national security apparatus in each of the Southern Cone countries. For the military rulers of these nations, intelligence and repression were inseparable. The FBI investigation of the Letelier assassination unwittingly revealed the nature of what national security had come to signify in the Southern Cone.

This exported national security model did succeed in repressing opposition. In fact, these regimes repressed everything, but Pinochet and some of the others also imported an economic model—the Chicago School or Milton Friedman, free-market paradigm. An up-dated version of the policies of economic obeisance that Washington had long imposed on Caribbean and Central American countries, Friedmanism aimed to produce optimal conditions for foreign cor-porations, thereby laying open natural resources and offering labor at bargain prices.

For a brief period of time, the combination of repression and renewed aid from the United States and U.S.-dominated multilateral development banks produced an "economic miracle" with dramatic growth in Gross Domestic Product and exports. But in the early 1980s, the Chilean economy collapsed; the miracle proved to be only a mirage. For example, some foreign corporations discovered that they had to close down their production facilities because Pinochet's artificial boosting of Chilean currency made imported goods cheaper than those produced locally.

Those Third World nations that adopted versions of monetarism, abandoned labor and environmental regulations, and reduced or abolished taxes for foreign investors did receive an inflow of foreign capital, both private and multilateral. But the funds that entered these countries did not correspond to the larger amount of capital that left. The military governments of Brazil, Argentina, and the Philippines, like Chile under Pinochet, had behaved as models for the International Monetary Fund's development notions; yet, the business class in these countries did not respond by reinvesting profits.

Instead, Third World capital was lured during the mid- and late 1970s to the high interest rate offered by U.S. banks. The economic results of the combined militarism and monetarism did not correspond to the "miracle" forecasts. The foreign debts of the most militarized Third World national security states rose to dangerous levels by the late 1970s, and the inflow of loans began to be used mainly to pay the interest on already acquired debts.

Just as Nixon struggled and failed to manage a rich and relatively flexible economy, so, too, did the generals fall prey to economic factors that they could not control. The Chicago Boys could not convert the teachings of Professors Milton Friedman and Arnold Harberger into a formula that could coexist with fascist military rule. Some of the very colonels and majors who had instigated coups to overthrow disorderly democratic regimes had little tolerance for beggars on the street, massive unemployment, and slums around their capital cities, which all were products of free-market economics.[13]

The national security model proved viable for short periods, as the scores of coups and countercoups among the South America military illustrated. Those military regimes that endured increasingly embarrassed the U.S. government with their continuing human rights abuses. National security exported to the Third World was cruder than the original U.S. product. A republican form of government based on a powerful economy could not be exported quite so easily as were its catchwords.

But U.S.-based multinational corporations and banks did benefit from the foisting of national security states on the Third World. Military rulers in some of these nations enabled the foreign exploitation of vast amounts of land and labor. These rulers opened up their domestic markets to foreign-made consumer goods. In the name of anticommunism and freedom, for example, Pinochet literally donated entire provinces of Chile to multinational corporations, with no regulations on labor policies, no taxes, and no oversight or even guidelines on environmental usage. The same military rulers abolished or crippled labor unions in order to reduce the cost of labor. Foreign capital, much of it from the United States, poured into the Third World as investments or loans. Investors felt that the regimes had been secured, if not insured, by the U.S. government.

By election time 1976, Chile, Argentina, Brazil, Uruguay, Bolivia, and Paraguay were governed by national security–type military regimes. In Central America, Nicaragua, El Salvador, Honduras, and Guatemala had similar governments. The U.S. national security state did not have to indulge in barbaric forms of behavior to control other nations. The export of national security meant in fact that the possible need for U.S. troops would be reduced in those countries. The native security forces would handle threats to U.S. interests.

The problem was, however, that the national security regimes did not work. They destroyed the economies and created such scandals through torture, murder, and violation of human rights that no matter how loyally these regimes behaved, the U.S. public would not tolerate them as allies. In the case of Bolivia, the military rulers were also the cocaine bosses. In other Latin American dictatorships, the military rulers also became deeply involved with crime.

In January 1977, as Gerald Ford was passing the mantle of presidential power to Jimmy Carter in Washington, revolutionaries in Central America had begun to win small but important victories over the local military in Nicaragua and to organize a challenge to the status quo in El Salvador. The U.S. "system" in Central America that had been so carefully constructed and modified for almost a century would be seriously tested.

## Notes

1. Report 220 of the Senate Foreign Relations Committee, June 1973, p. 2, cited in Marcus Raskin, *Notes on the Old System* (New York: David McKay, 1974), p. 86.

2. "Symposium: What Is to Be Done?" *The Nation,* November 22, 1980, p. 535.

3. Richard Cooper, Karl Keiser, and Mastake Kosaka, *Toward a Reconstructed International System* (New York: The Trilateral Commission, 1977).

4. Vice President Spiro Agnew, implicated in a financial scandal dating from his tenure as governor of Maryland, resigned October 10, 1973. Two days later, Nixon, acting according to Section 2 of the 25th Amendment to the Constitution, nominated Representative Gerald R. Ford (R-Mich.) as the new vice president. Ford was confirmed by the Senate on November 27 and by the House on December 6. He became president August 9, 1974, when Nixon resigned.

5. John Stockwell, *In Search of Enemies: A CIA Story* (New York: W. W. Norton, 1978). Also see *The CIA Case Officer* (Saul Landau, director, New Time Films, New York).

6. It also has been argued that Congress actually gave away more than it secured. During the debate, Senator James Abourezk charged that the War Powers Act would "set a dangerous standard which in fact expands, rather than contracts the President's warmaking powers" and "simply abandons the constitutional requirement that no war be entered without prior Congressional declaration." *Congressional Record,* 93d Cong., 1st sess., July 20, 1973, vol. 119, part 20, pp. 25052–25054. Also see Abourezk's insertion of an analysis by Senator Thomas Eagleton in the December 5, 1973, *Record,* p. 39594; and U.S. Senate, *War Powers Legislation: Hearings before the Committee on Foreign Relations,* 92d Cong., 1st sess., March 8, 9, 24, 25, April 23 and 26, May 14, July 26 and 27, and October 6, 1971. For further discussion, see Raskin, *Notes on the Old System.*

7. U.S. public opinion, as Leslie Gelb understood, was "the essential domino." See Leslie H. Gelb, "The Essential Domino," *Foreign Affairs* (April 1972):459–475.

8. Cyrus Eaton, Armand Hammer, Andy Young, and Ted Kennedy were examples, as were the aging George Kennan, John Kenneth Galbraith, and even Robert MacNamara, Paul Warnke, and McGeorge Bundy.

9. See Phyllis Schlafly and Chester Ward, *Ambush at Vladivostok* (Alton, Ill.: Pere Marquette Press, 1976).

10. See the discussion in Noam Chomsky and Edward Herman, *The Washington Connection and Third World Fascism* (Boston: South End Press, 1979).

11. Michael Klare and Cynthia Arnson, *Supplying Repression* (Washington, D.C.: Institute for Policy Studies, 1981).

12. John Dinges and Saul Landau, *Assassination on Embassy Row* (New York: Pantheon, 1980), pp. 237–239. In fact, the FBI agent correctly deduced that Letelier had been assassinated in a Condor operation. The cable also provided details about the Condor operatives' use of false names on third country passports, which in the Letelier case misled the FBI for nearly a year.

13. Colonel Manuel Contreras, the head of DINA, did not agree with the economic policies of the free-market Chicago Boys. As an ideological fascist, he was bothered by the notion of beggars on the street and the kind of anarchy he saw as the inevitable outcome of the Adam Smith model. See Dinges and Landau, *Assassination on Embassy Row,* pp. 136–137.

# CHAPTER 11

# Intervention
# and Human Rights

*The thought of military intervention seems remote after the domestic divisiveness of Vietnam. . . . Neither gunboat nor dollar diplomacy will work very well for the United States in the 1970's.*

—C. Fred Bergsten,
Assistant Secretary of the Treasury for International Affairs[1]

*The Carter approach to foreign policy rests on a belief that not only is the world far too complex to be reduced to a doctrine, but that there is something inherently wrong with having a doctrine at all.*

—Leslie Gelb[2]

*We have to restore faith in the system.*

—Edward Levi, U.S. Attorney General, 1976[3]

Jimmy Carter inherited a tainted presidency. The Vietnam War and the Watergate scandals hung over the Oval Office. In addition, Jimmy Carter faced a security bureaucracy that had lost the confidence of the public and a troubled economy that had been forced to pay for the longest, most expensive, and least popular war in U.S. history. The foreign policy bequeathed to Carter had been exposed by the media and Congress as confused and ineffective at best and possibly immoral.

Carter, a born-again Baptist, came into the presidency as Mr. Clean, a man who would transmit his religious convictions to the world, whose policies would carry an aura of morality, a man who could restore confidence and credibility to the post-Vietnam, post-Nixon United States.

Carter appointed to his cabinet leading members of the Trilateral Commission, including some who considered existing national security dogmas an encumbrance on U.S. trade and commerce, and others who remained staunch believers in the demonic nature of the enemy: Andrew Young on the left, Cyrus Vance in the center, and Zbigniew Brzezinski on the right. The Trilateral Commission dialogue had become elevated to policy debate.

## Carter and Human Rights

True to his image, Jimmy Carter declared that human rights would become the primary guideline for U.S. policy. As a consolation for the national security–minded members of the administration, Carter assured that the policy would be applied with equal rigor to abusers from the communist world and to pro-U.S. dictators.

Carter appointed Admiral Stansfield Turner to head the CIA.[4] Turner purged the CIA of many, although not all, of the "rogue elephants" that had rampaged through Southeast Asia during the Vietnam War period. Turner stressed instead the intelligence-gathering and analyzing function of the Agency. The reform of the CIA, like the emphasis on human rights, was part of a cleansing effort to restore faith in the old system and to demonstrate that legality and decency could reassert themselves after the scandalous decade of deceit and crime in government that spanned Vietnam, coups and assassinations, and the Watergate shenanigans.

Meanwhile, the immense national security apparatus did not sit idle. The defense contractors, bureaucrats, academics, and others who had bought into the national security state, and its supporting mythology, rallied to support it. In and out of government an assault began on the Carter administration's human rights policy as well as on the administration's continued pursuit of detente. To "destroy" the CIA covert action capability, the critics charged, strengthened the Soviet Union.[5]

Former CIA official Phillip Agee claimed that the CIA was criminal and named scores of its members publicly. The CIA had to do the dirty jobs, its defenders said, because the KGB was doing the same thing. Critics did not specify which foreign assassinations or coups d'etat the KGB had done, but simply asserted that the KGB did them. Members of the media rarely asked for details because the predictable answer was always, "That information is classified—national security."

A furious right-wing media campaign ensued to convince the U.S. public that detente stood for weakness, that human rights as a policy allowed the Soviets to achieve advantages in the Third World, and finally—the biggest lie of all—that the Soviets had far surpassed the United States militarily.

Some of the CIA operators removed in the Turner housecleaning became active in this campaign. They formed a group to combat the damage caused by the Agee revelations and the material discovered by congressional investigators. The Association of Former Intelligence Officers sponsored speakers to tour the country calling for a crackdown on "traitors" such as Agee and an end to national security "leaks."

A melange of right-wing ultras from the John Birch Society to the American Security Council joined with cold war liberals such as Senator Henry "Scoop" Jackson and his aide, Richard Perle, to sound the alarm. "The Soviets are winning," they cried, as they rode like modern Paul Reveres through town meetings and TV talk shows. "Build up the military," they wrote in newspaper columns. "Crisis in defense," said the direct mail solicitations. Organizations popped up, such as the Inter-American Defense Council, the Committee on the Present Danger, West Watch, and The Heritage Foundation. The far right, furious with Nixon and Kissinger for cutting deals with the Vietnamese communists and for secretly promising the North Vietnamese $3 to 4 billion of postwar aid pushed for ideological control of the Republican party.

Right-wing ideologues, such as Phyllis Schlafly and General Daniel Graham, later claimed that being first to spot the weak defense danger entitled them to a prominent place in the Reagan victory camp. Their policy guidelines—no deals with the Soviets, peace through space-based strategic superiority, roll back Third World revolutions—in fact had formed the foundation of Reagan's defense and foreign policy. In addition, the defense-gap lie was joined by right-wing evangelicals who had begun to see their future in linking "social issues," such as abortion and school prayer, with a "strong defense."

Just as Kennedy had successfully employed the spurious "missile gap" in his 1960 campaign, so, too, did a right-wing defense industry cabal sound the false alarm on Carter's defense and foreign policies. Human rights, the cabal maintained, was a naive, idealistic policy that allowed the diabolical Soviets to sow doubt and division, confound U.S. resolve, and replace pro-U.S. "authoritarians" with communist tyrants.

The human rights forces had their share of will and had as much courage and conviction as their ideological foes, but the former forces still were stuck with national security dogma. Although less vehement than the far right, the acquiescence of human rights advocates to the notion that the Soviet Union was the real enemy of the United States made them defensive if not vulnerable to the assault of the right wing, which also possessed more money, political power, and influence in the media than did the human rights liberals.

A further disagreement separated the national security mavens from the human rights advocates. Human rights, in part thanks to FDR's definition of the four freedoms during World War II, had come to mean more than the procedural rights guaranteed by the U.S. Bill of Rights and English Common Law. As the Third World nations began to express their economic and social needs inside the United Nations and other international forums, these nations also began to expand the definition of human rights to include food, housing, employment, medical care, and education, which were part of the program of the New Deal and European social democracy. The implications that would derive from endorsing substantive human rights were anathema to national security ideologues. If substantive as well as procedural guarantees were used as standards, regimes such as Castro's Cuba would compare favorably to those of the Third World national security models, such as Chile or El Salvador, which offered neither substantive nor procedural guarantees.

But after World War II, U.S. leaders began to deemphasize the four freedoms in U.S.–Third World relations. The communist enemy dominated the concrete barriers to freedom. The idea of freedom from hunger, FDR's concept, waned before the specter of communism.

By late 1978, those Rooseveltians in the Carter administration who saw the U.S. economy and culture as strong assets with which to compete ideologically and materially for the hearts, minds, markets, and resources of the Third World were removed gradually or neutralized effectively by cold warriors. When the "crises" hit, the voices of the Rooseveltians had lost the firmness of the early human rights honeymoon years. Jimmy Carter himself went with the trend. He tacitly approved the crisis managers' exaggerated claims about Soviet weapons advances by not backing his own SALT II Treaty in the Senate; he also approved claims emanating from national security adviser Zbigniew Brzezinski that the Soviets had placed a new combat brigade in Cuba. In fact, Carter became a victim of events far removed from the machinations of the national security apparatus.

On one issue Carter faced the right wing and held his ground: a treaty ceding the Panama Canal to Panama. Encouraged by Cyrus

Vance and Andrew Young, Jimmy Carter pursued the soft trilateralist route in Latin America, advocating acceptance of pluralism and seeking to improve relations and make amends for the past. The signing of the treaty was turned into a major diplomatic event, with every Latin head of state save Castro invited to Washington. Carter hailed the treaty as the beginning of a new era; in retrospect, the treaty was the high watermark of Carter's Latin policy.

Opposition to the treaty became a rallying point for the right wing, which blasted the pact as a near-treasonous giveaway. Better organized than the White House and protreaty forces, who made only feeble efforts to garner public support, the right wing came close to defeating the treaty in the Senate. The vitriolic nature of the antitreaty campaign—"We built it. We paid for it. It's ours."— surprised the Carter administration, and when the right wing began its attack on SALT II, the White House literally chickened out.

In fact, SALT II was a much better negotiated treaty than was SALT I. Arms controller Paul Warnke had extracted concessions from the Soviets far beyond anything Kissinger achieved in SALT I and gave away nothing substantial. But Carter succumbed to cold war pressure and at the crucial moment failed to push for ratification in a Senate besieged by American Security Council propaganda and an unprecedented military-industrial complex lobbying effort.

## Iran and Nicaragua

Carter and his inner circle danced, as liberals had since the Truman era, to the drumbeat of national security alarmism. The unofficial but persistent propaganda on "weakness" and the anti-Soviet rhetoric had their effect inside the government.

False reports from the "intelligence community" began to embarrass Carter as early as 1977, when he accused Fidel Castro of sponsoring an invasion of Shaba province in Zaire. Carter had to retract the charge when Castro convinced the U.S. media of Cuba's innocence in the affair and instead demonstrated that a former CIA client had been responsible for the military adventure.

In 1978, Carter announced, based on intelligence sources, that the Soviets had stationed a brigade of troops in Cuba contrary to the 1962 Kennedy-Khrushchev accords. It turned out that the brigade had been there in more or less the same strength since 1962. Castro then turned on Carter and accused him of fabricating the story in order to weaken Cuba during the meeting of a summit of nonaligned nations in Havana. Once again Carter had fallen for a national security ruse, which embarrassed him.

More important, however, were the distortions that national security agency heads or former national security buffs offered about Soviet nuclear strength and weapons buildup. The lie was oft repeated: The United States is weak; the Soviet Union is strong.

At the same time, U.S. arms control negotiating chief, Paul Warnke, had brought detente to its highest point when he reached agreement with the Soviets for the SALT II Treaty. It was at this point that the policy debate reached the point of decision: human rights and detente or reversion to the traditional national security dogmas, complete with weapons buildup and weakening of human rights policies in the Third World. Carter could still maintain the rhetoric, his national security adviser Brzezinski argued, but it could be focused primarily on Soviet abuses, not on those of Pinochet, Marcos, Somoza, and the shah.

By 1979, the human rights and detente factions were ill equipped to fend off the national security zealots when the Soviet Union invaded Afghanistan and anti-U.S. revolutions took place in Iran and Nicaragua. The human rights advocates had not organized a large constituency, or even key sectors of the Democratic party, to support their policy. Rather, they worked among policy elites in and out of government.

The evolution of events in the Third World pushed Carter into a choice, and, when faced with the weight of publicity, propaganda, and pressure from the well-organized national security sector, he bowed to its wishes. The key voice for a new foreign policy toward the Third World, Andrew Young, was forced to resign.[6] After Paul Warnke negotiated an agreement with the Soviets, as per the president's policy, Carter failed to back SALT II in the fight to get passage of the treaty in the Senate. Vance finally resigned when the people he saw as crazies carried the day for a "mission impossible" rescue attempt in Iran.[7] The human rights activists in the State Department remained influential in pressuring Third World dictators to release individual political prisoners,[8] but the ability of such activists to influence White House decisions had been seriously reduced by 1979.

Ironically, Carter's human rights policy helped to delegitimize the pro-U.S. Iranian and Nicaraguan regimes. Carter's belated pledge of loyalty to the shah and reluctant and tardy endorsement of Nicaragua's National Guard[9] hardly balanced the vulnerability suffered by Somoza and the shah because of human rights violations. When the choice appeared between the dictators and revolutionaries, Carter chose national security over human rights in both countries. But his human rights policies had delegitimized national security doctrine in Iran and Nicaragua, thus opening up those two regimes for internal and international attack and helping to convert both regimes into international pariahs. In so doing, the anti-Somoza and anti-shah opposition was legitimized. This turned into a boon for the Ayatollah Khomeini and the Sandinistas.

Both Iran and Nicaragua had been indelibly defined as vital to U.S. national security. With Nicaragua, the notion dated back to the Monroe Doctrine and with Iran, to 1946 when the Soviets were warned to keep out and to 1953 when the CIA arranged the overthrow of Mossadegh and the installation of the shah. The premise had become even more explicit when Carter announced his own doctrine, which extended U.S. national security perimeters to the Persian Gulf. Carter's inability to prevent the ayatollah and the Sandinistas from taking power and Carter's subsequent humiliation during the Iranian hostage crisis provided his enemies with the ammunition needed to effectively nullify the human rights advocates and reinstate the old doctrines.

The Carter presidency, its right-wing critics charged, had shown weakness, thereby proving that human rights policies could not substitute for the mysterious national security doctrine as an imperial guideline. Neoconservatives, who had coalesced in the mid-1970s, the old and new right wings, cold war liberals, and evangelical or fundamentalist right-wingers all began to merge into a political alliance whose purpose was to reinstate a new version of the old order. National security would reign again, and its key managers, in and out of government, felt well prepared for the victory of Ronald Reagan in 1980. For them, it presaged a return to the past, the known.

## The Decline of U.S. Power

No one has shown a direct correlation between loss of U.S. control over Third World countries and declines in the U.S. economy, but each piece of land lost nevertheless is seen by those inside the decisionmaking culture as less territory available for potential or future development. The mentality that gives birth to such thought is exacerbated when capital is not investing in productive enterprise. The state historically has assumed responsibility for providing appropriate conditions for capital. When interest rates rocket upward, inflation and unemployment climb; when trade balances worsen and deficits increase, a crisis mentality develops.

Under these conditions, "losses" in other sectors, foreign policy for example, tend to become magnified in the eyes of those who have defined themselves as trustees of the state. Kissinger succinctly wrote, "While there is undoubtedly an upper limit beyond which the injury to the budget would outweigh the gain in military strength, it is also the case that this theoretical ceiling has been consistently underestimated."[10] In other words, the empire is considered vital, and the economy must be pushed to the breaking point to maintain the empire. Since the end of World War II, no alternatives to U.S. government control of the currents of change and order were seriously considered by policymakers.

The problem was that U.S. power was not equal to such a task. The Iranian situation after the fall of the shah was not conducive to massive U.S. troop intervention. In 1979, Jimmy Carter paid for the Dulles brothers' coup of 1953. Ayatollah Khomeini, an Islamic fundamentalist who hardly fit the stereotype of the man that pro-Reagan national security ideologues would have designated for the spoiler role, helped defeat Jimmy Carter in the 1980 election.

As crises struck the old orders in Iran and in Central America, the societies responded in different ways. In Nicaragua, El Salvador, and Guatemala, an armed revolutionary response erupted anew; this response was grounded in a nationalist and radical ideology that called for the dismantling of the old order and the creation of a more just one based on an alteration of property relations, internally and with foreign investors and owners as well.

The ayatollah's movement sought to restore an imagined holy age of Muslim life, emulating the era that supposedly existed in the quarter century after the death of the Prophet. Like the Sandinistas, the Iranians were nationalistic and anti-imperialist. Both nations blamed the United States, and justly so, for intervening in their social affairs. As revolutionary Iranian guards made public captured CIA documents revealing massive U.S. involvement in the shah's internal repressive apparatus, the same guards also celebrated U.S. impotence. The mightiest power in the world could not rescue its hostage embassy personnel.[11]

The revolution in Nicaragua paled in comparison with events in Iran, at least in 1979–1980. Washington had used Iran as a platform country, a loyal military ally on the Soviet border, from where the CIA listened, infiltrated, and plotted. Yet, after Carter, as Iran engaged Iraq instead of the United States, the Sandinistas rose to high visibility on the enemies list of the national security elite.

The Carter experience, said the neoconservatives, proved the incompatibility of human rights and national security. Carter's swing from one to the other created dangerous situations, especially when he considered military responses in Iran, which borders on the Soviet Union.

In Central America, a new test was awaiting the national security managers. They faced not only a revolutionary Nicaragua, but also growing revolutions in El Salvador and Guatemala. The security managers' traditional allies, the ones that had long been the foundation of the "system," had committed atrocities that in 1980 became public knowledge throughout the world. Members of the Salvadoran security forces had murdered Archbishop Oscar Romero of San Salvador and had raped and then assassinated four U.S. Catholic missionaries, three of them nuns. In addition, mass graves were discovered shortly before Carter left office. The victims included opposition political and trade union figures.

National security doctrine assumed that the United States would forever control Central America. Native controllers were known to be murderers and torturers. Carter opted to continue aiding them while pushing gently for some moderation.

Ronald Reagan did not face any dilemma between two sets of values. He was a national security man all the way, and he chose Central America as his symbolic battlefield—the place where the United States would confront Soviet power, even though there was none to confront.


## Notes

1. C. Fred Bergsten, "The Threat from the Third World," *Foreign Policy* (Summer 1973):102–124.

2. Leslie Gelb, "National Security and the New Foreign Policy," *Parameters,* November 8, 1978, p. 10-F., cited in Alan Wolfe, *America's Impasse* (New York: Pantheon, 1981), p. 213.

3. The attorney general made this remark to the widow of Orlando Letelier, Isabel Morel, and to Michael Moffitt, Ronni Karpen's husband, in the presence of the author, October 1976.

4. Carter's first appointment choice was Theodore Sorensen, a former Kennedy adviser and critic of covert operations. After objections arose to Sorenson for being too soft, Carter asked TV newsman and former Johnson adviser Bill Moyers, who declined on the grounds that it would imperil his journalistic career, before settling on Turner.

5. Groups such as the Committee on the Present Danger and the Coalition for a Democratic Majority included cold warriors from both parties who believed that "the program of Soviet imperialism is based on a military buildup without parallel in modern history" and that the United States had to use both military and covert means to defend against this enemy. Among the Democrats in this crowd were Eugene and Walt W. Rostow and Dean

Rusk. Wolfe, *America's Impasse,* p. 138. Eugene Rostow's statement on foreign and defense policy was cited on p. 276.

6. Young horrified the national security intellectuals and operators early on in his tenure by referring to the Cuban troops in Angola as a "stablizing force." He advocated dialogue with the Palestine Liberation Organization, another national security taboo, and insisted that U.S. business could best be served by using the human rights guidelines for policy in the Third World. Young proved his case in Africa when he convinced the president to enforce and retain sanctions against Rhodesia, even though it was a key national security resource producer. Nigeria, observing the changed U.S. attitude toward racism in Africa, rewarded IBM, Kellogg, and other corporate giants by admitting them into its oil-rich market for the first time to compete with European transnationals.

7. Vance agreed to delay announcement of his resignation until after the attempt to rescue the hostages from Iran took place; he finally quit April 28, 1980, four days after the mission's spectacular failure. See Cyrus R. Vance, *Hard Choices* (New York: Simon and Schuster, 1983), pp. 388–392; Zbigniew Brzezinski, *Power and Principle* (New York: Farrar, Straus, Giroux, 1983); and Hamilton Jordan, *Crisis: The Last Year of the Carter Presidency* (New York: G. P. Putnam's Sons, 1982), pp. 252–253. Also see Gary Sick, *All Fall Down* (New York: Random House, 1985).

8. For a general assessment of the Carter human rights policy, see Lars Schoultz, *Human Rights and United States Policy Toward Latin America* (Princeton, N.J.: Princeton University Press, 1981), pp. 359–364.

9. William LeoGrande, "The Revolution in Nicaragua: Another Cuba?" *Foreign Affairs* 58, no. 1 (Fall 1979):36.

10. Henry Kissinger, *Nuclear Weapons and Foreign Policy* (New York: Harper and Row, 1956), p. 412.

11. The United States suffered humiliation in part because Carter had tried, too late, to prove to Third World national security allies that he would not abandon them. In fact, he abandoned them in power and then offered them charity, which was a deadly formula. When he allowed the hated shah to enter the United States for medical treatment, it was no more than a symbolic Christian gesture. The ayatollah answered by taking hostages. All the nuclear power and advanced technology could not bring them home, just as the same power and technology had been unable to defeat the Vietnamese a decade earlier.

# CHAPTER 12

# The Reagan Doctrine

*What I want to see above all else is that this country remains a country where someone can always get rich. That's the thing we have that must be preserved.*

—Ronald Reagan[1]

*I do not know how many future generations we can count on before the Lord returns.*

—James Watt, Secretary of the Interior[2]

*Deserting the Nicaraguan freedom fighters would be a national security disaster for the United States.*

—Ronald Reagan[3]

Ronald Reagan promised to restore the country's national pride after the "weakness" of the Carter presidency and the humiliation of the Iranian hostage crisis. Reagan resuscitated both the ideology and the policies of the cold war, portraying the Soviet Union as an implacable adversary and announcing plans to revive the arms race and intervention as basic policies.

Although his policies have been pragmatic, President Reagan nonetheless cultivated a domestic image of toughness. He ignored the objections of European allies to his virulent rhetoric and his aggressive "antiterrorism" measures, and he brushed aside the efforts of European allies and those of key Latin American nations to achieve a negotiated peace in Central America.

Central America became the arena in which the ideologues and the pragmatists in the administration concurred that they could play international hardball. Reagan's policy could be portrayed as an attempt to reverse the "communist inroads" made under the "weak and appeasing" Carter administration.[4]

## A Mélange of Doctrines

What has come to be known since 1984 as the Reagan Doctrine encompasses a variety of foreign policy elements loosely tied together by militant and ideologically intense rhetoric. True to his general presidential style, Reagan's doctrine combines Monroe's emphasis on Latin America, Theodore Roosevelt's interventionism there, Truman's emphasis on military support for anticommunist governments, Kennedy's belief in counterinsurgency, and Nixon's willingness to bomb other countries for symbolic purposes. When Congress objected to backing right-wing dictators in the Third World and stymied Reagan's attempts to supply them with almost limitless aid, he did not insist on his initial line, which was to support authoritarian anticommunist regimes.[5] Instead, Reagan even borrowed from the Carter lexicon by restoring democracy and human rights to the policy vocabulary.

The Reagan team cared less about facts than about ideological appearances. By grabbing newspaper headlines and lead stories on the TV news, Reagan officials defined the framework for public and congressional debate. In Central America, the president achieved his publicity goal by making dramatic headline claims about the communist threat that placed the Sandinista army close to Harlingen, Texas, and about the heroic "freedom fighters" that merited U.S. support. The most dramatic media ploy involved a "revelation" about the Salvadoran rebels.

The reinvigorated national security elite roared with righteousness as it presented to the public one of the most aggressive white papers ever to emerge from the government. A February 1981 white paper purported to prove beyond a shadow of a doubt that the Salvadoran guerrillas, the Front for National Liberation (FMLN), were part and parcel of a worldwide Moscow-based conspiracy, one whose tentacles stretched to Vietnam, Cuba, and, most pointedly, Nicaragua—the source of the FMLN's arms supply.

In support of their contentions, the authors of the white paper cited captured documents including a diary from Salvadoran communist leader Shafik Handal that allegedly tied Nicaragua to vast clandestine arms shipments into El Salvador. Secretary of State Alexander Haig and his assistants crowed about the white paper, which was accepted by most of the major media as a bona fide factual report.

Months after Reagan had accomplished his publicity goals, reporters for the *Los Angeles Times* and the *Wall Street Journal* discovered serious factual errors in the white paper, ones that rendered dubious the central thesis—that Nicaragua was a major supplier of arms to the Salvadoran guerrillas. The document's primary author, State Department official Jon Glassman, admitted to *Journal* reporter Jonathan Kwitny that he did not have the proof that the document claimed, that there were exaggerations in the paper, that some of the assertions were really speculations, and that in fact the government had no solid evidence that the Soviet Union, Cuba, or Nicaragua was a major arms supplier to the Salvadoran rebels.

The sensational Shafik Handal diary, when closely scrutinized, proved the opposite of what the white paper claimed. The Soviets had denied Handal's request for weapons, giving him only an airplane ticket out of the USSR. The "vast shipments from Nicaragua" turned out to be a trickle at best, and the much ballyhooed Cuban source was nonexistent. The U.S. ambassador to El Salvador, Robert White, testified to Congress on the spurious nature of the white paper, and the chief of the U.S. Mission in Cuba, Wayne Smith, verified that Cuba and Nicaragua both had notified the United States that they had stopped arms shipments as of January 1981 and indeed had done so.

The new U.S. ambassador to El Salvador, Deane Hinton, told a Senate panel in 1983 that "nary a pistola" had been interdicted between Nicaragua and El Salvador despite the CIA's allocation of more than $50 million to intercept such alleged shipments. A CIA official disputed Hinton by saying that some truckloads of material had been stopped at the Salvadoran border. When a senator inquired about the contents of the trucks, the CIA man admitted that the trucks contained cotton, which the Agency believed was intended for use as uniforms for the guerrillas.

In 1982, David MacMichael worked for the CIA as an analyst on Latin American affairs. After he resigned, he testified to Congress in 1983 that while he sat in Langley, reading the intelligence reports, he did not come across one piece of credible evidence of Nicaraguan arms transfers to the FMLN.

The importance of regional conflicts, such as the ones in Central America, reached beyond any specific economic or strategic relevance El Salvador or Nicaragua may have had. A more essential ingredient on the Reagan agenda was the rapid and significant escalation of arms buildup, and for that large jump in the defense budget to prove credible, an equally credible threat had to be demonstrated. Reagan, following Jimmy Carter's lead, discovered "windows of vulnerability" in U.S. nuclear defenses and a Soviet threat to national security in Central America.[6]

Reagan's policies were based on the presumptions that the Soviets had inherently aggressive intentions in the Third World and through Carter's weakness had managed to overtake the United States in both conventional and nuclear forces.[7] Reagan came to the White House with a right-wing ideology[8] that called for a crusade against what Reagan himself later termed "the evil empire." In content, Reagan's policies did not differ greatly from early cold war goals, such as containment and rollback, enunciated by Democrats such as Dean Acheson and George Kennan and Republicans such as John Foster Dulles.

The foreign policy guidelines that became known as the Reagan Doctrine assumed a permanent global conflict in which the United States would support "freedom fighters"—that is, insurgencies against "communist" governments. To distinguish "good" from "bad" guerrillas, the president said that one need only look at "what kind of government they are opposing."[9] These insurgencies would prove that "free people" could "undo the infamous Brezhnev Doctrine," which, according to Reagan, contended that "once a nation falls into the darkness of communist tyranny, it can never again see the light of freedom."[10]

The Reagan Doctrine would prevent new territory from leaving the "sphere of freedom" and falling into the communist world. The United States would rebuild its massive military apparatus, conventional and nuclear, to reverse the Red tide and in so doing force the Soviets to yield to the U.S. position or else spend themselves into bankruptcy. Along with this arms buildup, the Reagan team launched an expensive and vigorous propaganda war to preach and teach anticommunism and pro-Americanism.

Reagan's doctrine reaffirmed that the United States had a "moral responsibility" to accept "free world" leadership. Secretary of State George Shultz emphasized that support for "freedom fighters" went beyond U.S. "historical sympathy for democracy and freedom but also, in many cases, in the interests of national security."[11]

Shultz found the language to convert nationalist movements and their wars of liberation into an attack on U.S. national security. According to Shultz, they were "the pretext for subverting any non-communist country in the name of so-called 'socialist internationalism.'" The Brezhnev Doctrine supposedly prevented these nations from leaving the socialist camp once they are inside it; the Reagan Doctrine called for their removal.[12] Although Nicaragua became the focus, the symbol, the litmus test for the doctrine, the principles would be applied elsewhere as well.

Reagan's foreign policy rhetoric and policies had precedents. Truman had promised and given aid to anticommunist insurgents. Eisenhower sent troops to Lebanon and then pulled them out. Kennedy built up the military, based on a phony missile gap, and championed counterinsurgency. Nixon created a fanatic or madman image and a protected presidency, and he held fewer press conferences than did any modern president. The harassment of new revolutionary governments in the Third World was anticipated by Ford's attempt to put a covert operation to work in Angola, although Reagan has gone beyond him and actually has fostered five counterrevolutions simultaneously: Nicaragua, Cambodia, Ethiopia, Angola, and Afghanistan. Stylistically, Reagan has borrowed FDR's fireside manner, Kennedy's inspirational words, and Johnson's common-man approach and has added his own consummate skill as a television performer.

## The Terrorism Ploy

Even before winning the 1980 election, Ronald Reagan had begun to reinvent terrorism as a handy rhetorical device to scare hell out of the people, as Harry Truman had done with the Soviets in the late 1940s. The notion of international terrorism, a vague yet sinister sounding phrase, appealed to the Santa Fe Group (the group of right-wing intellectuals who prepared a policy guideline for Reagan in 1980) and the men who came to the center of foreign policymaking. Not only was there new wording, but the Soviets could be blamed for having caused the assorted skyjackings, kidnappings, and other acts of violence associated with a panoply of liberation movements and armed groups, mostly in the Middle East. Best of all, revolutionary and liberation movements could be stigmatized as "terrorist." The United States would be pitted not against patriotic nationalists seeking a homeland and freedom, but against vicious international terrorists linked to Moscow.

International terrorism became the new guideline for foreign policy. Moreover, the label "terrorist" was so pejorative that administration officials thought they they could get away with military adventures by invoking it. The administration also associated the word "terrorism" with Soviet behavior in general. Had terrorism been defined precisely to describe illegal violence against civilians or other states by governments or groups, the United States would have emerged as the leading terrorist force in the world due to its support of violent counterrevolutions and its clearly terrorist behavior against Nicaragua.

But President Reagan and his team excelled at defining the language and limits of debate.

In Central America, the "terrorists" were the Salvadoran revolutionaries and the Sandinistas, both backed by Cuba, which of course meant the Soviet Union. No proof needed to be offered when the names of archfiend nations were invoked. The major media reported uncritically the press releases and statements at news conferences. The "terrorist" label then became the wrapping for new CIA and military policies. New interventionist possibilities emerged with the ability to use terrorism as a new threat to national security.

Ronald Reagan set out to resuscitate covert action and rid the nation of the "Vietnam syndrome." International terrorism became an important vehicle to accomplish this. The label also permitted President Reagan to lump all of the disobedient nations of the world together as terrorist. Iran, Libya, North Korea, Cuba, and Nicaragua could be pushed into one pejorative pile.[13]

When the president ordered U.S. planes to bomb Libya as retaliation for alleged terrorism, this marked the second major military action he had undertaken. Seymour Hersh, a Pulitzer Prize–winning reporter, presented evidence to indicate that Reagan's real purpose for sending squadrons of F-111 bombers to attack Libya was to assassinate Libyan leader Muammar Khadaffi.[14] The claims that the Libyans had sponsored major acts of terrorism against U.S. and European citizens turned out to be flimsy.

The invasion of Grenada and the air strikes against Libya, both operations with little risk of failure, fanned the flames of patriotism. But the public was not disposed to allow the administration to pursue those "victories" with military escalation in Central America.

The president suffered a series of setbacks, mostly involving congressional opposition to his Central America plans. At the same time, public opinion did not correspond to the amount of energy spent in selling the new interventionism. By mid-1987, the public remained opposed to contra aid programs, adamantly against sending U.S. troops to Central America, and clearly still bound by the Vietnam syndrome.

In June 1986, the World Court ruled against the Reagan policies in Nicaragua. Aside from the weight of international legal opinion, the court's ruling symbolized the inclination of the international community to oppose the Reagan Doctrine in Central America. Lawlessness to achieve law was not an acceptable means. The United States was ordered to cease and desist in its aggression against Nicaragua. President Reagan dismissed the court's decision, maintaining that it had no jurisdiction in the case and was a body dominated by enemies of the United States.[15]

## Contadora and the Reagan Doctrine

Contadora, formed for the purpose of preventing a U.S. intervention in Nicaragua, was born as a result of the Reagan Doctrine. Contadora began when Panamanian, Colombian, Venezuelan, and Mexican leaders decided that if the Central America political scenario continued to develop alongside aggressive U.S. policies, military intervention would become inevitable. These leaders thought such a move would not only destabilize Central America, but all of Latin America as well.

The Contadora negotiators set out to insert themselves as a peace force between the United States and the Sandinistas. Despite repeated failures, the group has not only sustained itself but was joined in 1985 by the Lima Group, or "support group," composed of Argentina, Brazil, Peru, and Uruguay.

Despite repeated attempts by Lieutenant Colonel Oliver North and Assistant Secretary of State Elliott Abrams to sabotage Contadora efforts, the fear of U.S. troop intervention kept the peace process alive and indeed brought together the five presidents of Central America in a series of meetings. In August 1987, an agreement was announced in Guatemala on a plan that was named after Costa Rica's president, Oscar Arias.

Throughout the region, all of Latin America, and Western and Eastern Europe came thunderous approval for the idea of a negotiated peace in Nicaragua and El Salvador. The United Nations and the OAS backed the Arias Plan, as did the Soviets and Cubans. Arias won the Nobel Peace Prize for his work on the peace plan, albeit all five presidents had worked cooperatively on the process. President Reagan stood isolated in the world community and in the United States for his resistance to the plan. Speaker of the House Jim Wright declared strong support for the plan, while Ronald Reagan petulantly announced his intention to ask Congress for $270 million in contra aid in late 1987. Despite administration threats to reduce aid and impose import levies, Central American presidents held firm in their commitment to negotiate a peace, remove foreign troops and advisers from their countries, and build a democratic Central America.

Because it did not coincide with political reality, the Reagan Doctrine in practice has been less fierce than its rhetoric. During his first six and one-half years of militant anticommunism, Reagan could reclaim only one "piece of real estate" for the "free world":

the island of Grenada, with a population of roughly 100,000. Even there, Washington acted only because the revolutionary government consumed itself in a Jacobin frenzy and the population would not resist. The Reagan promises to roll back communism remained in the realm of rhetoric. But the president and his key ideologues had defined one area—Central America—as the symbolic key to the policy.

### Central America as the Key to the Doctrine

*The national security of all the Americas is at stake in Central America. If we cannot defend ourselves there, we cannot expect to prevail elsewhere. Our credibility would collapse, our alliances would crumble, and the safety of our homeland would be put at jeopardy.*

—President Ronald Reagan,
to a joint session of Congress, April 27, 1983

The system that historian Walter LaFeber described as the foundation for permanent U.S. control of Central America began to come apart in the late 1970s. Serious insurrections broke out in Nicaragua, El Salvador, and Guatemala. The pro-U.S. governments of all three countries were corrupt, brutal military dictatorships, on whose behalf there could be no persuasive arguments, except national security. But when human rights also counted, the national security argument was weakened. As a result, the Sandinistas squeezed through an opening in the system. Once aware of the perils, however, the national security apparatus swung into protective operation in order to seal the gap. By the end of 1980, the resolution had been made: No more Nicaraguas in Central America.

During the years of his administration, President Reagan has explained that Sandinista-dominated Nicaragua is a threat to the United States because it is a Soviet surrogate, a military threat to its neighbors, and a totalitarian regime. These charges are not only false, but absurd. This economically crippled nation, one-one-hundredth the size of the United States, has become an obsession for the Reagan administration.

Nicaragua has genuinely sought a nonaligned foreign policy, has armed only in an effort to stave off U.S. aggression, and is a very far cry from "totalitarian." President Reagan has grossly misused language in his campaign against the Sandinistas. Theirs is not a Marxist-Leninist government; the FSLN (Sandinista National Liberation Front) is not a communist party. More than 50 percent of the economy is privately owned; religion flourishes; opposition press, although censored, publishes harsh, antigovernment articles; and Western-style elections were held in late 1984, with reputable European observers attesting to the fairness of the elections.

The Sandinistas received less than two-thirds of the vote, hardly a Soviet-style election. The charge of totalitarianism has been used by the administration to obfuscate the positive reforms initiated by the Sandinistas in health, education, housing, sanitation, access to credit and technical assistance, and agriculture. The focus on civil liberties also masks the fundamental and historic concern of U.S. policymakers. The Sandinistas have changed the rules for foreign corporations doing business in Nicaragua. For the first time in Nicaraguan history, businesses must abide by occupational safety codes, respect labor unions, pay taxes, and remove only a portion of their profits from the country. The Nicaraguan state now runs export commerce and decides how to distribute the profits.

This model challenges the right of businesses to unrestricted access to labor and resources but does not challenge the national security of the United States. Following the overthrow of the Somoza dictatorship in 1979, the Sandinistas obtained substantial aid from Western Europe and the United States. Through 1981, 49 percent of its bilateral aid came from the West; less than 20 percent came from Soviet bloc countries.[16]

When the Reagan administration took office in 1981, it launched a multifront campaign to overthrow the Sandinistas. It employed tactics from economic strangulation and diplomatic isolation on the one hand, to ongoing military maneuvers, psychological operations, and propaganda war on the other. The kicker was a CIA-organized military force, the contras, that would operate as the lynchpin of the policy.

The CIA organized, trained, and equipped the Nicaraguan contras in 1981 in much the same fashion as it created the Cuban exile army in 1960. Like the Cuban prototype, the contras are led by former officers in the ex-dictator's National Guard. To make the rebels more palatable, the CIA created a cosmetic political leadership, although real power lies in the hands of the military commanders. Like the rebels that invaded Cuba's Bay of Pigs in 1961, the Nicaraguan contras have no popular base of support within their country and thus have been unable to take and hold one square inch of Nicaragua territory.

Washington's efforts to destabilize the Sandinistas have led to an increase in Nicaragua's economic dependency on the socialist bloc, particularly following the U.S. imposition of a trade embargo in May 1985. However, key U.S. allies have refused to join Washington's economic war against Nicaragua, and some have even increased their trade with and expanded their credit to the Sandinista government. In fact, of the $392 million in petroleum, lines of credit, and humanitarian aid garnered by Nicaraguan president Daniel Ortega's visits to socialist and Western European countries, $202 million was promised by the USSR and the socialist countries, while $190 million was granted by Western European countries.[17] This dependency on both the East and West is consistent with the desire expressed by Nicaraguan leaders to create a nonaligned but sovereign nation.

Administration claims that the Nicaraguan military "buildup" constitutes a threat of intervention and of "export of revolution" to neighboring Central American states are belied by the facts. Nicaragua has far less air and naval craft than does Honduras or El Salvador; Nicaragua's army is defensive in nature because it is designed primarily to deal with the U.S.-sponsored contra war. This statement is confirmed by a U.S. intelligence report prepared in late 1981. "The Nicaraguan defense establishment was swept away," the document concludes. "Nothing remains except for some small arms and the battered remnants of other equipment."[18] Thus, like the export of revolution accusation, so, too, the charge of massive Soviet and Cuban military involvement in Nicaragua is dubious.

The head of the Nicaraguan Democratic Front (FDN), the largest anti-Sandinista rebel force, told the New York Times that "his troops have seen little evidence of the major buildup of Soviet arms in Nicaragua that Reagan Administration officials have described."[19] The Soviet Union has shown little inclination to maintain "another Cuba," much less place costly and indefensible bases in Central America. On the charge of exporting revolution to El Salvador, aside from the difficulty of exporting a noncommodity, U.S. officials have not produced credible evidence that the Sandinistas have provided significant arms to the Salvadoran insurgents or any other rebel groups in the region.[20] Ironically, the U.S. government is engaged in exporting counterrevolution in Nicaragua as well as in Afghanistan, Cambodia, and Angola. This double standard has not been adequately discussed in Congress or in the press. Questions of law and international standards seem to dissipate with the mere mention of the words "national security."

By 1986, Nicaragua had become a fixation, an obsession, a kind of lurid image that blinded key policymakers. The professionals in the State Department, who had learned in Diplomacy School that governments always devise worst-case scenarios, or ways out, encountered an ideological determination among newly appointed men in the CIA, the Defense Department, and the NSC. The real American, these men argued, must go abroad to search for and destroy foreign monsters. The Sandinistas were transformed for policy purposes from a popular nationalist revolutionary group into a monster that symbolized the Soviet Union. Not to destroy the Sandinistas would show weakness and would allow the Vietnam syndrome to continue indefinitely.

## The Reagan Doctrine in Theory and Practice

Given that President Reagan never sat down and wrote an actual doctrine, the following points have been extrapolated from his and his advisers' key speeches and messages to Congress.

1. The United States will support freedom fighters throughout the world in armed struggles against economically weak or less than firmly consolidated Third World governments that are seen as pro-Soviet. The language used will reflect U.S. heroism and determination and will employ crisis metaphors as well as Hollywood grit.

2. Not one inch of new territory shall be allowed to fall into the hands of the communists.[21] This meant propping up governments threatened by revolution, such as Jose Duarte's in El Salvador, Ferdinand Marcos' in the Philippines until his ouster, and Gaafar Nimeiri's in the Sudan.

3. Points (1) and (2) will be accomplished with a minimum of visible costs to the U.S. public. The lesson that the Reagan administration has drawn from Vietnam is that prolonged involvements of U.S. troops on foreign soil are politically unsupportable. "Low intensity conflict," a 1980s version of counterinsurgency, signifies the conducting of long-term wars of attrition against guerrilla movements or vulnerable revolutionary governments without the extensive involvement of U.S. combat forces and with as much secrecy as possible. If U.S. forces are to have a high profile, as in the invasion of Grenada and the raid on Libya, overwhelming force is to be used for a very short period of time.

4. The right to use unilateral action has become a conspicuous element in the Reagan administration's evolving counterterrorist policy. Grenada was supposedly a threat to its neighbors, and therefore the U.S. justifiably responded to the calls from the eastern Caribbean nations, and Libya, labeled as "a Soviet client state," merited U.S. air strikes for its role in harboring, training, and fostering terrorism. Nicaragua also has been widely accused of harboring terrorists. The Reagan Doctrine has sought to identify the Soviet Union and regional Third World enemies of the United States as the prime sources of terrorism.

5. The most recent addition to the doctrine is the word "democracy." Just before a dictator is about to be overthrown by a popular uprising, Washington steps in to arrange a smooth ouster and transition to "democratic" government, thereby preventing radicals from taking power. The administration then claims it is only following the guideline of democracy, which, in order to prevail, requires a well-publicized, U.S.-style election.

6. The United States will rapidly build up its nuclear and conventional forces. This effort goes hand in glove with a vigorous propaganda campaign emphasizing both Soviet perfidy and military strength on the one side and U.S. goodness and vulnerability on the other. Such an institutionalized increase in military spending also results in the spreading of military culture. More U.S. citizens become directly dependent upon the military apparatus for their livelihood, which is supposed to translate into political behavior. Promilitary themes increase in commercial culture; the government legitimizes them through the amount allocated to the defense budget and through constant rhetoric. The military, which is portrayed as virtuous and heroic as opposed to the negative image created during and immediately after the Vietnam War, eventually will also help to overcome the Vietnam syndrome against interventions.

## Notes

1. From Robert Chesshyre, "White House Peddlar of an Ageless Dream," *Observer,* January 29, 1984. Also see Jeff McMahan, *Reagan and the World: Imperial Policy in the New Cold War* (New York: Monthly Review Press, 1984), pp. 1–25.

2. James L. Franklin, "The Religious Right and the New Apocalypse," *Boston Globe,* May 2, 1982.

3. *New York Times,* June 6, 1986, p. 5.

4. Carter had actually laid the groundwork for this policy when he sent emergency military supplies to El Salvador that earlier had been cut off because of egregious human rights violations.

5. Jeane Kirkpatrick differentiated totalitation regimes, which were communist and therefore permanent, from authoritarian ones, which were temporary and sided with U.S. policy objectives. "Dictatorships and Double Standards," *Commentary* (November 1979): 34–45.

6. In fiscal year 1977, the last of Gerald Ford's administration, the defense budget was $97 billion. Carter raised it to $158 billion in 1981, a rise from 5.2 to 5.5 percent of the country's Gross National Product.

7. See Alan Wolfe, *The Rise and Fall of the Soviet Threat* (Washington, D.C.: Institute for Policy Studies, 1979); Fred Halliday, *The Making of the*

*Second Cold War* (London: Verso, 1983); and Fred Kaplan, *Dubious Specter* (Washington, D.C.: Institute for Policy Studies, 1980).

8. See the Committee of Santa Fe, *A New Inter-American Policy for the Eighties* (Washington D.C.: The Council, 1980).

9. *Washington Post,* May 7, 1983.

10. Reagan radio address, February 6, 1985. There is no evidence that Brezhnev ever made such a statement. The "doctrine" was usually inferred from Moscow's invasions of Czechoslovakia in 1968 and Afghanistan in 1979, but these interventions, like Hungary in 1956, can be better explained (although hardly excused) as efforts by Moscow to hang onto its sphere of influence.

11. Commonwealth Club address, San Francisco, February 22, 1985.

12. Examples of the Soviets "losing" control after establishing "footholds" include China, Albania, North Korea, Egypt, Indonesia, Ghana, and Somalia.

13. Speech to the American Bar Association, reported in the *New York Times,* July 9, 1985, p. A1.

14. *New York Times Magazine,* February 22, 1987.

15. In fact, the majority of the court was composed of NATO countries and Third World nations, not members of the Soviet bloc.

16. Peter Kornbluh, *Nicaragua: The Price of Intervention* (Washington, D.C.: Institute for Policy Studies, 1987).

17. Daniel Siegel and Tom Spaulding with Peter Kornbluh, eds., *Outcast Among Allies* (Washington, D.C.: Institute for Policy Studies, 1985).

18. Department of State and Department of Defense Congressional Presentation Document, Security Assistance Program, FY 1981, at the National Security Archives. See Kornbluh, *Nicaragua,* p. 258, fn. 41. For an objective analysis of the lack of Soviet military presence in Nicaragua, see a study commissioned by the State Department, C. G. Jacobsen, *Soviet Attitudes Towards Aid to and Contacts with Central American Revolutionaries,* Department of State, Bureau of Intelligence Research Report (June 1984), p. 15.

19. *New York Times,* November 22, 1984.

20. The Sandinistas challenged the United States to present evidence to the World Court supporting the charge that Nicaragua was "exporting revolution," but the United States refused.

21. The definition of communism used here is loose and applies to regimes such as Nicaragua's and Angola's, even though the Sandinistas and the MPLA do not describe themselves as such, nor are they accepted by the Soviets as Communist party–led regimes. On the other hand, the administration has enjoyed relatively good relations with Mozambique and Zimbabwe. See Fred Halliday, *The Making of the Second Cold War* (London: Verso, 1983).

# CHAPTER 13

# Central America and the Fruits of Reaganism

*Central America is the most important place in the world.*
—Jeane Kirkpatrick,
U.S. Ambassador to the United Nations[1]

Central America may indeed become the most important place in the world if events there force a challenge to national security policies. As President Reagan escalates the war in Nicaragua, those opposed to his policies must address issues that go beyond Nicaragua and El Salvador to the heart of U.S. interests and security. By means of virulent anti-Soviet rhetoric, President Reagan had won a bare majority for his contra policy in the House of Representatives. But such simplifications do not explain the complex process that has caused so much of the Third World to erupt in nationalist and socialist revolutions, nor are these simplifications sound guidelines for foreign policy in this new international reality.

Washington policymakers still assume that they can and should exercise control over another nation and people, just as their ancestors did in 1898 when the marines landed in Nicaragua, Cuba, China, the Philippines, and elsewhere. U.S. policymakers see Third World countries as pieces of real estate to be acquired or reacquired, not as independent nations. The Reagan administration's methods to thwart Nicaragua's independence are familiar to the people of Central America and the Caribbean. These methods include surrogate warfare, trade and loan embargoes, propaganda, and threatening military maneuvers.

Since the end of World War II, the United States has shouldered the massive budget needed to sustain the policies of national security. In an era of skyrocketing deficits, the United States no longer can afford to maintain control of the Third World through massive military spending and at the same time escalate the nuclear and conventional arms race with the Soviet Union. Today's Latin American leaders, unlike their malleable predecessors, have warned U.S. leaders that they are pursuing a dangerous policy and that to escalate it by deploying U.S. combat forces would destabilize the entire continent.

While events in Central America move toward wider war, the debates in Congress about contra aid demonstrate the paucity of policy thinking in the Democratic opposition and among those Republicans who retain their respect for the law above the urgent cries of national security managers. Instead of challenging the Cold War premise of the policy, members of Congress debate peripheral issues: Were contra funds properly accounted for; did contra leaders use the war as a cover for drug dealing; did the contras consistently violate human rights? But the real issue is whether or not the United States ought to interfere in the affairs of another nation.

The contra policy epitomizes the abyss into which U.S. national security thinking has fallen as a guideline for policy in the modern world. The contra leaders are a dubious assortment of former Somoza National Guardsmen, criminals, and opportunists; the contras are responsible for repeated barbarities against civilians and are utterly dependent on U.S. aid. Although the national security elite claims that the contras represent freedom, democracy, and virtue, they have neither a social program nor popular support among Nicaraguans. The U.S. public, as polls constantly demonstrate, is overwhelmingly opposed to contra funding. The contras are a surrogate force for the national security state.

By pulling out the stops in a massive campaign of deception and intimidation, the Reagan administration has so far had its way in Nicaragua. In El Salvador, the Reagan administration has succeeded in averting a guerrilla victory but has encountered difficulty constructing a stable pro-U.S. regime capable of governing. A pattern of massive human rights abuses by military-sanctioned death squads, involving at least fifty thousand killings (including a number of U.S. citizens), radicalized the centrist Salvadoran politicians who survived and fueled congressional opposition to aiding the Salvadoran military; what power the current president, Jose Napoleon Duarte, has flows from his U.S. backers. The price of "holding the line" is more than $500 million a year in direct aid, in addition to the indirect costs of U.S. military support.[2]

El Salvador illustrates the high costs and fragility of national security regimes, something the Reagan administration has come to recognize. Moreover, the model Third World national security states that were constructed in the 1960s and 1970s in the Southern Cone, southern Europe, Iran, South Korea, the Philippines, Central America, and Haiti are increasingly unacceptable to the public. Only the far right wing clings to the notion that dictatorial regimes, such as those in Chile, Paraguay, and South Africa, are the hope for the future of capitalism and U.S. national security or even that these regimes are tenable.

Thus, the Reagan administration (perhaps mindful of the damage that the Iranian debacle did to Jimmy Carter) was eager to grease the skids under Ferdinand Marcos and Jean-Claude Duvalier, confident that it could retain its influence with their successors. But in Chile and South Africa, where it is not clear that a "third way" is possible, Washington has had difficulty arriving at a coherent policy.

## Finessing Revolution

In 1981, Reagan offered full and unequivocal support for Third World anticommunists. Vice President George Bush toasted Ferdinand Marcos in Manila; Jeane Kirkpatrick, the U.N. ambassador, praised Augusto Pinochet in Santiago. Indeed, the Argentine military leaders felt friendly and secure enough with Secretary of State Alexander Haig to attack the Malvinas (Falkland) Islands. In that contest, Great Britain and the loyal anticommunists of the Third World faced off, each expecting U.S. support. The pressure from the vast national security bureaucracy, which was invested heavily in the NATO partnership, forced a decision in favor of Britain.

The Falklands/Malvinas affair and Haig's failure to enlist support for a naval blockade of Cuba indicated that the Reagan national security elite in fact was more flexible than it sounded. Haig, who brought into a June 1981 cabinet meeting a plan to impose a naval blockade on Cuba, was almost laughed out of the room by other cabinet members and the president's key staff officers. Haig had taken seriously the rhetoric, and his plan indeed was designed to "go to the source" because Cuba was believed to be behind the revolutions in Central America and the Caribbean.

Because hard-line ideology could not convince the majority in Congress nor shape events in the Third World, a pragmatic policy emerged, one that would allow the State Department and the national security machinery to deal more realistically with political changes in the Third World. In the Philippines and Haiti, emissaries of the new policy helped to ease out pro-U.S. despots who were judged unable—or no longer suitable—to maintain control. By creating a high media profile for democratic changes—despite decades of support for the most barbaric dictators—the United States then could also claim some influence on the new moderate governments. With one hand U.S. diplomats held out enormous carrots, which were dangled in front of the new Philippine president, Corazon Aquino. With the other hand, U.S. diplomats brandished a stick—the threat that grave problems would ensue if the new government pursued anti-U.S. policies or, for that matter, allowed leftist forces to gain serious places inside the new coalition.

The Philippine solution was supposed to follow the Salvador model. Pro-U.S. generals inside the Aquino government pushed for an aggressive antiguerrilla program, while U.S. national security officials assured the Philippine president of unlimited support for pursuing such a line. President Reagan, the most rhetorically hard-line of all national security advocates, proved that the defense intellectuals could have their national security cake while they feasted on the rhetoric of democracy and human rights. Had the Salvadoran right wing, Duvalier, or Marcos remained in leadership, their nations might well have polarized, thus resulting in a clear advantage for left-wing insurgencies. With the new "democracy," or third way, option, U.S. military officials, not Soviets or Cubans, exercised influence in El Salvador, Haiti, and the Philippines.

As mentioned previously, however, there remain two stubborn flies in the new public relations ointment. Neither Chile under Pinochet nor South African apartheid can yield easily to a third way or, as in the case of El Salvador, to the facade of a third way.

### South Africa and Chile

The greatest industrial and military power on the African continent, the Republic of South Africa, developed into precisely the kind of a regional subpower that Nixon and Kissinger wanted as part of a worldwide antirevolutionary policy front. For years, with U.S. backing, South Africa launched and supported counterrevolutionary insurgencies against Zimbabwe, Mozambique, and Angola. In addition, the white-controlled minority government maintained its hold over Namibia and kept Botswana, Lesotho, and Swaziland in thrall. Using sophisticated technology and intelligence methods, South African forces have conducted raids on African National Congress (ANC) guerrilla offices as far away as Zambia, and South Africa has used its geographical advantages and substantial economic influence throughout black Africa to squash incipient independence and liberation movements.

South Africa itself is rich in natural resources and has an enormous industrial infrastructure and extensive foreign investment. Pretoria has relied on a combination of ideology and self-interest to ensure Western support and for years has portrayed itself as a bastion against communism and Third World socialism. The United States, Great Britain, and West Germany all have a strong interest in keeping the labor and resources of South Africa available, but all three nations also must deal with domestic pressures to oppose apartheid.

After both houses of Congress voted in favor of sanctions against South Africa, President Reagan vetoed the bill in September 1986, but not on national security grounds. Feeling the public opinion pulse, Reagan cited "harm" to blacks as his reason. The prevalent U.S. morality would not accept a national security reason for the veto. Activists from churches and campuses, along with minority communities, demanded divestment. These demands were met before they could become an issue in the 1986 gubernatorial and congressional elections. For example, California, led by a right-leaning Republican governor and the conservative regents of its universities, bowed to outraged public pressure and voted to sell its stocks in companies doing business in South Africa.

Despite Reagan's best efforts to maintain the illusion of "constructive engagement" and "quiet diplomacy," the U.S.–South African policy remained untenable in the prosanctions domestic climate. Reagan did his best to appeal to strategic interests, arguing that South Africa supplied the United States with important "national security resources" and that its government was threatened with Soviet designs. The opposition ANC, President Reagan claimed, was allied with, if not a front for, the South African Communist party. But references to anticommunism and national security gained the president little support; to the Congress and public at large, the issue appeared as one of right and wrong.

Likewise, the policy toward Chile changed as world and national sentiment began to be felt in Washington and as the precedent set in the Philippine case appeared applicable to Pinochet as well. In January 1986, a new U.S. ambassador, Harry Barnes, replaced the right-wing James Theberge, a staunch Pinochet backer. Barnes immediately raised with Pinochet the human rights issue. In June, a band of Chilean soldiers beat and burned alive a nineteen-year-old Chilean youth who resided in Washington, D.C. The death of Rodrigo Rojas focused world outrage against Pinochet and hardened the position of those in the national security apparatus who believed that unless Pinochet soon quit power, there mght well be no third path available and another leftist revolution would take place, this time in Chile.

In January 1987, former major Armando Fernandez Larios, one of three DINA officers accused of conspiring to murder Orlando Letelier in 1976, defected to the United States in order to confess his role in the assassination and provide U.S. authorities with other information on the matter. The importance of the defection was twofold. First, Fernandez asserted that President Pinochet was directly involved in the murder plot and the subsequent cover-up. Second, the involvement of the U.S. Department of Justice in making the defection both logistically possible and personally secure could not have been accomplished without the desire of the U.S. government to pursue the Letelier-Moffitt case; thus, by implication, the defection challenged the legitimacy of a supposed U.S. ally, General Augusto Pinochet.

By late 1987, the Letelier-Moffitt assassinations still stood as an impediment to normal relations between the United States and Chile.[3] At the same time, the defection of Fernandez was sowing seeds of doubt inside the officer corps about the Chilean dictator's integrity. The Reagan administration has sought to finesse the Chilean political situation, as in the Philippines under Marcos and El Salvador under the right-wing generals, by promoting the legitimacy of the civilian opposition while courting the loyalty of the army.

**Notes**

1. Stephen Kinzer, "Central America: In Search of Its Destiny," *Boston Globe Magazine,* August 16, 1981, p. 35.

2. See Joshua Cohen and Joel Rogers, *Inequity and Intervention* (Boston: South End Press, 1986), pp. 39–52.

3. The FBI discovered through evidence provided by Townley and later corroborated by Fernandez that the Chilean intelligence service had been responsible for the murder of the Chilean chief of staff, General Carlos Prats, and his wife in Buenos Aires in 1974 and of the wounding of Christian democratic leader Bernardo Leighton and his wife in an attempted assassination in Rome in 1975. In addition, the special agents of the FBI believed that DINA had planned to assassinate Swedish prime minister Olof Palme, who was later murdered in Stockholm and whose killer is still unidentified, and other European leaders who had led a campaign to isolate and punish the Pinochet regime for its consistent human rights violations.

# CHAPTER 14

# Behind the National Security Myths

*The United States must possess the ability to wage nuclear war rationally.*

—Colin Gray, Defense Department Consultant[1]

*Wise men will apply their remedies to vices, not to names. . . . Otherwise you will be wise historically, a fool in practice. . . . You are terrifying yourself with ghosts and apparitions, whilst your house is the haunt of robbers.*

—Edmund Burke[2]

*We have wasted our substance for thirty years and more fighting some phantom Russian. We've neglected America in favor of Russia. It's time we thought about America. I say get our own house in order. To thine own self be true.*

I. I. Rabi,
Nobel Prize winner in Physics, 1944,
key figure in making the first atomic bomb[3]

## Deceiving the Public

This book has argued that national security became the guiding doctrine for U.S. foreign and defense policy after World War II, although the doctrine's roots may be found in the expansionism of the nineteenth century. National security became a charged phrase, which, when used with proper gravity by presidents and other high officials, served in lieu of an imperial charter. The United States, whose gunboat diplomacy had secured a sphere of influence in the Caribbean, Central America, and parts of Asia, now became the

155

world's greatest power. But its leaders never acknowledged that they were amassing a world empire. Instead, they posed the issue for the public as one of defense, of freedom, of the free world, and, finally, of U.S. national security.

In the 1980s, either U.S. troops or forces paid by the CIA intervened in Grenada, Nicaragua, Angola, Lebanon, Afghanistan, Ethiopia, Cambodia, and the Persian Gulf. Those appointed to protect national security have assumed that U.S. freedom requires unimpeded access by U.S. business to shipping lanes as well as to labor and resources throughout the Third World. When George Shultz landed in Grenada after the 1983 military intervention, he commented on "what a lovely piece of real estate" the country was.[4]

Shultz was applying a metaphor he carried over from the corporate world. He, like most of the men who made up the national security apparatus, came from the ranks of the corporate and banking world.[5] Moving easily from the corporate world into the national security apparatus and back again, these men tended to see corporate and government interests through the same or a similar prism.

The quest of national security managers to maintain global economic control was couched in the rhetoric of "fighting for freedom," "keeping the world safe for democracy," maintaining "credibility," and preventing "falling dominoes." This book has argued that such euphemisms, while effective at tickling the most positive, patriotic, and benevolent parts of the U.S. conscience, also have obfuscated the more narrow and banal motives of policymakers; power, greed, and the desire to reproduce the national security state also have been important motivating factors. The idealistic language that inevitably preceded interventions framed the issues in precisely such forms as to avoid the tough questions: "In whose interest was the U.S. state operating?" Or, "was the national security elite's 'need' to perpetuate U.S. capitalism, or prop up individual corporations, worth the price that U.S. citizens and others had to pay for those goals?"

The notion that the United States should and could control vast overseas areas also has had its impact on military thinking and has defined U.S. interests in ways that high school students rarely encounter in their texts and lectures. Contrary to traditional assumptions about the task of the armed forces, the Joint Chiefs of Staff have viewed defense strategy as maintaining or gaining U.S. control over lands and resources often far removed from the territory that appeared on maps as demarcating the United States of America. The Joint Chiefs also, of course, have prepared to fight a nuclear war.

General William Westmoreland, U.S. military commander in Vietnam, said that strategic considerations, not "ideological dreams," drove President Lyndon Johnson to send troops to Vietnam.

> So just what were those strategic considerations? Well, the first one was simply control. If we could not stop the spread of communism . . . then Southeast Asia would inevitably fall, the so-called "domino theory" would have operated. . . . In addition to that, there was the oil of Indonesia and the tin of Malaysia. Most important of all, was the Malacca Straits, the waterway between the South Pacific and the Indian Ocean. If that area fell under the control of a hostile power, then we would have to go thousands of miles out of our way to get to the Indian Ocean.[6]

Even though the United States "lost" Vietnam, Laos, and Cambodia, no dominoes toppled on Thailand, Burma, Malaysia, Singapore, or South Korea.[7]

Such facts, however, do not appear to have altered the notion that U.S. security includes control over parts of the world far removed from its borders. A February 1986 article in the *Washington Post* noted that Secretary of State George P. Shultz had informed the House Foreign Affairs Committee of the "vital" importance of the Persian Gulf to "the economic and political security" of the free world as far back as 1983. In 1986, the article noted, in a presentation on the same subject to the same committee, Shultz did not mention the Persian Gulf. What had changed? According to the article, U.S. priorities had changed. The oil glut and the headlong tumble of petroleum prices from a high of $34 a barrel of crude oil in 1981 to about $16 five years later gave rise to a "new era, which promises an economic boon to many oil-consuming nations and economic woe to many oil-producing nations."[8]

By late 1987, the Iran-Iraq war that began in 1980 continued to rage in the waters of the Persian Gulf. Once again, U.S. national security was invoked as President Reagan announced that Kuwaiti oil tankers would fly U.S. flags. Reagan then ordered the U.S. Navy to protect the reflagged vessels. As hostilities began to involve U.S. ships, Congress debated whether or not the War Powers Act should apply to the situation, not whether the United States had vital security interests in the Persian Gulf. So deeply was the idea rooted of the United States as an interventionist power that the members of the Senate failed to raise the question of where it was mandated that U.S. forces had to take the lead in defending the right of free navigation 10,000 miles away.

## Excluding the Public

Key policy decisions in the five years after World War II—to "rearm," forge worldwide alliances, plot coups, fight a war in Korea, and repress dissidents at home—were not debated publicly, but announced or decreed in an atmosphere of crisis. National security was used to justify both the actions themselves and the lack of public discussion about them. The process forestalled not only relevant debate, but also definition.[9]

When Congress passed the National Security Act in 1947 and subsequent amendments to it, members of Congress did not insist on a definition of national security, nor did they ask the questions Senator Proxmire subsequently posed but to which he did not give or receive an answer: "What is security?" "How much defense spending is enough?"[10] Congress did not ask the Atomic Energy Commission why so many nuclear tests were needed, nor did Congress inquire about what was happening to the soil, water, and air as a result of atmospheric testing throughout the 1950s. Congress accepted, as did the public, that the country lived in a time of crisis, of genuine emergency, and instead of pushing for debate acquiesced to the sense of urgency invoked by national security spokesmen.

Congress, like the public, trusted the national security managers. The members of Congress believed that the motive of the grim officials who appeared before them was genuine patriotism, not personal or class interest. The periodic exposés of defense contractors bilking the public for hundreds of millions for overpriced goods, bribing foreign officials, and charging the Defense Department for lavish expense accounts were dismissed as aberrations, small prices to pay for protection against the ever-expanding Soviet threat.

## Anticommunism

The ideology of anticommunism has taken deep and firm root in the public mind. The demonization of communists makes it difficult for the U.S. public to see the citizens of communist or even so-called communist states as people, much less as patriots of their own nations in the Third World, as men and women responding to underdevelopment, colonialism, or neocolonialism—that is, to the domination of local or national economies by imperial powers. In fact, it is difficult to encounter any Third World communists who have expressed intentions or ambitions related to U.S. national territory. The ties of these supposed communists to the Soviet Union often have been ambivalent. Yet, national security doctrine defines movements containing communists as ipso facto threats to U.S. security. Indeed, all social change is perceived as threatening, unless that change is explicitly status quo or counterrevolutionary.

The focus on national security as a political adhesive has led to the development of a national security culture as well, one based on the myth of a perpetual mortal enemy. Anticommunism, as Richard Nixon phrased it, is not a policy, but an article of "faith." Nixon was correct. National security is a doctrine that is above the law.

When the World Court declared in June 1986 that the United States had acted criminally against the republic of Nicaragua, citing the mining of its harbors, the distribution of manuals encouraging assassination, and the terrorist acts against Nicaraguan civilians committed by the CIA's contras, the reaction from the U.S. Congress was muted. The Democratically controlled House did not assert itself and call for a massive investigation into the process that led to these criminal acts as well as into the kind of thinking that has replaced sober policy. The Senate did not open hearings about U.S. policy toward Nicaragua. Members of both Houses agreed that the mining was foolish or ill advised, but few questioned the process itself by which such terrorism was officially encouraged.

Some of the men who originally spread the myth of the impending Soviet threat knew better, or should have, but after repeating countless times the lies needed to sell the national security state to the public, even these men apparently became zealous believers of their own myths. Some, such as George Kennan, one policy architect, later admitted that he had gotten carried away. "The image of a Stalinist Russia poised and yearning to attack the West, and deterred only by our possession of atomic weapons, was largely a creation of the Western imagination." But those admissions of error were too few and came too late.[11]

In fact, President Reagan and his foreign policy advisers assumed that they could authorize almost any activity short of sending U.S. troops to Central America if they invoked the communist demon and cloaked the operations in the language of "top secret, ultra-classified" national security. Thus, the political process through which decisions were supposed to be filtered was bypassed, and although Congress did have monitoring committees, the result was and always has been, that the CIA could do almost as it wished as long as the president did not object.[12] At the same time, the corporate managers, some wearing cabinet hats and others close to the sources of political power, consented or at least acquiesced informally to the actions.

## A Society on Edge: National Security Culture Under Reagan

The national security–corporate marriage has not produced a healthy domestic culture nor encouraged the populace to link organically with its past. Indeed, the nation's leaders often have discouraged citizen participation in the major decisions of political life. Patriotism is as the national security managers define it. President Reagan, the greatest of national security communicators, offers cliches, slogans, and traditional symbols in lieu of substance about the meaning of the relationship of citizens to their country, to their neighbors at home and abroad. "Today," he proclaimed just before July 4, 1986, "America remains the standard-bearer for the cause of human freedom. . . . We share our wealth and technical expertise to relieve want and need in our own country and throughout the world. . . . God bless America."[13]

Reagan's communications style tends toward exaggeration. Although President Reagan is correct that the United States still stands as a symbol of freedom in certain parts of the world, it would surprise Third World people to hear him boast that either the U.S. government or its corporations share wealth and technology outside of the military and policy spheres. Indeed, during his reign polarization between the wealthy and the poor became more extreme. Millions of Africans, Asians, and Latin Americans as well as the U.S. poor desperately needed a share of what the wealthy had. But they did not get it. The public and private banks that held the markers for Third World debt showed no mercy for the starving of central Africa, northeast Brazil, or the Philippines. Just as he burlesqued the case for U.S. generosity in his sentimental July 4th mood, so, too, did the president reveal the ultimate mockery of the dangerous doctrine when he said, "Anything we do is in our national security interest."[14]

### Notes

1. *Washington Post,* April 16, 1982.

2. Cited in Raymond Williams, *Communications* (Middlesex, Great Britain: Pelican, 1982), p. 26.

3. *New York Times,* November 16, 1985, editorial page.

4. Shultz's comment to reporters as he alit on the newly "liberated" island was cited in "A Lovely Piece of Real Estate," *NACLA: Report on the Americas* 18, no. 6 (November-December 1984):19.

President Kennedy, using the same logic, saw Vietnam as a "piece of strategic real estate. It's on the corner of mainland Asia, across the East-West trade routes, and in a position that would make it an excellent base for further Communist aggression against the rest of free Asia." Cited by Paul Joseph, "The Making of United States Policy Towards Vietnam," *Socialist Revolution* 3, no. 3 (May-June 1973).

5. C. Wright Mills, *The Power Elite* (New York: Oxford University Press, 1956). See a critique of Mills by Paul Sweezy in *Monthly Review* (May 1957), and see G. William Domhoff, *The Higher Circles* (New York: Vintage/Random House, 1971). On this question, also see John Donovan, *The Cold Warriors: A Policy-Making Elite* (Lexington, Mass.: D. C. Heath, 1974). Also see Gabriel Kolko, *Main Currents in Modern American History* (New York: Harper and Row, 1976), pp. 245-270.

6. "Westmoreland," *The Washington Post Magazine,* February 9, 1986.

7. To those who clung to the domino theory in relation to the three "lost" Asian nations, Revolutionary Cambodian forces proved their independence from Vietnam by making incursions into Vietnamese territory. In 1975, the Vietnamese invaded and occupied Cambodia.

8. "Persian Gulf Slips Down Priority List," *Washington Post,* February 13, 1986, p. 1.

9. In national security language the unspoken assumptions are vital. The "need to know" mentality means "no need to know." Richard Barnet, Marcus Raskin, and Ralph Stavins, *Washington Wages an Aggressive War* (New York: Random House, 1971). The public is deprived of information without which intelligent debate is difficult if not impossible. The excuse is always that information will somehow help the enemy. Benjamin Bradlee, the *Washington Post* editor, responded to CIA director William Casey's threats to the media about revealing intelligence secrets allegedly passed on to Soviets in the June 8, 1986, issue. Bradlee, along with *Post* lawyer Edward Bennett Williams, decided that some stories about CIA covert actions should be published, while others should not because they would injure U.S. national security. Casey actually told *Post* reporter Bob Woodward details about several ongoing CIA operations. The *Post* executives in those cases decided on what was U.S. national security, a strange role for the media. See Bob Woodward, *Veil: The Secret Wars of the CIA, 1981-1987* (New York: Simon and Schuster, 1987), pp. 450-463.

10. Senator William Proxmire, *Hearing before the Joint Economic Committee,* 97th Cong., 2nd sess., April 27, 1982, p. 1.

11. George F. Kennan, "Overdue Changes in Our Foreign Policy," *Harper's* 213 (August 1956):27-33. *Vital Center* historian Arthur Schlesinger Jr. was one of the liberals who insisted that the Soviets had betrayed their pledges of freedom for Eastern Europe and, like Kennan, changed his mind some twenty years later.

One of the most bitter and unfortunately least read of the exposés of the CIA is Joseph Smith, *Portrait of a Cold Warrior* (New York: Putnam, 1976). See George Kennan, *Memoirs, 1925-1950* (London: Hutchinson, 1968).

12. See Woodward, *Veil*.

13. Ronald Reagan, "The Meaning of Liberty," *Parade Magazine,* June 29, 1986.

14. *New York Times,* July 16, 1986.

In fact, the policy agenda was expanded to encompass drugs as part of the national security domain. In mid-1986, President Reagan and Nancy Reagan declared war against drugs in the United States. With the advent of the president's antidrug campaign, national security became a war against the U.S. populace. The drug epidemic, like communism, was seen as a threat to U.S. health, lives, morality, and the economy and therefore became ipso facto a national security issue. Moreover, drugs were depicted by the Reagan rhetoric as a "foreign" threat, foisted upon the United States by corrupt or hostile Latins and Asians. Such rhetoric thereby fed U.S. nationalism and racism.

The diagnosis made by national security officials for the drug problem was predictable: Blame foreign criminals and increase police forces. U.S. agents infiltrated Mexican drug gangs and cracked down on Bolivian coca growers, Colombian processing laboratories, and Jamaican ganja farmers. The national security response to the drug problem was the same as the response to defense: Employ more "security" forces. In the process, the Drug Enforcement Agency assumed a police responsibility for a social problem.

Thus, terrorists, drug runners, and Third World revolutionaries were put virtually on a par with the Soviets as "threats to U.S. national security," and at times the president suggested that they were all part of one great communist plot. As a result, security in the late 1980s meant force, not safety; violence or the threat of it, not a sense of well-being.

# CHAPTER 15

# The Alternative

 *I don't make jokes—I just watch the government and report the facts.*

—Will Rogers[1]

*It is a great sin, to swear unto a sin;*
*But greater sin to keep a sinful oath.*

—*King Henry VI, Part II*

The doctrine of national security has served for forty years as an ambiguous and anxious guideline for defense and foreign policy. For several decades, a foreign and defense policy elite has used national security to justify U.S. intervention into other nations' economies and political systems. National security has become, in the minds of the U.S. elite, a permanent doctrine. But events overtook the narrow limits of U.S. national security ideology. Although national security terminology still dominates policy discussion, the United States has not been able to maintain its preeminence. Third World nations are diverse and no longer will submit to the industrially developed countries of the north. Some forms of independence have become a matter of survival for many Third World nations.

The immense nuclear arsenal and the mighty conventional forces at the disposal of the United States have not intimidated revolutionaries in Iran, Nicaragua, or other parts of the Third World. However, the cumulative cost of maintaining U.S. national security forces has inflated the U.S. budget and contributed to a massive deficit and debt. The U.S. debt and trade deficit hit new highs in 1987. The U.S. budget no longer has room for the escalating costs of maintaining an informal overseas empire. Following the guidelines of Gramm-Rudman-Hollings, the foreign aid budget will be cut by

$1 billion. Secretary of State Shultz argued that the sum "will not allow the United States to meet its commitments and will cripple U.S. ability to conduct foreign policy."[2] President Reagan argued that $12 billion to provide clean water was wasteful but that the $340 billion defense budget was "insufficient."

Even if the world had not changed so dramatically, the corrosive effects of the national security doctrine on U.S. democracy and on the national treasury should have been enough to spark domestic political opposition. The investigations by Congress and the media into the Iran-contra scandals revealed the existence of a secret, parallel government that had usurped not only the responsible agencies of foreign and defense policies, but also had devised a plan for domestic control, one that included police breakins at organizations supportive of the Salvadoran rebels and the Sandinistas.[3]

This scandal plus the burdensome costs of maintaining the imperial infrastructure should have provoked a serious mainstream policy debate. Old, new, and middle-aged leftist groups, anti-interventionists of various stripes, solidarity movements, and small political parties and groupings as well as New Deal liberals inside the Democratic party have been joined by members of the religious community who come to progressive politics out of a concern for human rights, for the poor and downtrodden. On foreign policy some traditional conservatives and libertarians who oppose interventionism could potentially ally with this group.

Such a political grouping lacks a national means of expression that would allow movement beyond individual or local actions and a yearly march on Washington to end intervention in Central America, for example. Even though some members of Congress have responded to militant constituents by actively blocking a consensus for Reagan's military push in the region, the public that opposes national security policy needs a program that goes beyond dissent in content and movement in form.

A jump from protest to a new phase of activism requires that there exist a mass alternative, one that embodies a sense of national interest, one that offers a plausible notion of security in place of the mythology that has embedded itself both in the public mind and the institutions of government. Such a politics also would try to appeal to some of the millions of adults who do not vote. Even for those who do enter minimally into the political process, the basic daily struggle to maintain life demands quantities and qualities of energy that leave little for the pursuit of liberty and happiness. As the federal government concerns itself with national security, personal and family security disintegrates.

The government's de facto definition of human rights ignores FDR's basic-needs formula and instead focuses on procedural rights, which the government then uses to attack leftist and communist governments. In the 1987 U.N. General Assembly, the U.S. delegate charged Cuba with human rights violations. The cases he cited, without proof, were on issues of prison behavior and legal procedure. The Cubans, while denying the procedural charges, trumpeted their version of substantive human rights, like infant mortality, which dropped below the rate of the District of Columbia. Ironically, in the USSR and Cuba, every person has a right to eat, to have shelter and medical care, while in the more prosperous and freer United States millions of homeless and hungry citizens have no legal claim to government for their basic needs.

Human rights, in the terms laid out in the U.N. covenants, constitute a solid basis for a political alternative to national security doctrine. The modern notion of human rights dates back to the works of Locke and Montesquieu and the Declaration of Independence; rights derive from political compacts and are inherent in natural law. In March 1977, Jimmy Carter acknowledged that these rights had the force of international law because the signers of the U.N. Charter had promised "to observe and to respect basic human rights." The president told the U.N. General Assembly in an address on March 17, 1977, that "no member . . . can claim that mistreatment of its citizens is solely its own business." A month later, Secretary of State Cyrus Vance told a Georgia Law School audience, "Since 1945 international practice has confirmed that a nation's obligation to respect human rights is a matter of concern in international law."[4] The issue that neither Carter nor Vance, nor indeed any president since Franklin Roosevelt has addressed, is the meaning of human rights.

In his Georgia Law Day speech Vance listed three human rights categories: (1) the integrity of the person, (2) vital needs such as food, shelter, and medical care; and (3) political and civil liberties. Despite the explicit recognition of vital needs, however, even the Carter administration officials most committed to human rights as a policy guideline showed clear preference for the rights of the integrity of the person and political and civil liberties. Indeed, most of the nongovernmental authorities cited by the media, such as Amnesty International and Americas Watch, monitor only the procedural freedoms, not the substantive ones.

The different standards in regard to development models also reflect the human rights criteria adopted by the socialist and capitalist nations. The Soviet Union stresses the substantive, the West the procedural, freedoms. The irony is that most Third World nations provide neither. Entire regions of the world are beset by famine and the plagues that accompany dire poverty. These people, according to the definition agreed to by the nations of the world, are being deprived of their basic human right—the right to life itself. Third World citizens also may suffer from arbitrary detention or the lack of free assembly. But the endemic poverty of Central America, for example, is not cited when the media or political authorities talk about human rights in the region.

This oversight also covers up the responsibility of U.S. policy for causing these disastrous conditions through U.S. support for military dictators and local oligarchies. The people charged with formulating human rights policies under Reagan, and even the more enlightened Carter officials, have not connected substantive and procedural rights, nor have they linked these rights to the historical process that led to the deformation of structures in the Third World. Much-heralded capitalist enterprise techniques have not produced development or democracy in the Third World. Yet U.S. aid programs and official ideology continue to insist that if a Third World state just allows the free market to operate, development will magically follow.

The most recent example of the failure of this magic to operate is Edward Seaga's Jamaica. Since his election to prime minister in late 1980, Jamaica has benefited from the largesse of multilateral lending institutions and private banks. In addition, U.S. aid to Jamaica has increased greatly thanks to Seaga's promise to put monetarism and other "free-market" features to work. After six years, Jamaica's economy is demonstrably worse off than when his capitalist experiment began. Despite the input of some $4 billion, unemployment actually has risen and standards of living have dropped for the majority. But Jamaica has repaid the high interest on its loans.

In other Third World experiments with capitalist development, political terror has accompanied the economic "miracle-makers." Indeed, through much of the 1970s in military-ruled South Korea, Chile, Argentina, Brazil, Uruguay, and the Philippines, political terror and economic freedom became partners in capitalist development experiments. Multinational corporations and banks were not concerned with human rights in the Third World. To corporate directors freedom meant free access to resources, markets, labor (nonunionized), and land. These business leaders invested in South Africa until public pressures against apartheid, not a code of ethics in the banking community, forced some to divest.

In order to make human rights a firm foundation for future policy, large publics must understand procedural and substantive elements as part of a bonded ethical doctrine. To become a moral guideline for policy, human rights, not welfare, must be internalized in the public mind. Welfare conjures up the notion of the government giving something to the unfortunate or to the lazy; of government as a public charity, not as the guarantor of rights.

According to the Declaration of Independence, governments are formed to secure life, liberty, and the pursuit of happiness. These rights or freedoms outlined in the modern era by President Roosevelt in 1944 and more recently by Pope John Paul have become the commonly accepted basis for international discourse and for judging the behavior of governments and movements in the world of nations. Many national constitutions carry explicit references to these rights or freedoms.

## The National Security Exemption
## and Anticommunist Dogma

*Who shall guard the guardians themselves?*

—Juvenal[5]

During "crises," national security doctrine assumes that its actions are exempt from divine and natural law. The doctrine's advocates maintain that they are singularly invested with the responsibility to fight the diabolical enemy and cannot be hampered by routine ethical and moral constraints. National security advocates claim, in effect, the right to suspend or circumvent law in order to deal with urgent threats to national security. By imposing this ostensibly "higher cause" above the Constitution and law, the national security elite limits the possibilities for practicing democracy and exercising the rites of republican government. Thus, a citizenry can never exercise fully its rights under national security rule.

If the public is to remove this fetter in the way of its self-realization, then each member of the public will have to confront the ideology of anticommunism, the all-encompassing mystique, the higher cause that has permitted, indeed encouraged, consistent lawbreaking. When stripped of its veneers, national security is nothing more than opposition to the Soviet Union and the ideology of socialism. If that is the only theme to which the United States as a nation is bound, then national security is a higher—albeit negative—cause. In effect, the Constitution and laws are secondary in import to the unwritten mandate to "rage forth into the night" against foreign monsters.

This expression of unrestrained anticommunist rage easily becomes national scandal, however, because the limits on national security activity remain vague, lodged in some wide-ranging gray area until the details are revealed. Then the public and the establishment react and recoil. So it was when it was made public that a marine corps lieutenant colonel inside the National Security Council felt that he had the authority—if indeed he was not granted it by superiors— to appropriate the taxpayers' money and reallocate it to contras in Nicaragua, aspiring pro-contra candidates, or other anticommunist "freedom fighters." He organized a shipping company that owned vessels, an airline, and several Swiss bank accounts. He commanded a team of government employees, civilians, and foreign nationals. He mixed private and public funds and retired and active military personnel and in effect ran entire foreign and defense policy programs. As the White House communications director, Patrick Buchanan, reminded enthusiastic crowds of anti-Castro Cubans in Miami in December 1986, Oliver North and the others who secretly sold arms to Iran and rechanneled the money for the contras were "national heroes" and true patriots.[6]

The definition of patriotism and heroism that lauds illegal behavior as long as it has anticommunist motives and goals derives from the acceptance of a higher morality, an uncharted crusade to destroy what is seen as a permanent ideological foe. George Washington might well roll over in his grave as would all those who had thought of themselves as conservatives, people who believed in the supremacy of law because it had withstood the test of history. However, some modern conservatives are national security zealots who scoff at law and see history as a series of frozen moments in which heroes and villains engage in the great contests of winning and losing.

In the name of preserving democracy, national security operatives violate the very fabric and texture of it. Because in their world all information is potentially dangerous, these operatives try to control it. By shaping news or information and controlling access to it, national security managers deprive the citizens of participation in life-and-death issues, for themselves and future generations. The national security elite has done devastating damage to the world's environment through nuclear testing and dumping as well as chemical and biological experiments that have produced horrendous contamination of people and places. On a global scale, national security priorities have deprived hundreds of millions of resources that could have been used for building solid infrastructure, for growing food, and for providing education. Instead, national security priorities go for weapons and violence.

National security as a permanent way of life has come to mean ongoing crimes against humanity, as defined in the Nuremberg Laws, and violations of the foundations of international law as conceived and agreed upon in Geneva. The sagacious advice of George Washington in his farewell address is a second practical guideline for a workable foreign policy. Washington warned future generations not only against forging permanent alliances, but also against permanent "antiparties," or enmities, as well. His advice was practical: Ideology should not govern international behavior because the world is too diverse to allow for such a limited criterion. Ideology, if allowed to rule, either results in damaging the economy or forcing the nation into a war, regardless of real interests.

## The Real National Interest

During the 1980s, the people of West Virginia watched their highway system deteriorate as federal and state legislatures cut budgets. Torn tires and broken axles were just one sign of a fiscal crisis that had forced immense cuts in the budget. But the West Virginia National Guard on duty in Honduras built a brand new road, one that connected U.S. and Honduran military bases to the Nicaraguan border. The irony of no new roads or even repair of old ones at home and unlimited expenditures abroad for the purpose of destroying foreign monsters should not be lost on the public. It is time to recall the warning John Quincy Adams uttered some one hundred sixty years ago:

> Wherever the standard of freedom and independence has been or shall be unfurled, there will be America's heart, her benedictions, and her prayers. But she goes not abroad in search of monsters to destroy. . . . [America] well knows that by once enlisting under other banners of foreign independence, she would involve herself, beyond the power of extrication, in all the wars of interest and intrigue, of individual avarice, envy, and ambition. She might become dictatress of the world; she would no longer be the ruler of her own spirit.[7]

Without foreign monsters and devil's agents, U.S. citizens might be able to fashion their own foreign policy for the last decade of the twentieth century—one that carries the nation well into the twenty-first century. National security is a mysterious doctrine, in that it holds up the banner of the higher cause, one that always manages to reach beyond the realm of divine or natural law. Yet, when national security policies are executed, they inevitably bring forth the worst kinds of greed and skullduggery known for millennia by the analysts of human nature. Congress can apply a majority-based wisdom and restore the system of law, which dictates that Congress and only Congress has power to declare war. The warmaking power is the ultimate trust that the citizenry can invest in its elected representatives.

## Notes

1. "A Rogers Thesaurus," *Saturday Review,* August 25, 1962.
2. "Foreign-Aid Purse Strings Tighten," *Washington Post,* December 16, 1986, p. A-17.
3. Alfonso Chardy, "Reagan Aides and the 'Secret' Government," *Miami Herald,* July 5, 1987, p. 1.
4. Cited in Peter Weiss, "Human Rights and Vital Needs," in *Orlando Letelier and Ronny Karpen Moffitt,* Transnational Institute Pamphlet Series no. 5 (Washington, D.C.: Transnational Institute, 1977), p. 70.
5. Juvenal, *The Sixteen Satires* (London: Penguin, 1967), Book 1, line 347.
6. The assumption that the Soviet Union is out to conquer the United States by any and all means underlies national security rationale, albeit motives often are less ideological. For White House communications director Patrick Buchanan, Lieutenant Colonel North did what he had to do. He was willing, in President Kennedy's words, to "let every nation know, whether it wishes us well or ill, that we shall pay any price, bear any burden, meet any hardship, support any friend, oppose any foes, in order to assure the survival and success of liberty. This we pledge—and more" (Inaugural Address, January 1961).
7. Address given on July 4, 1821, cited in William Appleman Williams, *The Contours of American History* (New York: World Publishing, 1961), p. 87.

# The Last National Security Scandal?

*Sometimes you have to go above the written law.*
—Fawn Hall, Secretary to Lieutenant Colonel North,
National Security Council, Testimony to Congress

*A fanatic is a man that does what he thinks th' Lord wud do if He knew th' facts iv th' case.*

Mr. Dooley in *Mr. Dooley's Opinions*[1]

On November 13, 1986, President Reagan addressed the nation. "We did not—repeat—we did not trade weapons or anything else for hostages." Less than two weeks later, Attorney General Edwin Meese disclosed that members of the National Security Council indeed had been selling weapons to Iran in exchange for Iranian help in freeing hostages held by pro–Ayatollah Khomeini groups in Lebanon. Funds, raised in part from the sale of weapons to Iran, had been secretly diverted to aid the Nicaraguan contras. Meese announced that the Justice Department had begun to investigate these activities to determine if they violated any laws. He also announced that President Reagan's national security adviser, Vice Admiral John Poindexter, had resigned and that another high NSC official, Lieutenant Colonel Oliver North, had been fired. The media also reported that Colonel North had shredded key documents before the Justice Department investigators had begun their probe.

One Washington wit commented that to the U.S. moviegoing public the news was as shocking as if John Wayne, in one of his westerns, had been selling liquor to the Indians and tried to justify it by appealing to both bad memory and national security.[2] The Iran-contra scandals of late 1986–1987 were part and parcel of national security policy doctrine. As Lieutenant Colonel North told the congressional inquiry, the illegal and even unconstitutional actions he carried out were done in the name of freedom and anticommunism—that is, national security. Ironically, Colonel North and his collaborators, who conspired to swap arms for hostages with the Iranian government and then divert some of the profits to the Nicaraguan contras, operated outside of the national security state apparatus. Indeed, the inability of the national security state to operate militarily in the post–Vietnam War period gave rise to the very military junta that operated covertly out of Reagan's White House, using the president's name but employing the "plausible deniability" mode that the CIA customarily used in the past. A small group of men in key national security posts conspired with others, many of them former national security officials, to violate the law in order to accomplish what they considered to be goals that transcended even the Constitution of the United States.[3]

While this junta was operating in secret, the president assured the public that he would never deal with terrorist governments and that he would not swap weapons for hostages. Reagan even scolded U.S. allies for being soft on the ayatollah's regime, for selling Iran weapons, and for trading with Iran. Zealous prosecutors in the Department of Justice arranged for an expensive "sting" operation in which seventeen "merchants of death" were accused of illegally selling arms to Iran. Among the group were four Israelis, who turned out later to be agents of MOSSAD (Israeli intelligence), and a variety of weapons dealers who thought that they were carrying out a secret U.S. policy. In fact, they were, but the prosecutors in the U.S. Attorney's Office did not know about the policy.

### National Security Scandals Past and Present

This was not the first national security scandal. The CIA sent a U2 spy plane over the Soviet Union just before a scheduled summit meeting in 1959. The Agency misinformed President Kennedy about key factors that might have influenced his decision to launch the disastrous Bay of Pigs expedition. President Johnson used national security officials to help him fabricate an "incident" in the Gulf of Tonkin in order to manipulate Congress into supporting a military adventure in Vietnam. In the 1970s, President Nixon tried to use national security as a pretext to cover up the investigation into the Watergate breakin. In 1975, the Church Committee reports offered details into a variety of the CIA's illegal activities, which ranged from assassination plots and coups to the use of journalists as agents and drug experiments on unwitting civilians.

But the joint congressional committee and the special prosecutor appointed to investigate the Iran-contra affair did not uncover just one more in a long series of illegal national security activities. Rather, investigators discovered a military junta inside the U.S. government that used the president's name and office as the source for the junta's authority. The group had covert action plans that went beyond the Iranian and Nicaraguan scenarios, and the full agenda of this group was never revealed to Congress.[4]

Whether or not the president knew about all the shenanigans undertaken by Colonel North and his superiors, national security advisers Robert MacFarlane and John Poindexter,[5] Reagan's name and rank were used to transact high-level U.S. government business. Director William Casey of the CIA and Oliver North, along with retired generals Richard Secord and John Singlaub, controlled major foreign and defense policy portfolios.[6]

With funds obtained from the Iran arms sale as well as from a variety of other public and private sources, Casey, North, and company raised a private navy and air force and hired crews to man the ships and fly the planes that carried U.S. weapons to Iran and supplies to the contras. The people chosen to carry out these tasks came from the corps of ex-agents, special forces personnel and ragtag mercenaries that the CIA had used for past secret operations. Such characters included Eugene Hasenfus, the "kicker" of supplies from the CIA supply plane to the contras on the ground. Hasenfus was the sole survivor of a contra supply plane shot down over Nicaragua. After he was captured in October 1986 by Sandinista forces, Hasenfus revealed to the public the existence of the complex resupply network that Casey and North had established, unbeknownst to Congress or even to key national security officials.[7]

The secretaries of state and defense, George Shultz and Caspar Weinberger, told Congress that they knew nothing of the contra resupply operations that were run out of the National Security Council, but both men claimed that they had opposed the arms-for-hostages swap and the government's funding of the contras during the period in which the congressional ban on such actions was in effect.[8] In their testimony to the congressional committee, Shultz and Weinberger stressed their commitment to law and indicated that although they were avid contra supporters, the notion of breaking the law to accomplish the resupply was beyond the pale. The assistant secretary of state for inter-American affairs, Elliott Abrams, however, admitted that he had lied to Congress about matters related to contra funding, but he excused his actions on the grounds that he had not been "authorized" to tell Congress the truth. He did not say who did not authorize him to give honest testimony to Congress, nor did he say who authorized him to lie.

Other witnesses supplied Congress with details of the methods used by the CIA to train troops, resupply the contras, and direct their military strategy. Veteran CIA operators such as Felix Rodriguez, who had participated in Agency affairs since the first attempts to overthrow the revolutionary government of Cuba (he was part of the 1967 operation to catch and kill Che Guevara), described how covert actions were and ought to be run, claiming that the infighting among the groups was about who would get the CIA's money supply.[9] Among those who worked with Rodriguez was Luís Posada Carrilles, a man accused by Cuba and Venezuela of having plotted the sabotage of a Cuban commercial airliner in October 1976 in which more than seventy passengers and crew perished. Posada, one of the world's most wanted terrorists, also had contacts with members of Vice President Bush's staff.[10]

Congress also discovered information that linked national security officials to a variety of terrorists, drug traffickers, and other unsavory characters.[11] The labyrinth of shady business activities and the "businessmen" that arranged for loans and Swiss bank accounts, and who, of course, made "fair" profits, also occupied Congress. Former generals Richard Secord and John Singlaub offered confusing information mixed with patriotic discourse about their roles in the informal military junta. Along with business partners and right-wing millionaire funders, Casey and North financed the secret operations so as to avoid congressional scrutiny and executive accountability. Given that the CIA already possessed thousands of secret Swiss bank accounts, the existence of a few more would hardly catch the attention of government watchdog agencies already primed to overlook "national security" activities.

The ex-military officers and their business partners wrapped all of their activities in the assumption of anticommunism, which became the operative definition of patriotism during the hearings because members of Congress did not challenge the rhetoric of the witnesses. Men whose profits ran to more than $1 million spoke contemptuously to Congress, as if real patriotism demanded those kinds of extralegal operations and not the timid vacillation of a legislature that responded to the flips and flops of public opinion.

## The Implications of the Scandal

The televising of the hearings and the focus on the "minutiae of the affair" obscured for Congress and the public at large the policy implications of the scandal. The months-long inquiry centered around questions of violation of laws, checks and balances, separation of powers, and the Constitution itself. What the facts of the Iran-contra scandal called into public scrutiny were the very processes of government, its accountability structure, and the relations among branches of government on the issues of controversial foreign and defense policies.

Congress avoided both the substantive and principled questions of policy. Members did not challenge the fairy-tale history told by Reagan officials to a national television audience. Nor did members take issue with Lieutenant Colonel North's claims that the contras were truly the "Nicaraguan democratic resistance" and that contra military commanders were not members of the Somoza National Guard. Several senators and representatives possessed ample documentation that proved that the contras had excelled only in the field of human rights abuse and that the vast majority of their military commanders indeed had worked for Somoza.

The policy implications in North's testimony also drew no opposition remarks from the committee members. Yet, behind the "facts" about the nature of the contras and the Reagan version of recent Nicaraguan history—the United States supported the Nicaraguan revolution, which was stolen by the bad revolutionaries, the Sandinistas, from the good revolutionaries, now called contras—there was an implicit policy that, if successful, would result in a contra victory—that is, in a return to power of Somoza officers.

Colonel North presented himself as a warrior of the Kennedy school willing to bear any burden, pay any price in the pursuit of liberty. His loyalty to other men, to a mission higher than law, his contempt for the vacillating Congress belied his stated love of democracy. North spoke like an early member of Germany's *Freikorps* (an association of World War I veterans, some of whom became Nazi activists) making a pitch for support from members of the National Rifle Association.

No other testimony had so dramatically brought both the substance and procedure of U.S. foreign policy into the public light. For forty years, Congress had ceded to the president the substantive issues of foreign policy. The dicey questions that underlay policy in the national security era were kept from the House and Senate floors.

Can the economy survive without an informal overseas empire? Will the U.S. public accept the fact that the country does have an imperial role, and will the public allow for institutional alterations that would make legal the operations that have been run as clandestine actions? Can the republic continue to survive covert actions that inherently violate law and the Constitution itself? Can policymakers elaborate a foreign policy and foreign policy guidelines that operate within the laws and treaties without abandoning the cold war assumptions? Is there a glue to hold this diverse nation together? Should the United States shed cold war ideology?

The Reagan officials that testified made it clear that they viewed Congress as an impediment to a successful anticommunist politics and that to the extent that the Constitution itself posed arcane barriers to current policy necessities, they were willing to circumvent it. Casey, North, and company justified their actions by appealing to a higher cause. North made clear his annoyance with the restraints imposed by Congress on the executive in light of what he perceived as a "crisis" situation, one that demanded rapid response unfettered by outdated provisions of an eighteenth century document.

The CIA and the national security advisers had stepped on congressional toes before, and there had been other investigations. None of the probes, however, from CIA assassination and coup attempts to Nixon's use of national security to try covering up the Watergate breakin, led members of Congress to debate the obvious. In order for the United States to manage affairs throughout the world, to have what historian Arthur Schlesinger, Jr., called "the imperial presidency," there would be agencies that Congress could not control, and these said agencies would commit crimes and breach the separation of powers, just as these same agencies did in the Iran-contra scam.

The United States has controlled directly or indirectly the politics, economics, and defenses of scores of other nations, a global position that has required an executive with powers well beyond what the Constitution offered the president. Nevertheless, Congress looked at the narrow issue, as if nothing had really changed in the basic partition of powers that the Founding Fathers had meted out to each branch. Instead of concentrating on the question of whether or not the United States could continue to function as a republic *and* as an empire, Congress asked: Did the president know about the unlawful activities carried out by members of the White House or NSC staff?

What the public glimpsed in the televised hearings was the cumulative impact of forty years of cold war battle veterans venting their frustrations. Even though the witnesses who participated directly in the arms-for-hostages swap and the diversion of the funds to the contras had operated outside of the national security state structure, these witnesses nevertheless presented a point of view that reflected the ideology of that structure, one that had grown weary of republican impediments to imperial posture.

In bars and poker parlors, living rooms and dens, people began to discuss again "who lost Vietnam?" and whether or not Ollie was a hero or a rogue. The man who deceived Congress had either "lied for our sins" or was the quintessential sinner. Those who had internalized cold war values wished that North truly had had freedom of action so that the United States would not "lose" more territory to the ever-encroaching Red encirclement. These national security doctrine addicts bought T-shirts that said "Ollie North for president." Protests arose demanding that the president issue pardons to those who might have engaged in illegal activities during the Iran-contra affair.

The issue became defined for the public as: Was Ollie not only right to do what he did, but a real national hero as well? Thus, the substance of the affair was lost. Was the ghost of empire fluttering around the congressional hearing room, or would it forever vanish and stop haunting the good order of the republic? Neither members of Congress nor opinion leaders in the media acknowledged that the language of the 1950s still prevailed in the political thought of the late 1980s and that the credibility of the president could be seriously weakened by his obsessive belief that Nicaragua posed a national security threat.

Under the guiding axioms of U.S. politics, Republican and Democratic aspirants call, as if programmed by the ancient cold war puppeteer, for a strong defense. Such political "necessity" remains unquestioned by mainstream politicians; the same holds true for the arcane notion that the Soviet Union still intends to conquer the United States or invade Western Europe. So ingrained has anti-Sovietism become that candidates and Congress members chant its tenets like catechism.

**The Real Enemies**

The United States of America does have enemies in the late 1980s, but they are mostly at home. The environment shows serious signs of decay, the cores of major cities need rebuilding, crime and drugs are rampant, and serious immigration problems exist. The time has come to question the Soviet "threat" upon which the United States has built its foreign and defense ideology. Seventy years after the Bolshevik Revolution, the Soviets are still unable to compete economically with the United States. The new Soviet leaders appear eager to reduce drastically the nuclear weapon stockpiles and sign accords to replace the threat of nuclear and even conventional war.

If this fictitious military threat can be disposed of and U.S. leaders and public alike can begin to see actions in the Third World as quite independent of the Kremlin, the United States can begin to deal with the real threats to its security—which are mostly at home— and derive a foreign policy that rings true to the advice of the Founding Fathers. Such a policy would benefit the internal, domestic needs of U.S. society and bid goodbye to the futile chase of foreign monsters.

Such thinking would require Congress to play a policy role that breaks the limits that have guided congressional inquiries into national security issues. Did Eisenhower, Kennedy, Johnson, and Nixon authorize assassination plots against Castro? Did the "rogue elephant" metaphor apply to the CIA's behavior? Similarly, the questions raised at the 1987 Iran-contra hearings focused on President Reagan's knowledge, or lack thereof, of the sale of weapons to Iran for the return of hostages and the diversion of funds from that sale to the contras.

Members of Congress have been reluctant to go beyond the limited questions of "responsibility" in order to investigate the theme that has provoked such scandals: the meaning of U.S. national security in the post–World War II period. Congress, after all, had accepted the cold war language that U.S. policymakers have used. Few members objected when President Reagan reactivated the moribund "Red threat" metaphors of the late 1940s. Congress passively allowed the president to transform the U.S.-Soviet conflict into a way of dealing with the issues of the Third World as well. The right wing, once inside the government, made use of the acceptable political culture. Cabinet members, assistant secretaries, and members of the NSC staff appeared before Congress and announced that the anticommunist struggle once again was invigorated with zeal and righteousness. Reagan ideologues utilized traditional U.S. hostility to revolutions and added to it the language of antiterrorism and those geopolitical theories that saw the United States and the USSR in eternal and mortal conflict. The United States undertook, with the consent of Congress at least to the euphemisms presented to it, to control the "free world."

## National Security—Above the Law?

The policies fashioned from the Truman era on defined U.S. security and global actions as one and the same. The Truman Doctrine called for operations in foreign countries that came into conflict with existing U.S. laws and treaties. These operations included orders to assassinate individuals, overthrow governments and install new ones, and plot and conspire with other governments to accomplish some of these deeds. Under the rubric of national security, the CIA and other secret agencies carried out a range of secret activities ranging from public-health-imperiling nuclear testing to drug experiments. These activities became part and parcel of what came to be called the imperial presidency.

This notion presumes that the president presides over an empire, not a mere republic, and that his office is therefore endowed—or should be—with the necessary prerogatives properly to exercise his duties, which are global in nature. The imperial president acts without more than a token glance at Congress. President Roosevelt attempted to send destroyers to England without congressional authorization and ultimately achieved the powers he sought once the Japanese attacked Pearl Harbor. Truman announced that he was committing U.S. military forces to Greece, Turkey, Iran, and, later, Korea. By the late 1940s, the national security apparatus had a foundation in law, and by the early 1950s, the existence of a secret state within an open state became not only an accepted fact but a matter of routine. But the routine was not smooth.

Covert action was devised so as to circumvent the law and offer the president "plausible deniability," while still maintaining policies designed to control other countries' destinies. Policymakers had to maintain international law and the principle of self-determination as operative norms, while practicing interventionism with a vengeance. A system of national security explanations was offered to cloud the contradictions that otherwise would become clear. Under guidelines of emergency, crisis, and "need" for rapid response—all of which were coincident with the existence of a terrible devil in the guise of international communism, or the USSR—a consensus was developed that postponed any serious scrutiny of the national security agencies and their international behavior.

Scandals erupted periodically because the agencies went "too far"; because secrets were leaked to the press; because Congress decided that it could not allow certain behavior on the part of executive agencies, lest congressional authority be lost; and, most importantly, because the national security policies themselves proved to be unrealistic, foolhardy, criminal, and downright dangerous to the real security interests of the United States. The Vietnam War was such a policy; so, too, was the decision and its augmentation to trade U.S. weapons for hostages and then divert to the contras the profits from the operation.

The cabal that operated behind both the congressional and the official national security scenes came out of the culture that national security doctrine and practice had produced. In this culture, a deadly enemy always existed whose defeat required breaking the law, violating the separation of powers, and misusing executive authority. This communist enemy was viewed from the vantage point of spy versus spy.[12]

## Forging a Foreign Policy Consensus

The facts of political life in the late 1980s have changed from the heyday of U.S. power at the end of World War II. Yet, foreign policy decisions appear to continue as part of a pattern whose origins and vital center are derived from cold war thinking. The cold war itself, as we look back on it, provided ideology for the expansion of U.S. power. The justification for the break in the traditional ways of carrying out policy was the communist threat, one that went beyond anything the Founding Fathers could have imagined. The communist threat involved, the policymakers declared, the national security of the country, a concept that had been fashioned during World War I and then revived with World War II.

National security should begin at home, to paraphrase Will Rogers, and the adventures that U.S. policymakers have embarked upon in the Persian Gulf and Lebanon, the "retaliatory" bombing of Libya, and the obsession with Central America have not satisfied the domestic desire to raise living standards or reduce tensions. The renegades who ran madly throughout the world carrying out secret missions, buying arms, organizing hostage releases, plotting coups and in-vasions, and keeping alive a bloody war in Central America for several years were like a tumor that grew naturally on the body of the national security state apparatus.

The national security mentality, the foreign policy doctrine that grew from it, and the larger culture that developed from the politics of the cold war no longer coincide even remotely with reality. The world of 1947 has faded and with it the presumptions that U.S. policymakers utilized in order to fashion the national security.

By 1990, as many as a dozen nations will possess nuclear weapons; and even with some twenty-five thousand nuclear weapons, the

United States cannot bend tiny Nicaragua to the U.S. will, nor can the Soviets subdue the Afghan rebels. Nuclear weapons, the weapons base for cold war thinking, are as obsolete as is the economic order conceived in Bretton Woods. NATO also exists on dubious premises some forty years after its creation, but the most inappropriate premise in the policy world, the one that has led to disasters and scandals, is the notion that Third World events can be placed into an East versus West context.

The containment of revolutions has succeeded in some places and for a certain length of time, but the costs have been high, and some of the bill is yet to be paid. Ollie North will leave a legacy and a persistent fan club long after he has ceased to be a trendy character. John F. Kennedy's promise to carry on a global crusade "in the pursuit of liberty" gave rise to the first military junta, which in turn generated both illegal policy and criminal activity.

The doctrines that arose after World War II to enable U.S. leaders to pursue global empire by citing the "clear and present danger" of the communist enemy have led to a true crisis: Neither the leaders of the state nor the prestigious sectors of society have been able to offer policies that fit the facts of the world and the limits of the U.S. budget. Revolutions in Iran and Nicaragua helped to bring down President Carter and unwittingly led to the weakening of the Reagan presidency as well. The forty-year accumulation of doctrine and weapons proved useless against Third World nationalism.

One other factor contributed to the events that led up to the creation of the first U.S. military junta. Beginning in a militant public, including members of religious communities under the sway of liberation theology, solidarity groups for Nicaragua and the Salvadoran resistance movement, and antiwar and anti-interventionist groups maintained consistent pressure on Congress and the administration. Indeed, the slogans of these groups often referred to the similarities between the Central American scenario and the one that led the United States into Vietnam.

This public not only countered the right-wing push for more intervention, but spread this noninterventionist consciousness throughout society. Even after the conclusion of the televised Iran-contra hearings, most of the public remained unsure of which side the U.S. government supported in Nicaragua and El Salvador. But the militant anti-interventionist public had successfully transmitted its political vibrations to a large sector of the general public: The contras were bad guys, and the United States should not be involved in the internal politics of Central America. The junta that carried out the illegal operations with Iran and the contras was sensitive, if not supersensitive, to the depths of opposition and to the latent antipathy to their tactics. Ironically, the so-called ignorant public, which in frequent public opinion polls consistently opposed contra aid, and the highly conscious community that set out to deter U.S. intervention caused the Caseys and the Norths to seek their goals through clandestine behavior, the very actions that led to the Iran-contra national security scandal. Will this public be able to push further for a long-term debate on the very nature of U.S. national security?

To forge a foreign policy consensus for the 1990s, U.S. society must divorce itself from the cold war, which has become a source of divisiveness. Cold war precepts do not conform to reality, and their costs are burdensome, if not exhausting. The informal U.S. pact with anticommunism has become a forced marriage. As the Duke of Suffolk declared at the end of *King Henry VI, Part I:*

For what is wedlock forced, but a hell,
An age of discord and continual strife?
Whereas the contrary bringeth force bliss,
And is a pattern of celestial peace.

## Notes

1. Finley Peter Dunne, "Casual Observations," in *Mr. Dooley's Opinions* (New York: Harper, 1901).

2. See *Washington Post,* March 5, 1987. "I told the American people I did not trade arms for hostages. My heart and my best intentions tell me that's true. But the facts and the evidence tell me it's not. . . . What began as a strategic opening to Iran deteriorated in its implementation into trading arms for hostages." President Reagan, March 4, 1987, address to the nation.

3. "Director Casey and I talked at length on a variety of occasions about the use of those monies to support other operations besides the Nicaraguan operation." Lieutenant Colonel Oliver North, testimony, July 8, 1987, before the Iran-contra committee.

4. "People with their own agenda . . . were doing everything they could to put this agenda into effect." Secretary of Defense Caspar Weinberger, testimony, July 31, 1987, before the Iran-contra committee.

5. The secret plans included channeling support to anticommunist "freedom fighters" throughout the Third World and a takeover scheme in which a "parallel government" under the aegis of the Federal Emergency Management Agency would "suspend the Constitution in the event of a national crisis, such as nuclear war, violent and widespread dissent or national opposition to a U.S. military invasion abroad." Alfonso Chardy in the *Miami Herald,* July 5, 1987, p. 1.

North also apparently directed a secret army unit called the Intelligence Support Activity, a navy unit, and a clandestine helicopter assault group, all of whom engaged directly in combat against "entrenched Nicaraguan troops." Frank Greve and Mark Fazlollah, *Miami Herald,* July 26, 1987.

6. The Christic Institute filed a lawsuit for reporter Tony Avirgan, who was injured in the 1985 assassination attempt against contra leader Eden Pastora. Christic claimed that the CIA and contra leaders conspired to murder Pastora because he had become a thorn in their side. When the bomb exploded at Pastora's jungle headquarters, several journalists were killed and wounded. Pastora recovered but never regained his stature inside the contra hierarchy. In material attached to the suit and in other presentations, the Christic Institute claimed that a covert network had existed for decades, one that involved drug dealing and a host of other criminal activities and that this old boys connection was revived with gusto when Reagan assumed office. William Casey was considered the chief coordinator of this covert gang, whose secret agenda was to wage covert wars throughout the world and finance them through traffic in illicit goods and services—a kind of modern Chinese tong.

7. North, apparently under Casey's command, hired former general Richard Secord to provide the aircraft and coordinate the resupply of the contras. Secord also had played a major role in the weapons sales to Iran.

8. In 1984, Representative Edward Boland (D-Mass) successfully sponsored an amendment to ban U.S. support for the contras. The diversion of funds from the Iranian arms sales and other illicit financing was designed to circumvent this law.

9. Rodriguez claimed that Secord and his gang were part of the criminal operation that involved former CIA official Edwin Wilson, who was convicted of unauthorized weapons sales to Libya and other "unfriendly" clients, and that North had "sold out" the integrity of the contra operation.

10. The evidence against Posada consisted of confessions by two of the perpetrators of the bombing. In addition, Posada had undertaken other clandestine CIA operations, including one in Jamaica that touched on the attempt to assassinate Prime Minister Michael Manley. Posada had met with a group of violent anti-Castro exiles in the Dominican Republic in June 1976, at which time the Cuban airplane bombing was plotted.

11. *In These Times,* December 10–16, 1986. The House and the Senate began to hold hearings in late spring 1987 into alleged connections between narcotics trade and contra activities. Senator John Kerry's subcommittee produced several witnesses that confirmed such connections, but as of September 1987, there was no direct evidence that traced the drug links to North or Secord.

12. In the Iran-Contra scandal the leader appeared to have been William Casey, a man who began his spying career in the Office of Strategic Services, where he ran another agent, John Singlaub, who graduated to become a general in the U.S. Army. The old cold warrior, Casey, brought his protégé into the contra operation. Other ex-military men, such as General Richard

Secord and Colonel Richard Gatt, also joined the secret war against the Sandinistas and became instruments—who made healthy profits—in the arms-for-hostages swap. These men knew the world of clandestine affairs and of business.

Lieutenant Colonel Oliver North and his bosses, former U.S. Marine Corps officer Robert MacFarlane and Admiral John Poindexter, ran the official side of the operation using the president's name and authority to get things done. The names of other officers appeared in the testimony, along with funders, fundraisers, and nonmilitary supporters from the ranks of the ultraright wing.

# Selected Bibliography

Acheson, Dean. *Present at the Creation.* New York: W. W. Norton, 1969.

Alperowitz, Gar. *Atomic Diplomacy.* New York: Penguin, 1985.

Ambrose, Stephen E. *Rise to Globalism.* New York: Penguin, 1985.

————. *Eisenhower, the President,* 2 vols. New York: Simon and Schuster, 1983–84.

————. *Ike's Spies.* Garden City, N.Y.: Doubleday, 1971.

Barnet, Richard. *The Alliance.* New York: Simon and Schuster, 1983.

————. *Intervention and Revolution.* New York: Meridian, 1980.

————. *Roots of War.* Baltimore, Md.: Penguin, 1973.

Barnet, Richard, Marcus Raskin, and Ralph Stavins. *Washington Wages an Aggressive War.* New York: Random House, 1971.

Beard, Charles A. *American Foreign Policy in the Making: 1932–1940.* New Haven, Conn.: Yale University Press, 1946.

————. *President Roosevelt and the Coming of War, 1941.* New Haven, Conn.: Yale University Press, 1948.

Bernstein, Carl, and Bob Woodward. *All the President's Men.* New York: Simon and Schuster, 1974.

Blackstock, Nelson. *COINTELPRO: The FBI's Secret War on Political Freedom.* New York: Vintage Books, 1975.

Blum, William. *The CIA: A Forgotten History.* London: Zed Books, 1986.

Borosage, Bob, and John Marks, eds. *The CIA File.* New York: Grossman, 1976.

Bottome, Edgar M. *The Balance of Terror.* Boston: Beacon Press, 1980.

Brenner, Philip. *From Confrontation to Negotiation: U.S. Relations with Cuba.* Boulder: Westview Press, 1988.

Brodhead, Frank, and Edward Herman. *Demonstration Elections.* Boston: South End Press, 1984.

Caute, David. *The Great Fear.* New York: Simon and Schuster, 1978.

Chomsky, Noam. *Turning the Tide: U.S. Intervention in Central America and the Struggle for Peace.* Boston: South End Press, 1985.

Chomsky, Noam, and Edward Herman. *The Washington Connection and Third World Fascism*. Boston: South End Press, 1979.

Cohen, Joshua, and Joel Rogers. *Inequity and Intervention: The Federal Budget and Central America*. Boston: South End Press, 1986.

——. *Rules of the Game: American Politics and the Central America Movement*. Boston: South End Press, 1986.

Dinges, John, and Saul Landau. *Assassination on Embassy Row*. New York: Pantheon, 1980.

Donovan, John C. *The Cold Warriors: A Policy-Making Elite*. Lexington, Mass.: D. C. Heath, 1974.

Draper, Theodore. *The Dominican Revolt: A Case Study in American Policy*. New York: Commentary, 1968.

Fagan, Richard. *Forging Peace: The Challenge of Central America*. New York: Basil Blackwell, 1987.

Fall, Bernard. *Last Reflections on a War: Last Comments on Vietnam*. Garden City, N.Y.: Doubleday, 1967.

Fleming, D. F. *The Cold War and Its Origins: 1917–1960*, 2 vols. Garden City, N.Y.: Doubleday, 1961.

Fonzi, Gaeton. "Who Killed John F. Kennedy?" *The Washingtonian* 16, no. 2 (November 1980):157–237.

Gardner, Lloyd. *Architects of Illusion*. Chicago: Quadrangle Books, 1970.

Girvan, Norman. *Corporate Imperialism: Conflict and Expropriation*. New York: Monthly Review Press, 1976.

Gleijeses, Piero. *The Dominican Crisis*. Baltimore, Md.: Johns Hopkins University Press, 1977.

Goldstein, Robert Justin. *Political Repression in Modern America*. Boston: G. K. Hall, 1978.

Halliday, Fred. *The Making of the Second Cold War*. London: Verso, 1984.

Halperin, Morton, Jerry Berman, Robert Borosage, and Christine Marwick. *The Lawless State*. New York: Penguin, 1976.

Hamilton, Nora, et al. *Crisis in Central America: Regional Dynamics and U.S. Policy in the 1980s*. Boulder: Westview Press, 1988.

Herman, Edward. *Demonstration Elections*. Boston: South End Press, 1984.

Hersh, Seymour. *The Price of Power*. New York: Summit Books, 1983.

Hinckle, Warren, and William W. Turner. *The Fish Is Red: The Story of the Secret War Against Castro*. New York: Harper and Row, 1981.

Immerman, Richard H. *The CIA in Guatemala: The Foreign Policy of Intervention*. Austin: University of Texas Press, 1982.

Jacobs, Paul, and Saul Landau. *To Serve the Devil: A Documentary Analysis of America's Racial History*. New York: Random House, 1971.

Kaplan, Fred. *Dubious Specter: A Skeptical Look at the Soviet Nuclear Threat*. Washington, D.C.: Institute for Policy Studies, 1978.

Kennan, George. *Memoirs, 1925–1950*. Boston: Little, Brown, 1967.

Kissinger, Henry. *Nuclear Weapons and Foreign Policy*. New York: Harper and Row, 1956.

Klare, Michael. *Beyond the Vietnam Syndrome: U.S. Intervention in the 1980s.* Washington, D.C.: Institute for Policy Studies, 1982.

Klare, Michael, and Cynthia Arnson. *Supplying Repression.* Washington, D.C.: Institute for Policy Studies, 1981.

Kolko, Gabriel. *Main Currents of American History.* New York: Harper and Row, 1976.

————. *The Politics of War.* New York: Random House, 1968.

Kolko, Joyce, and Gabriel Kolko. *The Limits of Power: The World and United States Foreign Policy, 1945–1954.* New York: Harper and Row, 1972.

Kornbluh, Peter. *Nicaragua: The Price of Intervention.* Washington, D.C.: Institute for Policy Studies, 1987.

LaFeber, Walter. *America, Russia, and the Cold War.* New York: John Wiley and Sons, 1967

————. *Inevitable Revolutions.* New York: W. W. Norton, 1984.

Levinson, Jerome, and Juan de Onis. *The Alliance that Lost Its Way.* Chicago: Quadrangle Books, 1970.

McMahan, Jeff. *Cracks in the Empire.* New York: Monthly Review Press, 1984.

Mankiewicz, Frank. *Perfectly Clear: Nixon from Whittier to Watergate.* New York: Quadrangle/New York Times Book Company, 1973.

Marks, John. *The Search for the "Manchurian Candidate": The CIA and Mind Control.* New York: New York Times Books, 1979.

Marzani, Carl. *We Can Be Friends.* New York: Garland Publications, 1971.

Matthews, Herbert L. *Revolution in Cuba.* New York: Charles Scribner's Sons, 1975.

Meyer, Karl E., and Tad Szulc. *The Cuban Invasion.* New York: Praeger, 1962.

Mills, C. Wright. *The Causes of World War III.* New York: Ballantine Books, 1959.

————. *The Power Elite.* New York: Oxford University Press, 1956.

Moffitt, Michael. *The World's Money.* New York: Simon and Schuster, 1983.

Molineu, Harold. *U.S. Policy Toward Latin America: From Regionalism to Globalism.* Boulder, Colo.: Westview Press, 1986.

Nixon, Richard. *U.S. Foreign Policy for the 1970s: Building for Peace. A Report to the Congress.* Washington: U.S. Government Printing Office, February 25, 1971.

O'Connor, James. *The Origins of Socialism in Cuba.* Ithaca, N.Y.: Cornell University Press, 1970.

Oshinsky, David M. *A Conspiracy so Immense: The World of Joe McCarthy.* New York: The Free Press, 1983.

Policy Alternatives for the Caribbean and Central America. *Changing Course: Blueprint for Peace in Central America and the Caribbean.* Washington, D.C.: Institute for Policy Studies, 1984.

Prados, John. *Presidents' Secret Wars: CIA and Pentagon Covert Operations Since World War II.* New York: Morrow, 1986.

Ranelegh, John. *The Agency: The Rise and Decline of the CIA.* New York: Simon and Schuster, 1986.

Raskin, Marcus. *Notes on the Old System.* New York: David McKay, 1974.

*Report of the National Bipartisan Commission on Central America.* Washington: U.S. Government Printing Office, January 1984.

Rice, Gerard T. *The Bold Experiment: JFK's Peace Corps.* Notre Dame, Ind.: University of Notre Dame, 1986.

Roosevelt, Kermit. *Countercoup: The Struggle for Control of Iran.* New York: McGraw-Hill, 1979.

Sayers, Michael, and Albert E. Kahn. *The Great Conspiracy Against Russia.* New York: Boni and Gaer, 1946.

Scheer, Robert. *America After Nixon.* New York: McGraw-Hill, 1974.

Schlesinger, Arthur M., Jr. *A Thousand Days: John F. Kennedy in the White House.* Boston: Beacon Press, 1965.

Schlesinger, Stephen, and Stephen Kinzer. *Bitter Fruit.* Garden City, N.Y.: Doubleday, 1982.

Schor, Juliet, and Daniel Cantor. *Tunnel Vision: Labor, Central America, and the International Economy.* Boston: South End Press, 1987.

Shoup, Lawrence, and William Minter. *Imperial Brain Trust: The Council on Foreign Relations and United States Foreign Policy.* New York: Monthly Review Press, 1977.

Sklar, Holly, ed. *Trilateralism.* Boston: South End Press, 1980.

Smith, Joseph B. *Portrait of a Cold Warrior.* New York: G. P. Putnam, 1976.

Smith, Robert. *The United States and Cuba.* New York: Bookman Associates, 1960.

Stavrianos, L. S. *Global Rift: The Third World Comes of Age.* New York: Morrow, 1981.

Stockwell, John. *In Search of Enemies: A CIA Story.* New York: W. W. Norton, 1978.

Stone, I. F. *The Hidden History of the Korean War.* New York: Monthly Review Press, 1952.

Summers, Anthony. *Conspiracy.* New York: McGraw-Hill, 1981.

Talbott, Strobe. *Deadly Gambits.* New York: Random House, 1986.

Walker, Thomas W., ed. *Reagan Versus the Sandinistas: The Undeclared War on Nicaragua.* Boulder, Colo.: Westview Press, 1987.

Weinberg, Albert. *Manifest Destiny.* Baltimore, Md.: Johns Hopkins University Press, 1935.

Whalen, Richard J. *Catch The Falling Flag.* Boston: Houghton Mifflin, 1972.

Williams, William Appleman. *American-Russian Relations, 1781–1947.* New York: Rinehart, 1952.

――――. *Contours of American History.* New York: World, 1961.

――――. *Empire as a Way of Life: An Essay on the Causes of Character of America's Present Predicament.* New York: Oxford University Press, 1980.

――――. *The Tragedy of American Diplomacy.* New York: Dell, 1967.

Wolf, Eric R. *Europe and the People Without History.* Berkeley: University of California Press, 1982.

Wolfe, Alan. *The Limits of Legitimacy*. New York: The Free Press, 1977.
———. *The Rise and Fall of the Soviet Threat*. Washington, D.C.: Institute for Policy Studies, 1980.
———. *The Seamy Side of Democracy*. New York: Longman, 1973.
Woodward, Bob. *Veil: The Secret Wars of the CIA, 1981–1987*. New York: Simon and Schuster, 1987.
Wyden, Peter. *Bay of Pigs: The Untold Story*. New York: Simon and Schuster, 1979.
Zeitlin, Maurice, and Robert Scheer. *Cuba, Tragedy in Our Hemisphere*. New York: Twayne Publishers, 1963.

# Index